世代間交流の理論と実践 2

世界標準としての
世代間交流のこれから

The Theory and Practices of Intergenerational Learning; Series 2
Future of the Intergenerational Exchange
as the World Standard

草野篤子・溝邊和成・内田勇人・安永正史 編著

三学出版

はじめに

　2015 年は、日本での世代間交流の研究や実践にとって、記念すべき年になった。日本における世代間交流の全国的な動きの歴史をたどれば、2003 年 3 月に、ピッツバーグ大学名誉教授のサリー・ニューマン氏が、オーストラリアでの国際会議の帰途、世代間交流について特に関心を抱いている人々に対して、東京で講演を行ったことが大きな契機となった。そこに集まった人々が、同年 11 月に信州大学や実践女子大学などで、講演とシンポジウムの会を開催した。それをきっかけに、同年暮れから Joyful Generations という研究会が組織され、2004 年 7 月に日本世代間交流協会が創立された。その後、2006 年 5 月には東京都から特定非営利活動法人の認可を受け、7 月末から 8 月初めにかけては早稲田大学の国際会議場で 10 か国 300 名余の参加者を得て、「世代間交流国際フォーラム　世代をつなぎ地域を再生するために」と「世代間交流についての国際研究集会」を開催するまでになった。世代間交流の実践が日本全国で草の根から繰り広げられる一方で、理論的な構築と発展が求められた結果、多くの準備会を経て 2010 年 6 月 6 日、日本世代間交流学会が設立された。日本学術会議から協力学術研究団体として認定されるのには、一般的には、数十年の歳月を待たなければならないなどといわれているが、当学会は、時代の緊要なニーズにも後押しされてか、学会設立から 5 年余をもって、日本学術会議を構成する協力学術研究団体となることができたことは、この上なく嬉しいことでもあり、今後、真摯に世代間交流の理論化や実践に精進することが求められている。

　一方、国際的な世代間交流についての動向に目を移してみると、ICIP（International Consortium for Intergenerational Programs)、米国の GU（Generations United)、ヨーロッパの EMIL（European Mapping of Intergenerational Learning）の存在を忘れることができない。特に ICIP の成立について日本ではほとんど知られていないので、ここにサリー・ニューマン博士が執筆し

た "Creating an 'International Consortium for Intergenerational Programs" ("Linking Lifetimes; A Global View of Intergenerational Exchange" edited by Matthew Kaplan, Nancy Henkin and Atsuko Kusano 所収）を参考に、少し詳しく述べてみたい。

　世界の多くの経済的、政治的に異なる基盤を持つ国々において、共通した問題が存在している。変動する社会構造、変容する家族の役割関係、そして世代間で異なるニーズが、これらの問題のいくつかを代表している。こうした変化する時代に、世代間に関する領域に対して、特に関心がもたれるものの中に、世界の多くの国々で、高齢者と子どもの劇的かつ急速に変化する役割関係がある。

　1999年4月、こうした全世界に及ぶ社会現象を認識して、ユネスコ、ヨーロッパ、アジア、アフリカ、北アメリカの人的サーヴィスの指導者グループが、ドイツのドルトムント大学（The University of Dortmunt）、ハウス・ボマーホルツ（Haus Bommerholz）校に集まり、人生という連続体の両極にある2つの世代が影響を及ぼしている普遍的な問題のいくつかに関して、世代間交流を通した解決に向けた討論を行った。討議は、オランダのファールス（Vaals）で行う第1回国際社会改革を促進する世代間交流プログラム会議（First International Conference on Intergenerational Programs to Promote Social Change）の組織化へとつながっていった。

　ハウス・ボマーホルツ運営会議（House Bommerholz Working Meeting）と、ファールス会議両者への参加者は、国際的世代間交流イニシアチブに対して、総括的信用を供する公式の組織を作ることの重要性を認めた。そうした組織があれば、様々な世代間交流イニシアチブについて意思疎通を図るための枠組が与えられ、またそうしたイニシアチブ創出のための推進力が得られるであろう。こうしたコンセンサスを得られたことで、国際世代間交流プログラム・コンソーシアム（International Consortium for Intergenerational Programs）、つまり、全世界規模にわたる社会改革を起こすものとして、世代間交流プログラムとその実践を促す為に計画された世代間交流組織が生まれることになったの

はじめに　iii

である。

　ハウス・ボマーホルツワーキング会議では、若者と高齢者が直面しているいくつかの問題に対する概念的及び現実的な解決法としての世代間交流プログラムに関連した理論的及び実践的な問題に取り組むために、10か国から25人が集まり、3日間にわたって基本的な問題について検討した。1つは、異なる国々、文化、政治組織という背景を持つ、お互いに知らない者同士の集団が、社会改革を推進するためのプロセスについて、コンセンサスを得られるだろうかという問題であった。もう1つは、もしそれが可能であるとすれば、望ましい社会改革を成し遂げるのに必要な世代間交流の概念とプログラムを効果的に利用することのできるパートナーシップを形成するために、どのような戦略が必要であろうかという問題である。これら2つの基本的な問題と取り組むに際し、ワーキング会議は、8つの問題点を考慮したが、ここに、そのいくつかについて言及する。

　世代間交流のプログラムは、若者、高齢者の生活を全世界規模で改革しようとした場合、文化的、経済的、政治的相違を超える普遍的な手段となりうるであろうか。

・世代間交流プログラムの、普遍的な定義づけが可能であろうか。

・世代間交流プログラムは、どんな社会的問題及び状況に、取り組むことができるのであろうか。

・世代間交流グループのメンバーは、国家的な共通点を入口のところに残して、児童、若者、高齢者の普遍的なニーズに焦点をおくことができるであろうか。

　ホストであるドルトムント大学ボマーホルツ校ルードガー・ヴィールケルン（Ludgar Veelkern）と、ピッツバーグ大学、サリーニューマン（Sally Newman）は、このグループがコンセンサスを得られるように、グループを先導していった。

　最初の課題は、世代間交流プログラムの理論と論理的根拠を議論し、それから共通の価値観を反映し、国境を越え、更なる意思疎通と交流を図るための基

盤として機能するような、グローバルな定義を作ることであった。こうした議論から、多様なニーズ、文化、社会構造を持つ国家群をまとめることのできるグローバルなミッション声明書が、創り出された。

「世代間交流プログラムとは、高齢者世代と若者世代との間に、意図的・継続的な資源の交換と学習を創出する社会的媒体である」と。

会議の参加国に共通の要素を検討するにあたり、参加者は、言葉、文化、下部構造の水準の違いにかかわらず、世代間交流活動によって効率的に取り込むことのできるいくつかの共通した普遍的な社会問題について慎重に考察した。断絶と排除、十分な雇用機会、識字能力、そして住みよい環境といったような問題が、いくつかの国々に共通していた。こうした問題のいくつかは、アメリカ、日本、イギリスにみられ、一方、中央ヨーロッパでは、これら同じ問題が、他所から入り込んできている移民に関連したものとなっている。高齢者と１０代の若者両者の雇用機会は、いくつかの国々で重要な問題として報告された。ヨーロッパ諸国は、高齢者に対する十分な支援を報告したが、その他の国の代表（南アフリカ共和国、日本、アメリカ）は、加齢する人口、特に十分な退職手当のない人たちのための、雇用機会のニーズを確認した。

こうした社会問題に関する議論は、いくつかの社会問題が、すべての国々に共通したものであるという認識を確証し、強化するものであり、また、これらの問題に対し、世界規模で世代間交流に解決を求めて、すべての国々が一緒になって取り組む必要性を強調することになったのである。

1999 年 10 月には、オランダのファールスで第 1 回国際社会変革を促進する世代間交流プログラム会議が開催された。会議の目的は、次のようなものである。

・世界のあらゆる場所における世代間交流プログラムに関する知識と情報を分かち合うこと。

・世代間交流の教育フォーラムとしてのプロジェクトを特定すること。

・社会の中に組み込むことを奨励し、社会改変を進める手段としての世代間交流プロジェクトの開発、評価、調査、公共政策を検討すること。

会議には、ユネスコと１２ケ国（ベルギー、カナダ、キューバ、フランス、ドイツ、イスラエル、日本、オランダ、南アフリカ共和国、スペイン、イギリス、アメリカ）を代表する 60 人余の人々が、出席した。出席者は、世代間交流プログラムの必要性について共通した関心と認識を持ったのである。

国際世代間交流協会（ICIP：International Consortium for Intergenerational Programs) は、1999 年 10 月 14 日に、オランダのファールスで、創設された。その目的は、次のようなものがある。

・世代間交流プログラムの研究と実践を促し開発していく。

・世代間交流プログラムの理論と実践の体系的な開発をコーディネートする。

その後、ICIP の世界大会は、第 1 回大会は、2002 年に英国キール大学で、第 2 回を 2004 年カナダのヴィクトリア大学、第 3 回を 2006 年オーストラリアのメルボルン、第 4 回大会を 2010 年にシンガポールで開催している。次回は、是非、日本でと期待されている。

本書には、米国の Generations United の代表幹事である Donna Butts 氏が、「世界標準としての世代間交流への理論と実践に関する寄稿」、スウェーデンのAnn Kristin-Bostrom 氏は「世代間学習とウェルビーイング」、ジョンズ・ホプキンス大学でエクスピリエンス・コア・プログラムを実践している Michelle Carlson 氏ほかの「神経認知的な健康の促進と加齢に対する『世代性的』介入プログラム：Experience Corps」、米国ペンシルヴァニア州立大学医学部のDaniel George 氏の「高齢者・認知症にやさしい都市への運動： 世代間交流の欠落と『世代間交流性的』機会」、米国テンプル大学で永年、世代間交流学習センター所長を務め現在、GU 理事である Nancy Henkin 氏による「世代間の共感を醸成する：エイジズムを克服し、世代間理解を強化すめるための戦略」、香港の Alan Lai 氏による「世代間交流ＥＳＬ活動：教訓とそれに対応する活動」、米国ハワイ元チャミネード大学教授 Mae Menderson 氏による「米国の格差を破壊する：パーソナルエッセイ」、スペイングラナダ大学の Pablo Galindo-Calvo 氏らによる「世代間交流がもたらす今日的課題とは」、シンガポール国立大学の Leng Leng Thang 氏による「世代間のつながりの促進と世

代間の接触空間（ICZ）の創造」、英国の Alan Hatton-Yao 氏による「年齢に
やさしいコミュニティー：つながりが強い世代間交流社会への戦略的アプロー
チ」、米国の認知症研究の権威であり、世代間交流学校を経営している Peter
Whitehouse 氏らによる「国際的世代間交流学校：年齢を超えた分かち合い」
など、海外で、世代間交流の研究や実践において先駆的に活躍している方たち
からの、まさに先見性のある示唆に富んだ論文が、盛りだくさん折り込まれて
いる。

　現在、重要なのは、高齢者が地域に積極的に関わり、子どもや若者、中年世
代の生活に有意義な貢献をするため、どの程度十分な機会があるのかという点
である。増え続ける高齢者が社会の向上に貢献する方法を考える際、日本で今、
世代間交流活動が盛んになりつつあることは心強いことである。「世代間交流
プログラム」とは、現在、ICIP によると、「高齢者と若者世代の間に意図的・
継続的な資源の交換と学習を創り出す社会的媒体」である。これには、学校、
保育園・幼稚園、地域社会、施設、病院などをはじめ、さまざまな場で見られ
るプログラムや実践が含まれる。世代間交流を目指すプログラムや方策が、高
齢者福祉と子育て支援の両方のニーズへの対応、教育制度の補強、高齢者の生
活の質の向上、祖父母と孫との関係の改善、文化遺産に対する人々の意識の向
上、地域の支援体制の強化を促す有効な手段となるのである。

　世代をつなぎ地域を再生するために、関連する社会問題への対応とすべての
世代の生活全般の質の向上のために、幅広い世代間交流プログラムが国内外で
実施され、さらに将来への、一段とした弾みとなっていってほしいものである。
日本では非常に革新的かつ精力的な世代間交流プログラムが実施されてきてお
り、生涯を通じて人々を支え、地域を力づけ、長年大切にされてきた文化的伝
統を守るために寄与していくことを切に期待する。

草野　篤子

引用文献

はじめに vii

Newman S., Creating an "International Consortium for Intergenerational Programs",
pp.263-272, Kaplan M. Henkin N. Kusano A., Linking Generations-A Global View of Intergenerational Exchange, 2002, University Press of America
サリー・ニューマン、国際世代間交流プログラム／コンソーシアムの創設、マシュー・カ
プラン、ナンシー・ヘンケン、草野篤子編著・監修、加藤澄訳、グローバル化時代を生き
る世代間交流、2008　明石書店

Preface

This year has become a distinguished one for the intergenerational research and practice field in Japan. When we look back at the nation-wide intergenerational situation in Japan, Dr. Sally Newman, professor Emeritus of the University of Pittsburg came to Japan in March, 2003 and held a study meeting with colleagues interested in intergenerational theories and practices. People who gathered at the meeting organized another conference and a symposium at Shinshu University and Jissen University in November in the same year. Those people organized a research group called "Joyful Generations" and established the Japan Intergenerational Unity Association in Sep of 2004. After that, JIUA became a non-profit organization in May of 2006. In the end of July and the beginning of August of the same year, JIUA, Penn State, Japan Foundation, Center for Global Partnership and Shinshu University held an international conference called "Uniting the Generations: Japan Conference to Promote Intergenerational Programs and Practices" and a post session called "International Academic Meeting on Intergenerational Issues and Initiatives."

While there was much grassroots progress with intergenerational practices emerging throughout Japan, there was limited attention to the construction and the development of intergenerational theories. On the sixth of July in 2010," The Japan Society for Intergenerational Studies (JSIS)" was established after a number of preparation meetings.

Usually it is said that it takes more than a decade or so to be admitted to be a member of Japan Academic Committee, but our JSIS was admitted in five years or so. This is probably, because of the urgent needs of intergenerational studies in recent times. It is our supreme pleasure to respond to the need for further theory construction and for continued work in developing new and effective intergenerational practices tailored to address societal needs.

While we pay attention to international intergenerational exchanges, we cannot underestimate the role of organizations such as the "International Consortium for Intergenerational Programs (ICIP), "Generations United (GU) in the United States, and "European Mapping of Intergenerational Learning" in Europe.

Since the establishment of ICIP is not known in Japan by any means, I would like to tell a little bit more in detail by following the article of Dr. Sally Newman in a book "Linking Lifetimes; A Global View of Intergenerational Exchange" edited by Matthew Kaplan, Nancy Henkin and Atsuko Kusano.

Throughout the world, in countries with many differing economic and political infrastructures, there are common challenges: changing social structures, shifting roles within families, and the differing needs of generations represent some of these challenges. Of par-

Preface ix

ticular interest to the intergenerational field in this time of challenge is the dramatic and rapidly altering roles of older adults and children in many countries of the world.

In April 1999, in response to perceptions of this malaise, a group of human service leaders representing UNESCO, Europe, Asia, Africa, and North America gathered at Haus Bommerholz, of the University of Dortmund, Germany, to discuss intergenerational solutions to some of the universal issues and problems affecting the two generations at the opposite ends of the human continuum. Their discussion led to the organization, in Vaals, of the First International Conference on Intergenerational Programs to Promote Social Change. Participants in both the Haus Bommerholz Working Meeting and the Vaals Conference acknowledged the importance of creating a formal organization that would give universal credibility to international intergenerational initiatives. Such an organization would provide both a framework for communication about diverse intergenerational initiatives and impetus for the generation of such initiatives. This consensus was the genesis of "the International Consortium for Intergenerational Programs," an intergenerational organization designed to promote intergenerational programs and practices as an agent for global social change.

From ten countries, 25 persons came together at Haus Bommerholz, University of Dortmund, Germany for three days to address both philosophical and practical questions related to intergenerational programs as a concept and a realistic solution to some issues confronting their young and old. The group faced two basic challenges: Could a group of strangers from different nations, cultures and political systems reach consensus on a process to promote social change? And if they could, what strategies would be needed to form a partnership that could effectively use intergenerational concepts and programs to achieve the desired social change?

The host in Bommerholz, Ludger Veelken of Dortmund University, and planning team member Sally Newman of the University of Pittsburgh, led the group in a three-day process that helped the group reach consensus in addressing these questions.

The first task was to discuss the theory and the rational for intergenerational programs and to develop a global definition that would reflect common values, extend beyond national boundaries, and function as the basis for further communication and exchange. From this discussion emerged a global mission statement able to accommodate nations with diverse needs, cultures, and social structures:

"Intergenerational programs are social vehicles that create purposeful and ongoing exchange of resources and learning among older and younger generations."

In examining the elements common to the participating countries, the attendees observed several shared social issues that, irrespective of differences in languages, culture or level of infrastructure, might be effectively addressed by intergenerational initiatives. This includes the following issues – social disconnection and isolation, and inadequate employment opportunities. Some of these issues are evident within the United States, Japan, and the U.K. and relate to their nationals, while in Central Europe these same issues relate to immigrants who are becoming integrated into the cultures of their new countries.

After that, international conferences were held in Keele University in England in 2002, in Victoria University in British Columbia, Canada in 2004, in Victoria University in Melbourne, Australia in 2006, and in Singapore in 2010 by the strong effort of Dr. Leng Leng Thang. Some people expect the next one will be in Japan.

This book consists of articles not only written by Japanese authors, but also from 11 scholars from the U.S., England, Spain, Sweden, China and Singapore who bring new theories, aspects, ideas and practices for our deliberation.

Donna Butts, the executive director of the Generations United from the U.S. has written "Contribution to the Theory and Practices of the Intergenerational Exchange as the World Standard", Ann-Kristin Bostrom, a researcher at Jonkoping University in Sweden has written "Intergenerational Learning and Wellbeing", Michelle Carlson, a professor at Johns Hopkins University, and colleagues authored "Designing Generative Intervention to Promote Neuro-Cognitive Health and his Aging : Experience Corps", Daniel George, an associate professor at Pennsylvania State University, wrote "The Age-and-Dementia -friendly cities" 'Movement: Intergenerational Omissions and Intergenerative Opportunities", Nancy Henkin, ex-director of Center for Intergenerational Learning of Temple University and a board member of G.U. from the U.S. talked about "Cultivating Intergenerational Empathy: A Strategy for Combatting Ageism and Strengthening Intergenerational Understanding", Alan Lai, an associate professor of applied psychology at BNU-HKBU United International College of Hong Kong in China, has written "Intergenerational –ESL Activities: Lessons Learned and Corresponding Actions", Mae Mendelson, Ex-Professor of Chaminade University in Hawaii, wrote "Disrupting Inequality in the United States: a Personal Essay", Pablo Galindo-Calvo an associate professor of Granada University from Spain and his colleague wrote "The Challenge Posed by Intergenerational Relationships Today", Leng Leng Thang, associate professor in the Department of Japanese Studies at the National University of Singapore, wrote about "Promoting Intergenerational Connection and the Creation of Intergenerational Contact Zone (ICZ)", Alan Hatton-Yao, Strategic Development Manager for Volunteering Matters Wales, has written "Age Friendly Communities: A Strategic Approach to a Connected Intergenerational Society", and Peter Whitehouse, a founder of Intergenerational schools and professor of neurology at Case Western Reserve University in the U.S., and his colleagues wrote "Intergenerational Schools International: Sharing Across the Ages."

Atsuko Kusano

CONTENTS

Preface

Atsuko Kusano ············· i

Abstract in English ········viii

Part 1　Messages from the World

Chapter 1　Contribution to The Theory and Practices of
Intergenerational Exchanges as the World Standard

Donna Butts··················· 2

Abstract in Japanese ········10

Chapter 2　Intergenerational Learning and Wellbeing

Ann-Kristin Bostrom ········14

Abstract in Japanese ········26

Chapter 3　Designing Generative Interventions to Promote Neuro-
Cognitive Health and Aging: Experience Corps®

Michelle C. Carlson, Linda P. Fried, George W. Rebok ···31

Abstract in Japanese ···········44

Chapter 4　The 'Age- and Dementia-Friendly Cities' Movement:
Intergenerational Omissions and Intergenerative Opportunities

Daniel George ················47

Abstract in Japanese ········59

Chapter 5　Cultivating Generational Empathy:
A Strategy for Combatting Ageism and Strengthening
Intergenerational Understanding

Nancy Henkin ···············62

Abstract in Japanese ········74

Chapter 6　Intergenerational-ESL Activities:
Lessons Learned and Corresponding Actions

Alan Lai ·····················77

Abstract in Japanese ········93

Chapter 7　Disrupting Inequality in the United States:
A Personal Essay

Maeona Mendelson············99

Abstract in Japanese ····· 105

Chapter 8　The Challenge posed by Intergenerational Relationships
Today

Pablo Galindo-Calvo, Mariano Sánchez-Martínez ····· 108

Abstract in Japanese ································· 119

Chapter 9　Promoting Intergenerational Connection and the Creation
of Intergenerational Contact Zone (ICZ)

Leng Leng Than············ 126

Abstract in Japanese ····· 133

Chapter 10　Age Friendly Communities:
A Strategic Approach to a Connected Intergenerational
Society?

Alan Hatton-Yao············ 136

Abstract in Japanese ····· 141

Chapter 11　Intergenerational Schools International:
Sharing across the Ages

Peter Whitehouse, Yachneet Pushkarna,

Qinghong Wei, Richard Owen Geer············· 144

Abstract in Japanese ································· 154

目　次

はじめに

　　　　　　　　　　草野篤子 ……………………… i

　　　　　　　　　　要約（英語）…………………… viii

第1部　世界からのメッセージ

第1章　世界標準としての世代間交流の理論と実践に関する寄稿

　　　　　　　　　　ドナ・バッツ ………………… 2

　　　　　　　　　　要約（日本語）……………… 10

第2章　世代間学習とウェルビーイング

　　　　　　　　　　アン‑クリスティン・ボストロム ……………… 14

　　　　　　　　　　要約（日本語）……………… 26

第3章　神経認知的な健康の促進と加齢に対する「世代性的」介入プログラム：Experience Corps®

　　　　ミッシェル・C・カールソン、リンダ・P・フリード

　　　　　　　　　　ジョージ・W・リボック ……………… 31

　　　　　　　　　　要約（日本語）……………… 44

第4章　高齢者・認知症にやさしい都市への運動：世代間交流の欠落と「世代間交流性的」機会

　　　　　　　　　　ダニエル・R・ジョージ ………… 47

　　　　　　　　　　要約（日本語）……………… 59

第5章　世代間の共感を醸成する：エイジズムを克服し、世代間理解を強化するための戦略

　　　　　　　　　　ナンシー・Z・ヘンケン ………… 62

　　　　　　　　　　要約（日本語）……………… 74

第6章　世代間 ESL 活動：教訓とそれに対応する活動

アラン・レイ　……………………77

要約（日本語）……………………93

第7章　米国の格差を破壊する：パーソナルエッセイ

メイ・メンダーソン　……………………99

要約（日本語）……………… 105

第8章　世代間交流がもたらす今日的課題とは

パブロ・ガリンド・カルボ、

マリアーノ・サンチェス・マルティネス　……………… 108

要約（日本語）……………… 119

第9章　世代間のつながりの促進と世代間の接触空間 (ICZ) の創造

リン・リン・タン　……………… 126

要約（日本語）……………… 133

第10章　年齢にやさしいコミュニティ：つながりが強い世代間交流社会への戦略的アプローチ

アラン・ハットン・ヤオ　……………… 136

要約（日本語）……………… 141

第11章　国際的世代間交流学校：年齢を超えた分かち合い

ピーター・ホワイトハウス、ヤクニー・パッシュカーナ

クインホン・ウエイ、リチャード・オーウェン・ギア　……………… 144

要約（日本語）……………… 154

第2部　世界へのメッセージ

第1章　現下の社会保障としての世代間交流
──「社会」をつくる「学び」の観点から

牧野　篤　…………… 160

要約（英語）…………… 167

第2章　世代間交流学とエリクソン及びヴィゴツキーの概念
──「第9段階」及び「他者」概念の考察を通して

佐々木　剛・草野　篤子　…………… 168

要約（英語）…………… 176

第3章　伝統文化の世代継承に対する世代間交流学からのアプローチ

内田　勇人　…………… 177

要約（英語）…………… 184

第4章　都市部の新規分譲集合住宅における多世代交流プログラム導入の試み

高橋　和也　…………… 186

要約（英語）…………… 193

第5章　高齢者ボランティア活動によるソーシャルキャピタル醸成に関する日米比較
──REPRINTS と Experience Corps の比較より

安永　正史　…………… 195

要約（英語）…………… 202

第6章　高齢者を取り巻くシームレスな世代間交流

藤原　佳典　…………… 203

要約（英語）…………… 219

第7章　子どもとふれ合うことによる高齢者の感情体験

村山　陽　…………… 220

xvi

要約（英語）………………… 233

第8章　リ・ラーニングをひらく学校

溝邊　和成　……………… 234

要約（英語）……………… 244

おわりに

（溝邊和成）　……………… 246

要約（英語）……………… 250

Part 2　Messages to the World

Chapter 1　Intergenerational Interaction as Current Social Security: From the Perspective of "Learning" that Builds "Society"

Atsushi Makino　………… 160

Abstract in English　…… 167

Chapter 2　Discussion of Intergenerational Studies and the Concepts of Erikson's "Ninth Stage", and Vygotsky's "More Knowledgeable Others"

Tsuyoshi Sasaki and Atsuko Kusano … 168

Abstract in English……………… 176

Chapter 3　Approach from Intergenerational Studies for the Succession of Traditional Culture

Hayato Uchida…………… 177

Abstract in English　…… 184

Chapter 4　A Trial of Intergenerational Exchange Programs Introduced in the newly Developed Collective Housing in an Urban City

Tomoya Takahashi……… 186

Abstract in English ⋯⋯ 193

Chapter 5 **Comparison between Japan and the US on Social Capital Fostering through Elderly Volunteer Activities: Comparison between REPRINTS and Experience Corps**

Masashi Yasunaga ⋯⋯⋯ 195

Abstract in English ⋯⋯ 202

Chapter 6 **Seamless Social Participation and Intergenerational Relationships for the Elderly: A Viewpoint from Multiple Support System in Accordance with One's Life Course**

Yoshinori Fujiwara⋯⋯⋯ 203

Abstract in English ⋯⋯ 219

Chapter 7 **Emotional Experiences of Elderly through Intergenerartional Exchange with Children**

Yoh Murayama ⋯⋯⋯⋯ 220

Abstract in English ⋯⋯ 233

Chapter 8 **Re-Learning System for the Elderly in the Elementary/ Junior High School**

Kazushige Mizobe ⋯⋯⋯ 234

Abstract in English ⋯⋯ 244

Afterword

Kazushige Mizobe ⋯⋯⋯ 246

Abstract in English ⋯⋯ 250

第１部

Part 1

世界からのメッセージ

Messages from the World

Chapter 1

Contribution to The Theory and Practices of Intergenerational Exchanges as the World Standard

Donna M. Butts

1. Abstract

America's changing demographics raise concerns about the strain on public systems. As the population ages, some view longer life as a burden taxing pensions, Social Security and health care delivery. With the growing racial and ethnic diversity of the younger population, some express concern about overtaxing public education and the ability to absorb a younger, diverse workforce. Rather than focusing on burden, societies would be better served shifting the conversation to benefit. The duel changing demographics are, in fact, America's greatest asset. This paper will touch on those demographics and explore the key role intergenerational exchanges, structured and unstructured, play in strengthening the commitment between generations.

2. America's Changing Demographics

Americans are living longer and healthier lives. By 2043, one in five U.S. residents will be age 65 or older. At the same time, the younger population is becoming more racially and ethnically diverse. By 2042, more than half of the nation will be people of color. This points to the potential for a growing racial and generational gap. Today, more than half of Americans under the age of five are people of color compared to less than one in five Americans over 65. (Generations United & the Generations Initiative, 2013)

The country is "age advantaged" which bodes well for its future. While America's aging population increases, its younger generations continue to grow and come of working age. With the right investments and encouragement, this younger cohort will contribute to their communities' economic health and well-being. At the same time, as the population ages the country needs to harness the life-stage appropriate capabilities and goals of people in later life, recognizing that investments across the full lifespan can pay dividends. (Rowe, 2015) The generations, however diverse, are interconnected. Those connections should be reinforced whenever possible in order all ages to survive and thrive.

3. Concern about Fragmentation and Social Isolation across Generations

The population is becoming more fragmented with housing, recreation and social service delivery often age-based and therefore age segregated. Anthropologist Margaret Mead said "If you associate enough with older people who do enjoy their lives, who are not stored away in any golden ghetto, you will gain a sense of continuity and the possibility for a full life." By creating artificial 55+ communities, the so called Grandparent Advantage has been lost. Instead the recycled knowledge, wisdom and culture is passed on not to the next generation but contained within a monochromatic age group. For example, a recent newspaper story described a gated senior-only housing community whose residents benefitted from their highly accomplished neighbors. A regular lecture series fueled by former professors and successful business people provided stimulating learning and discussion opportunities for the community. But only among the community members.

They were sorely lacking the opinion and voice of other ages and missing the opportunity to pass their learning to the next generation.

The same is true for most schools which are divided into grades based on age and infrequently benefit from older adult volunteers or oral histories. When elders are in the classroom they become not just mentors or tutors but time tellers and witnesses to the history lessons that are taught.

Age isolation is increasing at the same time there is a growing concern about social isolation among older adults, children and youth. At the 2015 Generations United International Conference, Dr. Robert Putnam spoke about poor kids in America saying social isolation is the most fundamental feature of their lives leading to a lack of savvy and the "airbag" protection they need to grow up to be healthy, contributing adults. (Putnam, 2015) Without that extended network of caring adults, they may face a dead-end instead of a step up when they need doors opened.

Among older adults, perceived social isolation or loneliness is linked to increased risk of chronic disease and mortality. (Lahey & Lahey, 2015) Technology-based solutions such as remote monitoring, social media and robots have been deployed in an attempt to find ways to increase social inclusion for homebound seniors and those hoping to age in place. However, nothing seems to top in-person social contact with friends and family as a preventive strategy for older adult depression. This includes friends of all ages.

Intergenerational solutions can and should play a prominent role in connecting generations to the betterment of each age group providing purpose and protection.

4. Intergenerational Programs Promote Exchange

Over the past 50 years, the concept of intentionally bringing generations together to serve as resources to each other and to their communities has become increasingly popular as a vehicle for addressing critical societal needs and strengthening cross-age relationships. Beginning with the Foster Grandparent and Retired Senior Volunteer (RSVP) Programs in the 1960's, early intergenerational programs focused primarily on dispelling age-related stereotypes, fostering cross-age understanding, reducing social isolation, and providing financial support for low-income elders. (Kaplan, Henkin & Kusano, 2002)

As interest in intergenerational solutions increased, they were generally categorized by direction of service. These are described as follows:

- Young Serving Old: Friendly visiting in homes or senior living facilities; home services; teaching computer skills or English as a second language; delivering meals to homebound elders and service learning projects such as oral histories.
- Older Adults Serving the Young: Mentoring programs; childcare centers with older adult staff or volunteers; teen parenting guidance; tutoring and vaccination education.
- Older Adults and the Young Serving Together: Performing/visual arts programs; family support programs; environmental preservation, meal delivery and community service.
- Older Adults and the Young Sharing Sites: Intergenerational community centers; childcare centers in senior housing, intergenerational playgrounds and senior centers in schools and libraries. (Generations United, 2007)

When thoughtfully planned and executed, intergenerational programs benefit the participants and the greater community and promote exchange across the ages. Quality intergenerational programs share distinct character-

6

istics. They are:

- Reciprocal-each age gives and receives through the interaction.
- Respectful-valuing the strength and contribution of each generation.
- Purposeful-providing meaning for each age group.
- Intentional-thoughtfully planned with preparation and reflection allowing for mid-course corrections and celebrations.

The following example of a successful intergenerational program illustrates these qualities in action.

For 10 years, the Retired Senior Volunteer Program (RSVP) in central Texas educated and deployed older adults as childhood vaccination champions in a network of health care organizations. They focused on educating parents who did not have firsthand experience with the devastation of diseases that were now vaccine preventable. The older adult volunteers remembered and had lived through these diseases and watched their decline.

The program linked two generations – parents and older adults – to protect a third generation – children. The older volunteers educated new mothers about the importance of vaccinations and following through on all the inoculations needed for immunization. They also developed a system to follow up and remind the young parents. The program was made even stronger by its design to engage older adults of all ages and abilities. In some instances the older adults would drive the parents and children to their appointments while more frail or homebound seniors would make the follow up phone calls to the families from their homes.

The program incorporated another essential component of high quality intergenerational programs-fun. Regular recognition events were held throughout the year culminating in an annual celebration elevating the contributions and impact of the older adult volunteers. The project's results demonstrate the trifecta that can be generated by intergenerational

Chapter 1 Contribution to The Theory and Practices of Intergenerational Exchanges as the World Standard   7

solutions. In the 10 years the program operated over 250,000 infants were enrolled and 500,000 reminders were sent to parents. Ninety percent of the senior volunteers reported positive reviews of the program and their role in it. The professional medical staff, though reluctant at the beginning of the program, said they had strong positive feelings about abilities and contributions of older adults. (Dreyer & Ingman, 2004)

5. Facilitating Quality Exchange Between Generations

Policies and programs promoting sound intergenerational relations and intergenerational solidarity play an important role by promoting social cohesion, national unity and shared responsibility (Hatton-Yeo, 2002). Intergenerational programs also play a key role developing positive relationships across age groups and have been shown to strengthen the quality of ties between family members (Thang, 2006).

To be truly effective however, intergenerational exchanges need to be ongoing and not one time events. To help understand the level of encounters between generations, Dr. Matt Kaplan developed a scale that has been adapted for use by various groups implementing intergenerational programs.

The Depth of Intergenerational Engagement Continuum helps organizations and communities understand the current level of contact between generations. It ranges from learning about other generations to occasional contact to ongoing intergenerational exchange. By understanding where an activity lands on the scale, goals can be set and steps can be taken to increase engagement among and between generations. (Generations United, 2015)

8

6. Conclusion

Intergenerational cohesion is fundamental to civil societies. In order to protect and deepen the engagement and exchange among generations, policy makers, academics and other community leaders should use an intergenerational lens when planning for the future. Are all generations considered and their unique contributions included in the equation? Are resources being better used to connect generations rather than separate them? Cities, towns and villages are strengthened when the human capital asset of all ages is fully leveraged. Combining the wisdom of elders with the energy and new ideas of the young, will lead to healthier, more vibrant societies for years to come.

References

Dreyer, K. & Ingman, S. 2004. *Seniors and Volunteers for Childhood Immunization: A Generational Link Addressing a Societal Problem.* New Delhi, India: Indian Journal of Gerontology Vol.18 Nos 3&4 pp 423-431.

Generations United & The Generations Initiative. 2013. *Out of Many, One: Uniting the Changing Faces of America.* Washington, DC: Generations United and The Generations Initiative.

Generations United. (2002). *The Benefits of Intergenerational Programs.* Washington, DC: Generations United.

Generations United. (2015). *Creating An Age-Advantaged Community: A Toolkit for building Intergenerational Communities that Recognize, Engage and Support All Ages.* Washington, DC: Generations United.

Hatton-Yeo, A. (2002). *Connecting Generations—A Global Perspective.* International Consortium of Intergenerational Programmes International Conference. Keel University, England. p.19.

Kaplan M., Henkin N., & Kusano, A. (2002). *Linking Lifetimes: A Global View of Intergenerational Exchange.* Lanham: University Press of America.

Lahey, J. & Lahey, T. 2015. *How Lonliness Wears on the Body.* http://www.theatlantic.com/health/archive/2015/12/loneliness-social-isolation-and-health/418395/?utm_source=SFTwitter accessed 1 2 2016

Putnam, R.D. 2015. *Our Kids The American Dream in Crisis.* New York: Simon & Shuster.

Rowe, J.W. (2015). *Successful Aging of Societies.* Cambridge, MA. Daedalous Journal of the American Academy of Arts & Sciences. Vol144 No2 pp 5-12.

Teo, A.R., et all. (2015). *Does Mode of Contact with Different Types of Social Relationships Predict Depression in Older Adults? Evidence from a Nationally Representative Survey.* Journal of the American Geriatrics Society. Vol63 No10 pp 2014-2022.

Thang, L.L. (2006) *The Necessary Connection: Intergenerational programmes in the context of Singapore.* IMEMGS Research Paper Series, 1. Tokorozawa: Institute for Multi-ethnic and Multi-generational Societies, Waseda University.

第1章　世界標準としての世代間交流の理論と
　　　　 実践に関する寄稿

ドナ・M・バッツ

1．アブストラクト

　アメリカの変わりつつある人口統計学は公共システムの負担について考えを挙げている。人口の高齢化にともない、いくつかの視点として、課税年金の負担、社会保障と健康ケアの受け渡しがある。若年世代人口の人種や民族の差異の増加に伴って、公教育を酷使することや若くて差異のある被雇用者集団を吸収する能力について考える主張もある。負担に焦点を当てることよりもむしろ、社会は利益についての話にシフトする方が良いであろう。変わりつつある人口統計学の決闘は、実際、アメリカのもっとも優れた強みなのだ。この論文はこうした人口統計学に触れ、世代間交流のもっとも重要となる役割を調査し、世代間のかかわり合いを強固にしていくだろう。

2．アメリカの変わりつつある人口統計学

　アメリカ人はより長くより健康に生活している。2043 年にはアメリカ在住者の五分の一が 65 歳以上になる。同時に、若年層はより人種的民族的差異が大きくなる。2042 年には国民の半分以上が有色人種となる。これは人種的そして世代間的ギャップを大きくする可能性を指摘している。今日、5 歳以下のアメリカ人の半数以上が有色人種で、65 歳以上のアメリカ人と比較すると五分の一に満たない。(Generations United & the generations Initiative, 2013)

　この国は "の国は "rations Uni であり、その未来の前兆となる。アメリカの加齢人口の増加の一方で、若年の人口は増加しつづけ、働き盛りの世代となる。正確な投資と奨励を以て、この若年者集団は彼らのコミュニティの経済的安定と福利に貢献する。同時に、国がライフステージでの相応しい能力と人生の後半にある人々の目的を利用することを必要とする世代の人口として、全人生を越えての投資という認識が分け前を払いうるのだ。(Rowe, 2015)この世代、しかしながら差異は、相互に連絡しあう。こうした連絡がすべての世代が生き残り成長していくためにいつでも可能であることを補強する。

3．世代を越えた分裂状態と社会の孤立について考える

　人口は住宅、レクリエーション、そして社会サービスデリバリーからより分離されるようになり、それゆえ世代が分裂される。人類学者の Margaret Mead はこう述べている。「もし

第1章　世界基準としての世代間交流の理論と実践に関する寄稿　11

人生を全うし、golden ghetto にしまいこまれていない老人と十分に関わると、全人生の連続性や可能性の感覚を得ることができるだろう」人工的に 55 歳以上のコミュニティを作ると、Grandparent Advantage は失われる。そのかわりに再生利用される知識、知恵、文化は次世代につたえるだけではなく単調な世代グループを含む。例えば、最近の新聞記事はかなり熟練した隣人から利益を得た住居をもつ a gated senior-only housing community について述べている。通常のレクチャーシリーズは、非常に興味のある学びと討論の機会をコミュニティに提供した先の専門家や成功したビジネスマンによって動いた。しかしそれはコミュニティのメンバーだけに限ったことだ。彼らは痛ましいほど意見やほかの世代の声に欠落していて、彼らの学びを次世代に伝える機会に乏しかった。

　ほとんどの学校でも同様に年代に基づいて級を分け、まれに高齢者ボランティアや口述歴史史料の恩恵をうける。高齢者が教室にいるとき、彼らは助言者やチューターだけでなく、授業で教わる歴史の語り手や目撃者となる。

　年齢の分離が増加すると同時に、高齢者や子ども、青年の社会的分離についての考えを大きくする。2015 年 Generations United International Conference では、Robert Putnam 博士がアメリカの貧しい子どもについて話し、社会的分離はもっとも基本的な彼らの人生の特徴であり、彼らが健康に成長し、貢献できる大人に育つために必要としている理解やエアーバッグ保護に欠けるというものだ（Putnam, 2015）。世話をする大人の広範囲なネットワーク無しでは、彼らはおそらくドアを開ける必要があるときにのぼるステップの代わりに限界に直面するだろう。

　高齢者のあいだでは、認知された社会的分離や孤独は慢性の病や死の危険性を高めることと直結している（Lahey & Lahcy, 2015）。遠隔監視や社会メディア、ロボットなどのような情報機器主体の解決策は、家に引きこもった高齢者やそこで年をとることを望んでいる高齢者を社会に包含することを増加させる方法を見出す試みとして配置されている。しかし、高齢者の失望を防止する計画として友人や家族と連絡を取ることに優れるものはなかった。すべての世代において友人が含まれている。

　世代間の解決策は、それぞれの世代グループが提供されている目的や保護の改善につながる世代間のかかわり合いにおいて目立った役割を果たすべきであり、果たしうる。

4．世代間プログラムは交流を促進する

　過去 50 年以上、世代それぞれの互いの、コミュニティの資源のために尽くすための故意の世代交流の概念は、ますます批判的、社会的ニーズを話すことや世代間の関係を強化するための乗り物として人気になっている。1960 年代の里親の祖父母や定年退職した高齢者ボランティアプログラムに始まり、初期の世代間プログラムは主として、年齢による固定観念を晴らすこと、年代を越えた理解を育成すること、社会的孤独を減らすこと、そして低所得の高齢者への福祉的サポートを供給することに焦点を当てた。（Kaplan, Henkin & Kusano, 2002）

12

　世代間の解決策の増加に興味をもつにつれて、それらはサービスの方向性によってカテゴリーに分けられた。以下の通りである。

・若者は高齢者に尽くす：親切に家を訪れたり居住施設を訪れること；家事サービス；コンピュータ技術を教えたり第二外国語として英語を教えたりすること；引きこもりの高齢者に食事を宅配し、口述史料のような学習プロジェクトサービス

・高齢者は若者に尽くす：プログラムを助言すること；高齢者やボランティアスタッフを伴った託児施設；10代への親になることについてのガイダンス；ワクチン予防接種教育のチューター

・高齢者と若者が共に尽くす：演じることや視覚芸術のプログラム；家族サポートプログラム；環境維持；食事配達やコミュニティサービス

・高齢者と若者が場所を共有する：世代間コミュニティセンター；シニアハウスでの託児センター；世代間活動場や学校、図書館でのシニアセンター（Generations United, 2007）

　考え込んで計画し実行したとき、世代間プログラムは参加者やコミュニティにとって利益になり、年代を越えての交流を促進する。世代間プログラムの質ははっきりとした特徴に分けられる。それらは、

・年代が相互に触れ合いを通じて与え、与えられる。

・丁寧な提供は各年代のグループに意味がある。

・意図的に考え込んで準備しリフレクションをした計画は訂正と祝賀の中間軌道であると認める。

　次の成功した世代間プログラムの例はこれらの質を行動で示している。

　10年間、テキサス中心街の定年退職高齢者ボランティアプログラム（RSVP）は高齢者を保健組織のネットワークで幼少期ワクチン接種擁護者として教育し、動員した。彼らは、現在ではワクチンで予防できる病気の荒廃の直接経験のない両親の教育に照準をあてた。高齢者ボランティアはこうした病気を思い出し、生き延び、病気の衰退を見てきたのだ。

　プログラムは二世代―両親と高齢者―子どもたちという三代目の世代を守るために―を結合させた。高齢者ボランティアは新米の母親たちにワクチン接種の重要性やすべての予防接種が免疫のために必要であることを教えた。彼らはまた若い親をフォローし思い起こすためのシステムを発達させた。プログラムは高齢者をすべての世代や能力に従事させるためのデザインをより強いものにした。いくつかの例では、高齢者は両親や子どもたちを彼らのアポイントメントに運ぶ一方、より弱い引きこもった高齢者は自宅から家族にフォローを求める電話をした。プログラムはほかの高品質な世代間プログラムのおもしろさの重要な構成要素を合併する。通常認識されるイベントは年中行われていて、結果的に高齢者ボランティアの貢献や影響を高めている年中祝賀会になっていた。プロジェクトの結果は世代間解決策によって生み出される三連単を証明する。10年間でプログラムは行われ、250,000人以上の幼児が登録され、500,000ものリマインダーが両親に送られた。90パーセントの高齢者ボランティアがプログラムと自身の役割について肯定的なレビューを報告した。医療の専門家は、プログラムの初期は乗り気でなかったけれど、彼らが高齢者の能力や貢献について強い肯定

的感覚をもった。（Dreyer & Ingman, 2004）

5．世代間の交流の質を促進すること

世代間の関係性と世代間の団結を促進するような政策やプログラムは、社会的つながりを促進すること、国の調和や共有された責任によって重要な役割を果たす。（Hatton-Yeo, 2002）世代間のプログラムはまた年代のグループを越えた肯定的な関係性を発達させるうえで重要な役割を果たしており、家族間のつながりの質を強化することも示している。（Thang, 2006）

しかしながら実に効果的に、世代間交流は進行し、一回きりのイベントであってはならない必要がある。世代間の体験レベルを理解することを助けるために、Matt Kaplan博士は世代間プログラムを実行しているさまざまなグループによって使用のために適合させている規模を発達させた。

世代間契約の連続体の深さは組織やコミュニティに最近の世代間の接触の度合いを理解することを助ける。それはほかの世代について学ぶことから時々の進行している世代間交流へ及ぶ。活動がその規模に着陸するところを理解することによって、目標は設定され、世代間の契約を増加させるステップが取られる。（Generations United, 2015）

6．まとめ

世代間のつながりは一般社会において必須である。世代間の契約と交流を守り、深くしていくために、政策を作る人、大学機関やほかのコミュニティは未来を計画するときに世代間のレンズを使うべきだ。すべての世代は相関関係に含まれる独自の貢献を考えているだろうか？よりよく使われる資源は世代をつなぐよりむしろ分けていないか？市町村はすべての世代の人間の主な強みが十分に影響するとき、強固なものになる。高齢者の知恵を熱意とともに合併させることと若者の新しい考えはより健康で、活気に満ちた社会が何年もくることにつながるだろう。

Chapter 2
Intergenerational Learning and Wellbeing
Ann-Kristin Boström

1. Introduction

This chapter will discuss a possible model for the relationship between intergenerational learning, wellbeing and social capital. In this context the article will deal with intergenerational learning as defined as a learning taking place between different generations which involves benefits in terms of possible increased social capital for all parts involved. The model as well incorporates the concept of lifelong learning. As social capital is sometimes described in relation to wellbeing and quality of life, the chapter sets out to clarify this connection and this will be included in the model.

2. Lifelong learning and social capital

Cropley introduced a model of lifelong learning in 1980. His model included an aspect of learning which takes place "from the cradle to the grave", as a lifelong process, and life-wide learning that included the aspects of formal, non-formal and informal learning. A historic perspective of Lifelong learning is referred to by Tuijnman and Boström (2002). Social capital is included in the model (Boström, 2014), see figure 1. The definition of social capital that will be used in this chapter is Coleman's (1988:98) where he describes that social capital is composed of several entities and involves individuals working together, trusting each other, having good communication between each other, share their values and are working towards the same goal. He argues

Chapter 2 Intergenerational Learning and Wellbeing   15

that social capital is a compilation of various components that have the following in common: they consist of some form of social structure, they facilitate certain aspects of social structures and they facilitate certain responses
on the part of various actors within the structure. These three entities consist of:

The level of *confidence and trust*, which is found in the actual social environment

The second entity consists of those *information channels*, which are
found there, and how information is passed between actors

The third entity are the *shared norms and structures* that are found
when people are working towards the same goal, when they are doing
this on the basis of common, unselfish interests. (1988:98)

Intergenerational learning is a form of lifelong learning as it is a learning
taking place between different generations. Learning of attitudes and values
in these relationships between younger and older persons or vice versa is
a form of informal learning. Informal learning is also taking place in formal
settings, as in adult education. The entities of social capital are therefore included in the lifelong/life-wide learning model (see figure 1). One researcher
who has studied these entities in depth is Fukuyama (2000). He discussed
values and trust and he described both formal values and informal values.
Formal values are the values that are decided by law and regulations in a
society, while informal values are the values that you find in every society
as the attitudes, codes and acceptance of how people should behave towards
each other. In figure 1 the continuum of values are included in the model of
lifelong learning. The arrows included in the model represent other entities
of social capital; communication between individuals, relationships and trust.
Thus, this can represent a model of intergenerational learning as these enti-

ties of social capital are working in a context where young and old people meet. This can happen in a school setting where older people work as a benefit for young students, but can also take place in adult education when young teachers and older students meet. The model shows that intergenerational learning depends on the shared values and attitudes and is therefore cultural bounded to the context in the community and specific country depending on local culture and historic background and the values and attitudes developed out of this. The model has shown a possibility to create social capital in a programme called class granddads in school. The work of the class granddad (Boström 2002, 2003, 2009) consists of many different parts. The pupils most often refer to the fact that he talks to the children and comforts them when this is needed (*communication* = a part of social

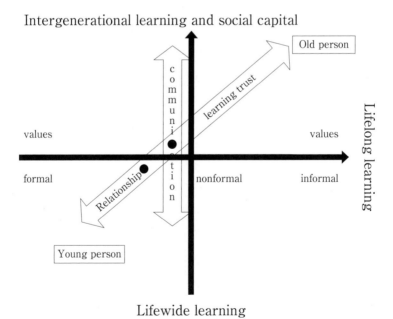

Figure 1. Developed from Boström, 2002,2014. Social capital included in the lifelong/lifewide model

Chapter 2 Intergenerational Learning and Wellbeing   17

capital), that he assists everyone (*security, trust* = a part of social capital) and that he sets limits for what is allowed (*norms and structure* = a part of social capital). In other words, the work of the class granddad contains all the parts that constitute social capital, according to Coleman's definition (Coleman, 1988:98). The work of the class granddad, both together with the teacher and outside during the breaks, also influences in a positive way, the social capital between the pupils and the teacher which contributes to both intergenerational solidarity and community development.

3. Quality in life and happiness

Quality in life has been used since the 1990s. In Sweden the concept was explicitly used in a study by Bang (1995). This study dealt with retirement and quality of life. Network and health were found to be the most important dimensions for the people in the Malmö longitudinal study in this qualitative study. Almost at the same time the Division of mental Health and prevention of substance abuse (World Health Organisation 1997) developed a program on mental health. The goal was to measure Quality in Life, a definition was needed and resulted in the following:

"WHO defines Quality of life as individual's perception of their position in life in the context of the culture and value systems in which they live and in relation to their goals, expectations, standards and concerns. It is a broad ranging concept affected in a complex way by the person's physical health, psychological state, level of independence, social relationships, personal beliefs and their relationship to salient features of their environment."p.1

WHO was also responsible for the construction of a tool for measuring overall quality of life and general health. There were indicators constructed

18

for six areas: Physical health, Psychological, level of independence, social relationships, environment and spirituality in the form of religion and personal beliefs developed from the definition. Relationship to other people was stressed as important in this tool.

Another way to measure the wellbeing is made by the World Happiness report (Helliwell, Layard and Sachs, 2013). They are using the word "happiness" to measure how people rate both their emotions and their lives as a whole. They found that mental illness is the single most important cause of unhappiness. They are also looking at the many beneficial consequences of wellbeing rather than its cause. The report gives evidence for that people who are emotionally happy, who have a more satisfying life and who live in happier communities are more likely both now and later to be healthy, productive and socially connected. Also here we can see the importance of social relationships. Having supportive relationships boosts subjective wellbeing. Having high subjective wellbeing leads to better social relationships so happiness increases a person's level of sociability and improves the quality of social interactions. Although high subjective wellbeing can help people function better, it does not solve everything. Happiness is like any other factor that adds health and functioning. Many other factors such as personality, intelligence and social capital are also important for good functioning

4. Social thinking

We receive social rewards when others let us know they like, respect, or care for us as well as when we care for others (Lieberman 2013). The capacity for mindreading allows us to consider the goals, intentions, emotions and beliefs of others. In all cases the neuropeptide oxytocin is a criti-

Chapter 2 Intergenerational Learning and Wellbeing   19

cal driver of our caregiving motivations. Within the brain's reward system, oxytocin also motivates within the brain's reward system and it diminishes the personal distress we ordinary feel of approaching someone else in distress. Being cared for promotes opioid-based pleasure processes in the brain. Lieberman (2013) expressed the fact that our social imagination is processed via the mentalizing system, primarily in the dorsomedial prefrontal cortex and the tempoarietal junction. Even though social and nonsocial thinking are structurally and experimentally similar, the brain handles these two kinds of thinking using very different neural systems. Heightened activity in the regions of the brain involved in working memory, nonsocial reasoning and fluid intelligence are almost never observed in studies of social thinking.

5. A model for social capital and wellbeing

Recently wellbeing has been used in policy when trying to measure and compare societies. To be able to do this there have been needs for indicators that have been used in several policy sectors as health care, public health, social services, parks and recreation, work life, transportation families and the environment. Diener (2005) have been working with indicators for wellbeing. He argues that they are not exact but they are useful and they fulfill a need. He means that individual's personal subjective wellbeing can have an impact of society as a whole. The definition of subjective wellbeing according to Diener (2005) is:

Subjective wellbeing refers to all of the various types of evaluations, both positive and negative, that people make of their lives. It includes reflective cognitive evaluations, such as life satisfaction and work satisfaction, interest and engagement and affective reactions to life events, such as joy and sadness.

There is also a definition of quality in life that explains the difference between the two concepts.

Quality in life usually refers to the degree to which a person's life is desirable versus undesirable, often with an emphasis on external components, such as environmental factors and income. In contrast to subjective wellbeing, which is based on subjective experience, quality of life is often expressed as more "objective" and describes the circumstances of a person's life rather than his or her reaction to those circumstances (Diener 2005).

There are several international reports that are using indicators for wellbeing. One of these is the European Quality of life survey, EQLS, (European commission, 2013). The third wave of this study was conducted during 2011-2012. The study covered 27 European Union Member states at the time of the study and seven candidate or pre-accession countries. The survey was conducted with face-to-face interviews and had representative estimates at

Wellbeing

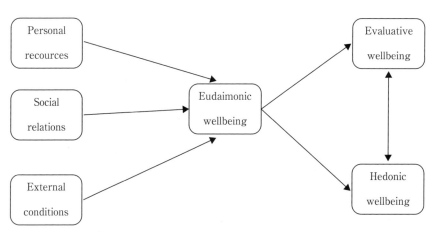

Figure 2. Adapted from Thomson and Marks 2008

the national level. It covered the population 18+. There was a need for a definition of subjective wellbeing and a framework when trying to measure the outcome of wellbeing in Europe. Subjective wellbeing in this case is referred to as "experienced wellbeing to highlight that it reflects people's experiences of their lives" p.12.

There was also need for a framework and a conceptual model and this was adapted from Thomson and Marks (2005) and is displayed in figure 2.

There are three main aspects in this model. The hedonic wellbeing refers to people's day-to-day feelings and moods. The evaluative wellbeing refers to how satisfied people are with their lives as a whole nowadays and the eudemonic wellbeing refers to concepts that are believed to be important to wellbeing. Some of these are people's sense of autonomy, relationships meaning and self-esteem. These concepts are sometimes also seen as preconditions for wellbeing. Examples of questions for these aspects are for the hedonic aspect; I have felt cheerful and in good spirits, I have felt downhearted and depressed. For the evaluative aspect the questions among other were; How satisfied are you with following items? Your education, standard

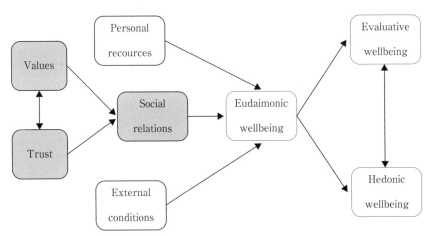

Figure 3. Social capital within the framwork of wellbeing (Boström 2014)

of living, your present job, your family life, your health, your social life? The eudaimonic aspect had the following statements that they had to consider; I am optimistic about the future; I feel I am free to decide how to live my life; I feel left out of society.

The results from the measurement of quality in life show that face-to-face contact with friends had a strong impact on wellbeing while indirect contact (by phone or e-mail) had almost no impact. The strongest predictor of wellbeing were material deprivation, health, work-life balance, lack of time, and satisfaction with public services. The predictors varied according to the measure being used. For example, the strongest predictor of loneliness was being widowed, while the strongest predictor of stress was work-life balance. The data also highlights the importance of protecting social networks and relationships.

This highlights the importance of considering the unintended social consequences associated with increasing geographical labor mobility, or the falling social cohesion and trust associated with increased inequality. Therefore the author of this article suggests an additional part in the conceptual model of measuring wellbeing (see figure 3). "Social relations" is already one part of the model and is important regarding the concept of wellbeing. Social capital as a concept involves relationships but but also values, communication and trust are important entities in this concept as a whole. If the three entities of social capital are included in the model, social capital can be part of the framework. This could place social capital in the context of wellbeing. As social capital is used (Coleman, 1988:98) within family or defined groups of agents there is a possibility to measure social capital in networks or relationships but it could also be compared in a broader perspective. This model illustrates the fact that social capital is connected to the actual context and culture. In the model the perspectives of "external conditions" and "personal resources" held by the individual represent these parts.

6. Summary

Intergenerational relationships have possibilities to increase social capital and wellbeing among the individuals from different generations that connect, meet and learn from each other. Recent research from biology show that our brains reward us for caring and being social to other people. Research from sociology show increasing social capital among those involved in intergenerational relationsships. The benefits of learning and the impact of education on health, family life and social capital is researched and the important effects of learning to self-esteem Schuller et.al (2004). Within the EQLS survey the subjective wellbeing is measured from different perspectives. Social relations are reported regarding relationships, networks, face-to-face communication and trust.

Social capital is connected to context that sets the base for what can be achieved. Personal resources and external conditions are the preconditions for the possibilities of increased social capital. This becomes even more evident in intergenerational meetings. As social capital is related to culture, intergenerational learning will be adapted differently and have different possibilities to grow in countries dependent of policies regarding volunteering, social benefits and historical background. It is important to consider that the concept of social capital and the concept of wellbeing are not the same and cannot be used interchangeably as the concepts are differently defined. Health is an important part of wellbeing but even if you are in bad health you can enjoy relationships that give you increased social capital and learning that can take place "from the cradle to the grave".

24

Happiness, quality in life and mindreading are all part of intergenerational relations.

Recent research from the areas of social thinking from biology supports research from pedagogy, psychology, andragogy that intergenerational meetings, projects, and learning between generations give the individuals involved a possibility for increased wellbeing for themselves and their relationship.

References

Bang.H. (1995). *Retirement and the quality in life*. Stockholm: Institute of international Education, Stockholm University.

Boström, A-K. (2014). Learning Across Generations in Europe: Contemporary Issues in Older Adult Education / [ed] B. Schmidt-Hertha, M. Formosa, & S. Jelenc Krasovec, Rotterdam: Sense Publishers, 2014, 191-201 s.

Boström. A-K. (2009). Social capital in intergenerational meetings in compulsory schools in Sweden. *Journal of Intergenerational relationships*, 7: 425-441.

Boström, A-K. (2003). *Lifelong learning, intergenerational learning, and social capital: From theory to practice*. Stockholm: Institute of International Education, Stockholm University.

Boström, A-K. (2002). Informal learning in a formal context: Problematizing the concept of social capital in a contemporary Swedish context. *International Journal of Lifelong Education. Volume 21*, 510-524.

Cropley, A.J. (1980). *Towards a system of lifelong education*. Oxford: Pergamon Press.

Coleman, J.S. (1988). Social capital in the creation of human capital. *American Journal of Sociology*, Vol.94, S95-S120.

European Commission (2013). *Quality of life in Europe: Subjective well-being*. Luxembourg: Publications Office of the European Union.

Diener. E. (2005). http://internal.psychology.illinois.edu/~ediener/Documents/Guidelines_for_National_Indicators.pdf, retrieved 2013.12.17.

European Commission. (2013). *Quality of life in Europe: Subjective well-being*. Luxembourg: Publication Office of the European Commission.

Fukuyama, F. (2000). *The great disruption, human nature and the reconstitution of social order*. New York: Touchstone.

Helliwell, J.,F., Layard, R., & Sachs, J.,D eds. (2013). World Happiness Report. New York: UN Sustainable Solutions Network.

Lieberman, M.,D. (2013). *Social: Why our brains are wired to connect.* New York: Broadway Books.

Schuller, T., Preston. J., Hammond.C., Brasset-Grundy.A., & Brynner. J., (2004). *The impact of education on health, family life and social capital.* London: RoutledgeFalmer.

Thompson, S. and Marks. N. (2008). Measuring well-being in policy: Issues and applications. London: nef.

Tuijnman, A., & Boström, A-K. (2002). Changing notions of lifelong education and lifelong learning. *International Review of Education,* Vol. 48, 93-110.

World Health Organization. (1997). *WHOQOL Meauring Quality of life.* Geneva: World Health Organization.

第2章　世代間学習とウェルビーイング

アン‐クリスティン・ボストロム

1．イントロダクション

　本論文は、世代間学習、ウェルビーイングと社会関係論の関係性の実行可能なモデルを論じ、その文脈において、増大した社会関係資本の観点から利益を伴う異世間で起こる学習と同じ定義として世代間学習を取り扱う。このモデルは生涯学習の概念も含む。社会関係資本はときにウェルビーイングや生活の質に関連して論じられるので、本章はこの結びつきを明らかにすることから出発し、それをモデルに含めることにする。

2．生涯学習と社会関係資本

　Cropley は、1980 年に生涯学習のモデルを紹介した。彼のモデルは、生涯過程としての「ゆりかごから墓場まで」の間に起こる学習と、公式、非公的・非公式な生涯にわたる (life-wide) 学習を論じていた。生涯学習の歴史的な観点は Tuijnman と Boström によって言及された。社会関係資本は Boström のモデル（2014）に見られる（図 1 参照）。本章で使われる社会関係資本の定義は Coleman のもの（1988-98）である。彼の定義によると、社会関係資本は、幾つかの実体（entity）からなり、ともに協力し、信頼しあい、優れたコミュニケーションを行い、価値観を共有し、同じ目標に向かって努力する複数の人からなる。彼は、社会関係資本は次のことを共通にもつさまざまな要素のまとまりである、とする：これらの実体は①ある社会組織を構成し、②その社会組織のある働きを円滑にし、③その組織内のさまざまな行為者側にたって種々の対応を円滑に行う。そして次の性質をもつ。
・信用（confidence）と信頼（trust）のレベルに関わる：実際の社会環境でみられる
・複数の情報チャンネル（information channels）から構成される：情報の行為者の間の伝わりかた
・共通の規範や組織をもつ：人々が同じ目標に向かって努力し、利他的利益に基づき行動するときの共有される規範や組織（shared norms and structures）
　世代間学習は、異世代間で行われる学習なので生涯学習の一つの形態である。若者と高齢者の間の関係における価値観や態度の学習は非公式の学習形態である。非公式の学習は成人教育のように公式の場所で行われる。社会関係資本の実体はそれゆえ生涯 / 学習のモデルの中に含まれる（図 1 本書 p.16）。この実態を深く研究したのが Fukuyama（2000）である。彼は価値観と信頼を論じ、公式と非公式の価値観の両者を述べた。公式の価値観は社会の法や規則で決まるのに対し、非公式の価値観は、人がお互いにどのように行動すべきかの態度、規範、受容としてあらゆる社会でみられるものである。図 1 では、価値観の連続は生涯学習

のモデルの中に含まれることを示す。モデルの中の矢印は「社会関係資本の他の実体 —コミュニケーション、関係性と信頼—」を表す。このことは生徒たちのために高齢者が働く学校で起こりうるが、若い教師と高齢の教師が出会う成人教育の場でも起こる。モデルは、世代間学習が共有される価値観や態度に依存しており、それゆえ、地域や特定の国で取り組まれる文化や歴史的背景に左右される場合が多いことを示している。モデルは、学校の「クラスのおじいちゃん」と呼ばれる事業が社会関係資本を作りだす可能性を示した。この事業（Boström 2002, 2003, 2009）は Coleman の定義（1988-98）による社会関係資本のすべての事項を含んでおり、教師と一緒に休憩時間に外で、世代間の連帯と地域の発展の両者に貢献する生徒と教師の社会関係資本に肯定的な影響を与えている。（図1：本書 p.16）

3．生活の質と幸福

「生活の質」は 1990 年代から使われている。スウェーデンでは、この概念は Bang（1995）の研究ではっきりと使われている。ネットワークと健康は、この質的研究の中の Malmo の縦断的研究によれば、人々の最も重要な要素であることが発見された。ほとんど同時期に、WHO の精神衛生と薬物乱用の防止の部門（WHO 世界保健機関 1997）が精神衛生について事業を開発した。WHO は、生活の質を、人々が住む所の文化や価値観の状況の中で、目標、期待、基準、心配事の観点から生活の立ち位置についての個人の認識と定義している。これは、肉体的健康、心理状態、自立水準、社会的関係性、個人的信念、周りの環境の特色との関係性によって複雑に影響される幅広い概念である。また、WHO は総合的な生活の質や健康を測る道具の開発も担当している。6つの分野のために開発された表示器（肉体的健康、心理状態、自立水準、社会的関係性、環境、定義から開発された宗教や個人的な信条における精神性）がある。他人との関係性はこの道具で重要なものとして強調される。

幸福度（wellbeing）を測るもう一つの方法は、「世界幸福レポート（World Happiness Report）（Helliwell, Layard and Sachs, 2013）」によって作られている。彼らは、総じて人が感情と生活をどのように評価するかを測る「幸福(happiness)」をいう用語を使っている。レポートは、心情的に幸福で、より充実した生活を送り、より幸せな地域に住んでいる人々が現在または以後も健康的、生産的で社会的に結び付いている可能性が大きい、という証拠を提示している。またここで、社会的関係性の大切さを見ることができる。支え合う関係性は主観的なウェルビーイング（subjective wellbeing）を押し上げる。高い主観的なウェルビーイングをもつことはよりよい社会的関係性につながり、それゆえ幸福は人の社交性のレベルを上げ、社会的交流の質を高める。幸福は健康と機能を増進させる一つの要因である。個性、知性、社会関係資本のような他の多くの要因もまた優れた機能発揮に大切である。

4．社会的思考

私たちは、他人が好きなことを教えてくれたり、尊敬したり、世話をしたり、逆に私たち

が他人の世話をしたときに社会的な報酬を受ける（Lieberman2013）。読心術（mindreading）で私たちは、他人の目標、意図、感情、信念を考えることができる。すべての場合、神経ペプチド・オキシトシン（neuropeptide oxytocin）は人の世話をするモティベーションに影響を及ぼす重要な要因である。脳の「報酬システム（reward system）」の内部でオキシトシンはやる気を出させ、私たちが苦しんでいる人に近づいて個人の苦悩を減らす。世話をしてもらうことは脳の中のオピオイドに基づいた快楽プロセス（opioid-based pleasure process を促進させる。Lieberman（2013）は私たちの社会的想像力は精神作用システム、最初に視床下部前頭葉の皮質（dorsomedial prefrontal cortex）と側頭頂接合部（tempoarietal junction）の中で処理される。社会的および非社会的思考は構造的に実験的に同じだが、脳は非常に違った神経系統を使って2つの種類の思考をつかさどる。

5．社会関係資本と幸福

　最近、ウェルビーイングは、社会を測り比較するときに政策面でも使われてきている。Diener（2005）は、個人の主観的ウェルビーイングは、概して社会的インパクトをもつとしている。彼によれば、主観的なウェルビーイングは、人々が営む生活上のプラスであれマイナスであれ、さまざまなタイプのすべての評価に言及する。生活や仕事の満足度、興味や契約のような内省的認識評価（reflective cognitive evaluations）、喜びと悲しみといった生活上のできごとや、興味・約束への情動反応（affective reactions）を含む。

　また、次の2つの概念の間の違いを説明する生活の質の定義もある。生活の質は、ある人の生活が「望ましい」対「望ましくない」の度合いについて、しばしば環境要因や所得のような外部的要素に強調点をおいて言及される。経験に基づく主観的ウェルビーイングに対比して、生活の質はより客観的なものとして表され、状況への個人の対応というよりむしろ個人の生活の状況について述べる。

　ウェルビーイングの指標を使っているいくつかの国際的な報告もある。一つは「ヨーロッパ生活の質調査(European Quality of Life Survey（EQLS）(European Commission, 2013)（第3部：2011 ～ 2012年実施）。この調査は当時の27のEU加盟国と7の加盟候補または未登録国1億8千万強の人を対象にした。この調査での主観的ウェルビーイングは「人々のそれまでの生活体験の反映を強調する"体験型ウェルビーイング"」とされた（p.12）。枠組みと概念的モデルの作成が求められ、Thomson and Marks（2005）から応用し、図2に表している。（図2：本書 p.20）

　このモデルには3つの主要な側面がある。「快楽的ウェルビーイング」は、人の日常の感情や気分に言及する。「評価的ウェルビーイング」は、人が最近、概して自分の生活にどれだけ満足しているか、「ウェルビーイング観に基づくウェルビーイング」は、ウェルビーイングに大切だと思われる概念に言及する。これらの中には自治感覚、関係性の意味、自尊心が含まれる。これらはしばしばウェルビーイングの前提条件としてもみられる。快楽的幸福に対する質問例として「私は明るく上機嫌だった」「私はがっくりして落ち込んでいた」が

ある。「評価的ウェルビーイング」での特徴的な質問は「次のような点に満足しているか？
――教育、生活の質、現在の仕事、家族生活、健康、社会生活」。「幸福論の側面」は、次の
ような言葉を考えなければならない。「――私は将来について楽観的である」「自分の人生をど
う生きるか決めるのは自由だ」「社会からのけ者にされているように感じる」。

　生活の質の測定の結果では、友人との対面インタビューはウェルビーイングについて強い
インパクトがあったが、間接的コンタクト（電話またはEメールによる）はほとんどインパ
クトを感じられなかった。ウェルビーイングの最も強い予見材料（predictor）は、物質的欠
乏、健康、仕事と生活のバランス、時間の不足、公共サービスの満足度であった。予測材料
は使われる尺度により変化した。たとえば、孤独の最強の予見材料は配偶者を亡くしたこと、
ストレスの予見材料は仕事と生活のバランスであった。データでは、社会ネットワークや関
係性の重要さが強調されている。（図3：本書 p.21）

　調査データでは、増大しつつある地理的な労働力の可動性に関連した意図されない社会的
結果と、拡大する不平等に関連した社会的結合や信頼の低下を考慮する大切さを指摘してい
る。それゆえ、この論文の著者はウェルビーイングの測定の概念的モデルに部分的追加（黒
い四角）を行った（上記の図3参照）。「社会的関係（social relations）」がモデルの一部に
追加され、ウェルビーイングの概念については重要な部分となっている。概念の一つとして
の社会関係資本は関係性を含むが、価値観、意思疎通と信頼はこの概念の全体として大切な
存在である。社会関係資本の3つの実体がモデルに含まれれば、社会関係資本は枠組みの一
部になりうる。これにより社会関係資本をウェルビーイングの文脈の中におくことができる
ようになる。社会関係資本は家族や定義されたグループの中に使われているので（Coleman,
1988:98）、ネットワークの中の社会関係資本を測定する可能性は存在するが、より広い視野
の中で比較することもできる。このモデルは社会関係資本が現実の状況や文化と結びついて
いる点を図示し、個人の「外部的条件」や「個人的資源」の考え方も図示されている。

6．まとめ

　世代間の関係性は、結びつき、出会い、お互いに学びあいの異なった世代の人々の間での
社会関係資本や幸福度を増す可能性を秘めている。生物学の最新の研究によれば、脳は人が
他人のケアをしたり、社交的になったりすると、それに報いるとされている。社会学の研究
では、世代間の関係性に関連する人たちの間の社会関係資本が増加することを表している。
健康、家族生活、社会関係資本についての学習の利益や教育への影響が研究され、自尊心の
学習の重要な効果を産みだしている（Schuller et.al, 2004）。EQLSの調査の中では主観的ウェ
ルビーイングが異なった観点から測定されている。社会的関係については、関係性、ネット
ワーク、対面による意思疎通、と信頼に関して報告がある。

　社会関係資本は達成されるものの基礎をおく状況に関連している。個人的資源と外部的条
件は増大の可能性がある社会関係資本の前提条件となっている。これは世代間交流の会議で
さらに明らかになっている。社会関係資本が文化と関連しているので、世代間学習がボラン

ティア、社会的利益や歴史的背景について政策をもつ国々で違って応用され、異なった形で発展する可能性をもっている。社会関係資本の概念やウェルビーイングの概念は一様でなく、その概念が異なって定義されるように、取り替えても同じようには使えないということを考えるのが大切である。健康はウェルビーイングの大切な一部分であるが、たとえ健康を害しても、増大する社会関係資本と「ゆりかごから墓場まで」できる学習の機会を与えてくれる関係性を楽しむことができる。

　幸福、生活の質と読心術が世代間関係のすべてである。社会的思考の分野、生物学、教育学、心理学、世代間交流学の会議、プロジェクト、世代間交流学習、成人教育学（andragogy）の最近の研究はその関係者に、彼ら自身と関係性に対してウェルビーイングの増大の可能性を示している。

Chapter 3

Designing Generative Interventions to Promote Neuro-Cognitive Health and Aging: Experience Corps®

Michelle C. Carlson

Linda P. Fried

George W. Rebok

1. Overview

We have witnessed two key findings that shift our understanding of human brain aging in new directions. First, we learned that the adult brain remains plastic beyond childhood development, generating new neurons in response to activity and new experiences. The second emerging finding is on the importance of physical activity and social engagement to cognitive aging. The integration of these findings with our understanding of brain development over the life span leads us to consider the importance of the "social" brain in later life and exemplified by the developmental need to be generative through the fulfillment of socially valued roles and the transfer of knowledge to a younger generation. We then describe the design and evaluation of a generative model of volunteer service, entitled Experience Corps®, that seeks to increase physical, cognitive, and social activity to promote cognitive and mental health.

2. Brain Development

One region of the brain is particularly integral to interpreting and navigating complex social relationships, the prefrontal cortex. The prefrontal cortex (PFC) is the brain's planning center, or, "executive" and integrates past information with present information to predict and control future actions. Put in day-to-day terms, executive processes involve the initiation, planning, coordination and sequencing of actions toward a goal.

Evidence from brain imaging and cognitive testing studies in early life shows that lower socioeconomic status (SES) in children is associated with developmental lags in language and executive function and their associated brain structures (Bunge, Dudukovic, Thomason, Vaidya, & Gabrieli, 2002; Durston, 2006). We do not yet know if these maturational lags make the brain more vulnerable to the effects of additional insults that accumulate with age, nor do we know how modifiable or reversible these impacts are in a fully developed adult brain. SES may have long etiologic pathways in mediating neurocognitive resilience important to cognitive aging and risk for neuropathologies of aging, including Alzheimer's disease (AD) (M. Carlson, Seplaki, & Seeman, 2012).

The PFC and associated executive functions also appear to be more vulnerable than other brain regions with increasing age. In longitudinal observation, we have found that components of executive function decline earlier than memory in older community-dwelling adults, suggesting that executive function may represent a target for intervention to delay and mitigate memory declines that may lead to AD (M. Carlson, Xue, Zhou, & Fried, 2009). Consistent with this finding that age-related declines in executive function precede declines in memory, studies of the aging human brain show that loss of brain volume is greater in the PFC than in posterior areas of the cortex (Buckner, 2004; Head, Raz, Gunning-Dixon, Williamson, & Acker, 2002; Madden, 2000; Resnick, Pham, Kraut, Zonderman, & Davatzikos, 2003).

Nonetheless, aging is not synonymous with survival and the avoidance and management of chronic diseases (Rowe & Kahn, 2004). According to Erik Erikson, the third act of life represents an opportunity to realize a purpose-driven life through the transfer of a life-time of accumulated knowledge, the kind of knowledge that is not easily memorized in books, classroom lectures, or online searches (Erikson, Erikson, & Kivnick, 1986). This type of knowledge comes from decades of interpreting and understanding unpredictable social behaviors in order to predict and shape future rewards; not one's own future, but that of succeeding generations through the legacy of transfer.

3. Reversibility of Cumulative Environmental Risks in Later Life

Having summarized the brain's potential vulnerability in response to chronic environmental deprivation and disadvantage, we return to the environment to consider how such vulnerability may be reversed over the life course through these same plastic pathways. Animal models show that enriched environments elicit neurogenesis or synaptogenesis (i.e. growth of new neurons or formation of new synapses between neurons), and reduced neuronal death, especially in hippocampal structures important to memory and dementia risk (Desikan et al., 2009; Killiany et al., 2002). There is now ample evidence that enriching environments physically, cognitively, and socially, leads to the emergence of new neurons in animals throughout the life course (Kempermann et al., 2010). However, little of this work has been directly translated to human cognitive intervention studies.

Physical fitness and walking activity have been definitively linked to increased efficiency of executive function and associated activity in the PFC (Colcombe et al., 2006).Higher fitness levels have also been associated with greater hippocampal volume, suggesting that exercise may help maintain memory function (Erickson et al., 2009). However, while older adults represent the group with the most to gain from regular physical activity, they are also among the least physically active. Exercise programs have been difficult to promote adherence to in any long-term, large-scale way and are typically most successful among those who are already fairly active and who have access to resources. Those who are physically inactive are also often those with lower SES, and for whom opportunities to exercise regularly is restricted by neighborhood factors (Hillsdon, Panter, Foster, & Jones, 2007).

4. How Do We Enhance Physical Activity in Later Life? Known Benefits of Social and Volunteer Activities

A growing body of evidence in middle-aged and older adults suggests that low social activity is associated with increased risk for AD (Kondo, Niino, & Shido, 1994) and that mid- and late-life social engagement are associated with better cognitive and physical health, and greater longevity (Fratiglioni, Paillard-Borg, & Winblad, 2004; Saczynski et al., 2006). Both social integration and social activity predict better functioning and reduced risk for declines in cognitive functioning.Social engagement through volunteer activity has been associated with lower mortality and disability rates and improved self-assessed health and cognition (Harris & Thoresen, 2005; Lum TY, 2005; Morrow-Howell, Hinterlong, Rozario, & Tang, 2003). Ironically, at the same time, transitions to post retirement may serve to reduce opportunities for such activity with the resulting loss of routine contact with co-workers, and increasing tendencies for adult children to live remotely. As a result, opportunities for social activity and engagement may become more restricted and sporadic.

With this information, we face new opportunities in the design of programs to enrich and maintain cognitive and brain health as we age. Rather than focusing on ways in which to protect and buffer the aging brain's inevitable decline, we reframe aging through the developmental lens of Erikson (Erikson et al., 1986). To do so, we return to a theme articulated earlier, harness a lifetime of accumulated knowledge and wisdom and the late-life desire to be generative. As originally conceptualized by Erik Erikson, generativity is an expression of our desire to feel that we are fulfilling socially valued, functional roles – the "need to be needed," to be of some important use to other people and to "give back." The generative adult nurtures, leads and promotes the next generation, and in doing so, generates products that benefit the social systems and promote its continuity from one generation to the next.

5. The Design of a Generative Intervention to Promote Neuro-cognitive Health

We have outlined the beneficial associations between physical and social, cognition, and underlying neural pathways into later life. These findings collectively argue for the design and implementation of effective cognitive health programs to promote ongoing adult development and the maintenance of executive functions and memory. The very pathways by which inactivity and environment adversely affect childhood and adult development can serve as the same pathways by which to intervene to delay and remediate deficits.

The Experience Corps® Program represents the realization of these goals by embedding social, physical and cognitive activity into generative volunteer service to target increases in day-to-day activity. Specifically, Experience Corps® trains older adults in volunteer service in neighborhood elementary schools as mentors of children in grades Kindergarten-3 for 15 hours a week over an academic year. The goal of this program is to simultaneously improve the academic performance of children in underserved urban areas, including Baltimore City, and older volunteers' health through increases in a variety of activities. Many volunteers live near the schools they serve, meaning that physical walking activity occurred naturally through daily walks to and from, as well as, within the schools. We further incorporated cognitive activity through the intentional design of a variety of roles in reading, math, library support, and modeling positive communication that required flexibility, problem solving, and other executive functions. Socially, volunteers engage with other volunteers, teachers, and children. The program was designed to be cost-effective by simultaneously supporting the academic success of young children while promoting cognitive and physical function for older adults to prevent disability (Frick et al., 2004). Fried envisioned this program as one approach to decreasing the "structural lag" between the needs and opportunities of an aging society and our social institutions.

Results of the pilot trial of Experience Corps® revealed substantially increased rates of walking activity (blocks walked), improved physical, lower-limb strength, and, executive functions among African-American community-dwelling older adults with poor executive function at baseline (M. C. Carlson et al., 2008; Fried et al., 2004; Rebok GW, 2011). Our promising short-term findings suggested that this type of high-impact activity intervention might be a successful approach to help ameliorate executive deficits. We next turned to examine whether Experience Corps® intervened on the PFC pathways that regulate executive function through a 6-month, pilot neuroimaging study. We again observed program-specific improvements in executive function that were accompanied by improved functional activity in regions of the PFC (M. C. Carlson et al., 2009). These at-risk individuals exhibited measurable brain plasticity in direct response to such environmental enrichment, providing initial evidence of this program's potential to reverse cognitive and corresponding neural deficits. In summary, those at greatest risk for executive deficits showed substantial and clinically meaningful improvements in these and other cognitive functions as a result of participating in this program over a short exposure interval and suggest that those with the most to lose have the most to gain from environmental enrichment.

Similarly, preliminary evidence from the trial over one academic year showed that Experience Corps® improved academic and behavioral performance in kindergarteners and third graders compared to students at the control schools (Rebok et al., 2004). Participating schools further observed a 34 to 50% reduction in the number of office referrals for behavioral issues. These effects were expected to magnify over multiple years of program exposure and to further result in an improved school climate.

6. Summary Findings of Baltimore Experience Corps Trial

A large-scale evaluation of the Baltimore Experience Corps® program was supported by the National Institute on Aging (NIA) and entitled, the Baltimore Experience Corps Trial (BECT). (Fried et al., 2013) A Brain Health Substudy (BHS) was nested within the trial under separate funding (Chuang et al., 2013; Jonnassaint et al., 2014). The results showed that volunteer service in EC over 2 years led to increases in daily lifestyle activity (e.g., shopping, walking, visiting friends) and improvements in brain, psychological, cognitive and physical functional health. Following the first year of exposure, we observed increases in generativity (Gruenewald et al., 2015) and in rates of cognitive, physical and social activity (Parisi, Kuo, et al., 2015), and over 2 years in objectively measured daily physical activity (Varma et al., 2015; In Press). Health benefits accrued over 2 years in hippocampal and cortical brain volume (M. C. Carlson et al., 2015) and in both executive function and memory, both of which are important to independent function and dementia risk (M. Carlson et al., 2015 Under Review). Further, findings in men and women suggest that differences in the magnitude of health benefits may be related to baseline differences in levels of activity and health (obesity, chronic diseases). Given the generally lower and more variable levels of baseline physical activity and function among women relative to men, we hypothesize that the benefits of Experience Corps® would take more time to accrue during and after program exposure in women. These findings are the first, to our knowledge, from an RCT of a real-world volunteer activity intervention that led to generalized benefits across indices of activity, cognition, psychosocial well-being, and brain plasticity (Barnes et al., 2009; Davatzikos, Xu, An, Fan, & Resnick, 2009; Fjell et al., 2009; Jiang et al., 2014).Moreover, we observed that Experience Corps® volunteers significantly and positively impacted the school climates in which they served (Parisi, Ramsey, et al., 2015; Ramsey et al., 2015).

These findings offer initial evidence that older adults at high risk for executive dysfunction maintain great potential for brain "plasticity" and cognitive resilience. The high bolus of enrichment offered by Experience Corps® led to immediate short-term gains in brain regions vulnerable to aging. We do not yet know if these short-term effects translate to longer-term benefits and whether this experience can help overwrite or mitigate the impact of a lifetime of accumulated social and economic disadvantage. Through ongoing follow-up of those in the BECT, we will be better able to determine whether programs such as this can help delay risk for Alzheimer's disease (AD) and functional disability. The availability of large-scale activity promotion strategies that can even modestly delay the onset and course of cognitive aging and risk for dementia and disability by 6 months to 1 year have tremendous potential to reduce burden at the level of the individual, the family, and society (Brookmeyer et al., 2007). The work summarized above leads us to consider a new generation of "real world" interventions that target and enrich physical and cognitive activity in daily life in ways that matter to the individual, in the service of goals that are societally valued.

7. Summary and Conclusions

The point of view presented here moves emphasis away from aging as a time of managing inevitable biological declines to a period of continued development through the realization of a purpose-driven life. This revision of emphasis requires us to think differently about health care by building population-level public health infrastructures designed to create health. Rather, we can reconfigure health care programs and policies to incentivize generative giving and in so doing, capitalize on and value what only a lifetime of experience can provide. At the same time, data presented here indicate that valuing and exercising life experience will lead to health benefits in those systems that become vulnerable with increasing age. We now know that these systems, although vulnerable to aging, are the same systems that sought out novelty throughout early and mid- life and remain plastic and ready to be exercised. We also know that humans are particularly social. This desire to engage with others may be the vehicle or glue by which to make a social contract with others (e.g., school children; peers) to promote activity and brain health in everyday life. This approach may offer health rewards that outweigh reductionist approaches focusing solely on cognitive or physical exercises.

References

Barnes, J., Bartlett, J. W., van de Pol, L. A., Loy, C. T., Scahill, R. I., Frost, C., . . . Fox, N. C. (2009). A meta-analysis of hippocampal atrophy rates in Alzheimer's disease. *Neurobiol Aging*, 30(11), 1711-1723.

Brookmeyer R, Johnson E, Ziegler-Graham K, Arrighi HM. Forecasting the global burden of Alzheimer's disease. Alzheimer's and Dementia : *The Journal of the Alzheimer's Association.* Jul 2007;3(3):186-191.

Buckner, R. L. (2004). Memory and executive function in aging and AD: multiple factors that cause decline and reserve factors that compensate. *Neuron*, 44(1), 195-208.

Bunge, S. A., Dudukovic, N. M., Thomason, M. E., Vaidya, C. J., & Gabrieli, J. D. (2002). Immature frontal lobe contributions to cognitive control in children: evidence from fMRI. *Neuron*, 33(2), 301-311.

Carlson, M., Gross, A., Betz, J., Xue, Q. L., Chuang, Y. F., Varma, V. R., . . . Rebok, G. (2015 Under Review). Generalized Benefits of a Social Engagement Program on Cognition: The Baltimore Experience Corps Randomized, Controlled Trial.

Carlson, M., Seplaki, C., & Seeman, T. (2012). Reversing the impact of disparities in socioeconomic status over the life course on cognitive and brain aging. In B. Wolfe, W. Evans & T. Seeman (Eds.), *The biological consequences of socioeconomic inequalities* (pp. 215-247): Russell Sage Foundations Publications.

Carlson, M., Xue, Q. L., Zhou, J., & Fried, L. P. (2009). Executive decline and dysfunction precedes declines in memory: the Women's Health and Aging Study II. *The Journals of Gerontology. Series A, Biological Sciences and Medical Sciences*, 64(1), 110-117.

Carlson, M. C., Erickson, K. I., Kramer, A. F., Voss, M. W., Bolea, N., Mielke, M., . . . Fried, L. P. (2009). Evidence for neurocognitive plasticity in at-risk older adults: the experience corps program. *The Journals of Gerontology. Series A, Biological Sciences and Medical Sciences*, 64(12), 1275-1282.

Carlson, M. C., Kuo, J. H., Chuang, Y. F., Varma, V. R., Harris, G., Albert, M. S., . . . Fried, L. P. (2015). Impact of the Baltimore Experience Corps Trial on cortical and hippocampal volumes. *Alzheimers Dement.*

Carlson, M. C., Saczynski, J. S., Rebok, G. W., Seeman, T., Glass, T. A., McGill, S., . . . Fried, L. P.

Chapter 3 Designing Generative Interventions to Promote Neuro-Cognitive Health and Aging: Experience Corps® 41

(2008). Exploring the effects of an "everyday" activity program on executive function and memory in older adults: Experience Corps. *Gerontologist*, 48(6), 793-801. doi: 1758-5341 (Electronic)

Chuang, Y. F., Eldreth, D., Erickson, K. I., Varma, V., Harris, G., Fried, L. P., . . . Carlson, M. C. (2013). Cardiovascular risks and brain function: a functional magnetic resonance imaging study of executive function in older adults. *Neurobiol Aging*.

Colcombe, S. J., Erickson, K. I., Scalf, P. E., Kim, J. S., Prakash, R., McAuley, E., . . . Kramer, A. F. (2006). Aerobic exercise training increases brain volume in aging humans. *J Gerontol A Biol Sci Med Sci*, 61(11), 1166-1170.

Davatzikos, C., Xu, F., An, Y., Fan, Y., & Resnick, S. M. (2009). Longitudinal progression of Alzheimer's-like patterns of atrophy in normal older adults: the SPARE-AD index. *Brain*, 132(Pt 8), 2026-2035.

Desikan, R. S., Cabral, H. J., Fischl, B., Guttmann, C. R., Blacker, D., Hyman, B. T., . . . Killiany, R. J. (2009). Temporoparietal MR imaging measures of atrophy in subjects with mild cognitive impairment that predict subsequent diagnosis of Alzheimer disease. *AJNR, American Journal of Neuroradiology*, 30(3), 532-538.

Durston, S., Casey, BJ. (2006). What have we learned about cognitive development from neuroimaging?. *Neuropsychologia*, 44, 2149-2157.

Erickson, K., Prakash, R., Voss, M., Chaddock, L., Hu, L., Morris, K., . . . Kramer, A. (2009). Aerobic fitness is associated with hippocampal volume in elderly humans. *Hippocampus*, 10, 9.

Erikson, E., Erikson, J. M., & Kivnick, H. (1986). Vital involvement in old age: *The experience of old age in our time*. London: W. W. Norton & Company, Ltd.

Fjell, A. M., Walhovd, K. B., Fennema-Notestine, C., McEvoy, L. K., Hagler, D. J., Holland, D., . . . Dale, A. M. (2009). One-year brain atrophy evident in healthy aging. *J Neurosci*, 29(48), 15223-15231.

Fratiglioni, L., Paillard-Borg, S., & Winblad, B. (2004). An active and socially integrated lifestyle in late life might protect against dementia. *Lancet Neurology*, 3(6), 343-353.

Freedman, M., & Fried, L. (1999). *Launching Experience Corps: Findings from a two-year pilot project mobilizing older Americans to help inner-city elementary schools*. Oakland, CA: Civic Ventures.

Fried, L. P., Carlson, M. C., Freedman, M., Frick, K. D., Glass, T. A., Hill, J., . . . Zeger, S. (2004). A social model for health promotion for an aging population: initial evidence on the Experience *Corps model. Journal of Urban Health*, 81(1), 64-78.

Fried, L. P., Carlson, M. C., McGill, S., Seeman, T., Xue, Q. L., Frick, K., . . . Rebok, G. W. (2013). Experience Corps: a dual trial to promote the health of older adults and children's academic success. *Contemp Clin Trials*, 36(1), 1-13.

Gruenewald, T. L., Tanner, E. K., Fried, L. P., Carlson, M. C., Xue, Q. L., Parisi, J. M., . . .
Seeman, T. E. (2015). The Baltimore Experience Corps Trial: Enhancing Generativity via
Intergenerational Activity Engagement in Later Life. *J Gerontol B Psychol Sci Soc Sci.*

Harris, A. H., & Thoresen, C. E. (2005). Volunteering is associated with delayed mortality
in older people: analysis of the longitudinal study of aging. *Journal of Health Psychology,*
10(6), 739-752.

Head, D., Raz, N., Gunning-Dixon, F., Williamson, A., & Acker, J. D. (2002). Age-related differences in the course of cognitive skill acquisition: the role of regional cortical shrinkage
and cognitive resources. *Psychology and Aging,* 17(1), 72-84.

Hillsdon, M., Panter, J., Foster, C., & Jones, A. (2007). Equitable access to exercise facilities.
American Journal of Preventive Medicine, 32(6), 506-508.

Jiang, J., Sachdev, P., Lipnicki, D. M., Zhang, H., Liu, T., Zhu, W., . . . Wen, W. (2014). A longitudinal study of brain atrophy over two years in community-dwelling older individuals.
Neuroimage, 86, 203-211.

Jonnassaint, C., Varma, V., Chuang, Y., Harris, G., Yasar, S., Polinder-Bos, H., & Carlson, M.
(2014). Lower hemoglobin is associated with poorer cognitive performance and smaller
brain volumes in older adults. *Journal of the American Geriatrics Society,* In Press.

Kempermann, G., Fabel, K., Ehninger, D., Babu, H., Leal-Galicia, P., Garthe, A., & Wolf, S.
A. (2010). Why and how physical activity promotes experience-induced brain plasticity.
Frontiers in Neuroscience, 4, 189.

Killiany, R. J., Hyman, B. T., Gomez-Isla, T., Moss, M. B., Kikinis, R., Jolesz, F., . . . Albert, M. S.
(2002). MRI measures of entorhinal cortex vs hippocampus in preclinical AD. *Neurology,*
58(8), 1188-1196.

Kondo, K., Niino, M., & Shido, K. (1994). A case-control study of Alzheimer's disease in
Japan--significance of life-styles. *Dementia,* 5(6), 314-326.

Lum TY, L. E. (2005). The Effects of Volunteering on the Physical and Mental Health of
Older People. *Research on Aging,* 27(1), 31-55.

Madden, D. J. (2000). Neuroimaging of memory. Introduction. *Microscopy Research and
Technique,* 51(1), 1-5.

Morrow-Howell, N., Hinterlong, J., Rozario, P. A., & Tang, F. (2003). Effects of volunteering
on the well-being of older adults. *The Journals of Gerontology. Series B, Psychological
Sciences and Social Sciences,* 58(3), S137-145.

Parisi, J. M., Kuo, J., Rebok, G. W., Xue, Q. L., Fried, L. P., Gruenewald, T. L., . . . Carlson, M.
C. (2015). Increases in lifestyle activities as a result of experience Corps(R) participation. *J
Urban Health,* 92(1), 55-66.

Parisi, J. M., Ramsey, C. M., Carlson, M. C., Xue, Q. L., Huang, J., Romani, W. A., . . . Rebok, G.
W. (2015). Impact of Experience Corps Participation on School Climate. *Prev Sci.*

Ramsey, C. M., Parisi, J. M., Rebok, G. W., Gross, A. L., Tanner, E. K., Carlson, M. C., . . . Spira, A. P. (2015). Attendance and Retention of Older Adults in School-Based Volunteer Activities: The Role of School Climate. *Journal of Intergenerational Relationships*; Under Review.

Rebok, G. W., Carlson, M. C., Glass, T. A., McGill, S., Hill, J., Wasik, B. A., . . . Rasmussen, M. D. (2004). Short-term impact of Experience Corps participation on children and schools: results from a pilot randomized trial. *Journal of Urban Health*, 81(1), 79-93.

Rebok GW, C. M., Barron JS, Frick KD, McGill S, Parisi J, Seeman T, Tan EJ, Tanner EK, Willging PR, Fried LP. (2011). Experience CorpsR: A Civic Engagement-Based Public Health Intervention in the Public Schools. *Enhancing cognitive fitness in adults: A handbook for the development of community-based programs.*

Resnick, S. M., Pham, D. L., Kraut, M. A., Zonderman, A. B., & Davatzikos, C. (2003). Longitudinal magnetic resonance imaging studies of older adults: a shrinking brain. Journal of Neuroscience, 23(8), 3295-3301.

Rowe, J. W., & Kahn, R. (2004). Health promotion in the urban elderly. Experience Corps commentary. *Journal of Urban Health: Bulletin of the New York Academy of Medicine,* 81(1), 61-63.

Saczynski, J. S., Pfeifer, L. A., Masaki, K., Korf, E. S., Laurin, D., White, L., & Launer, L. J. (2006). The effect of social engagement on incident dementia: the Honolulu-Asia Aging Study. *American Journal of Epidemiology,* 163(5), 433-440.

Varma, V. R., Tan, E. J., Gross, A. L., Harris, G., Romani, W., Fried, L. P., . . . Carlson, M. (2015; In Press). Effect of community volunteering on physical activity: a randomized clinical trial. *Am J Prev Med.*

第3章　神経認知的な健康の促進と加齢に対する「世代性的」介入プログラム：Experience Corps®

ミッシェル・C・カールソン
リンダ・P・フリード
ジョージ・W・リボック

1．はじめに

　今日、私たちは脳の機能のエイジングに関する新しい2つの研究成果を目の当たりにしている。一つ目は成人の脳は可塑性を有しており、日常の活動や新しい経験により発達しえること。二つ目は身体活動と社会的なつながりは、認知機能の保持を考える上で重要になることである。このような生涯にわたる脳の機能の発達に関する新しい知見は、高齢期において社会的な部分を担う脳の機能の重要性を示しており、社会的に価値ある役割の実現や若年世代への知識の伝承といった「世代性的」重要性を示すものとしてとらえることができる。私たちは本稿において、ボランティアサービスによる一つの「世代性的」モデルとして、認知機能や精神的健康度の増進、および身体、認知、そして社会的な活動の向上を目的として開発されたExperience Corps®（EC）のデザイン、および実施効果について論述したいと考える。

2．神経認知の促進と高齢期における健康増進を目指した「世代性的」介入プログラム

　ECプログラムは、「世代性的」ボランティアサービスといった日々の社会、身体、認知的活動を通して、これら目的の実現を図るものである。特に、ECは近隣の小学校において1年生から3年生に対する指導者・助言者として、一週間あたり15時間、ボランティアサービスを行う高齢者を養成するプログラムである。このプログラムの目標は、様々な活動を通してボルティモア市を含むサービスが十分ではない都市部の子どもの学業成績と高齢ボランティアの健康のそれぞれの向上を同時に目指すものである。多くのボランティアは学校の近くに住んでいるため、活動への参加を通して自然と歩く機会や時間が増え、このことは学校内においても同様の効果が見込まれる。

　私たちは、朗読、算数、図書館業務、必要に応じた柔軟な対応、問題解決、および実行機能といった意図された種々の役割といった認知的な活動を組み合わせた。社会的には、ボランティアは他のボランティア、教員、子どもたちとつながり、交流を持つ。本プログラムでは、高齢者の障害予防を目的とした認知および身体的機能の増進を図りながら、子どもたちの学力の向上を同時に図る費用対効果が考慮されている（Frick et al., 2004）。Friedは高齢化社

第3章　神経認知的健康の促進と加齢に対する世代継承型介入プログラム：Experience Corps®　45

会のニーズ・機会と私たちの社会的施設の間に横たわる「構造的なラグ」を減少させる一つのアプローチになることを想定した。

ECに関するパイロット研究の結果は、地域在住のアフリカ系アメリカ人の歩行活動の割合の上昇、身体、下肢筋力、および実行機能の向上を明らかにした（M. C. Carlson et al., 2008; Fried et al., 2004; Rebok GW, 2011）。同様にプログラム実施後の最初の1年間の成果として、介入を受けた幼稚園児と小学3年生は対照群として設定した子どもたちより、学力と行動上のパフォーマンスが向上した(Rebok et al., 2004)。参加した学校においては、子どもの行動上の問題による職員室への届出数が34％〜50％減少したことがわかった。これら効果はプログラムの実施年数を重ねることで、さらなる改善が見込まれる。

3．ボルティモアECにおける研究成果のまとめ

2年間にわたるECにおけるボランティアサービスは日常の生活習慣（買い物、ウオーキング、友達を訪ねるほか）を向上させ、健康にかかわる脳の機能や心理、認知、身体の各機能を改善させることが明らかになった。私たちは、はじめの1年間においてはジェネラティビティ（generativity）（Gruenewald et al., 2015）ならびに認知、身体、社会の各活動の向上（Parisi, Kuo, et al., 2015）、そして2年間の追跡により、日常の身体活動の向上を客観的な評価により確認した（Varma et al., 2015; In Press）。脳の海馬と大脳皮質の容量（M. C. Carlson et al., 2015）および自立機能や認知症のリスクに関して重要になる実行機能や記憶機能において、健康上の効果が2年間にわたりみられた（M. Carlson et al., 2015 Under Review）。

さらに男性と女性における健康上の効果の相違は、プログラム実施前の活動や健康のレベル（肥満、慢性疾患の既往）の違いに関係していることが示唆された。女性は男性よりも、一般的に身体活動や身体機能のレベルが低く変動しやすいことをふまえると、女性の場合、プログラム実施中、および実施後のECによる効果が得られるまでに時間がかかると私たちは推察している。

これら私たちの研究成果は初めて明らかにされたことであり、私たちが得た研究成果については、実社会のボランティア活動に対する無作為化比較対照試験研究により、活動、認知、心理社会的に良好な状態、および脳の機能の可塑性といった全般的な恩恵が得られることがわかっている（Barnes et al., 2009; Davatzikos, Xu, An, Fan, & Resnick, 2009; Fjell et al., 2009; Jiang et al., 2014）。さらに私たちは、ECボランティアにおいては、彼らが参加した学校の環境や雰囲気に有意義、かつポジティブな効果を与えることを明らかにした（Parisi, Ramsey, et al., 2015; Ramsey et al., 2015）。

これら研究成果により、実行性機能不全リスクの高い高齢者であっても脳の可塑性と認知的回復力に大きな可能性を有していることが初めて明らかになった。ECは老化に弱い脳領域に即効性のある短期的な改善をもたらした。この短期間の効果が長期間にわたる効果に変わるのか、そして社会経済的困難が積み重なった人生による影響をECでの経験が変えるこ

とができるのか、あるいは軽減することができるのかについてはまだわからない。このようなプログラムがアルツハイマー病や機能障害のリスク軽減に寄与するかについては、継続中のボルティモア EC トライアルのフォローアップを通して今後判断可能となる。

ECのような大規模な活動促進戦略により、認知機能の老化の発現と進行、および認知症障害のリスクを6か月から1年間遅らせることが可能となり、これには個人、家族、社会の負担を軽減する大きな可能性が認められる（Brookmeyer et al., 2007）。上述の研究を通して、私たちは新たな「実社会」への介入手段について考えていくことになる。つまり、社会的価値のある目標に向けて、個人にとって重要な方法にもとづき、日常生活における身体および認知活動の向上を目指していくのである。

4．まとめと結論

本研究が示しているのは、老化を生物的に避けられない衰退を管理する時間としてではなく、目標のある人生の実現のための継続的な成長期間として着目点を変えるものである。着目点を変えるためには、私たちは健康管理に関する考え方を変え、健康を作り出すための集団レベルでの公衆衛生のインフラストラクチャーを作り出す必要がある。

私たちは、人間とは社会的な存在であることを理解している。他者とつながりたいという願望を持っていることが、学校の子どもや仲間などと社会的な結びつきをもたらすもとになり、それにより日常生活における活動や脳の健康が促進されるのではないかと考える。ECのようなアプローチは認知や身体活動にのみ焦点をあてたアプローチより価値があり、健康上の恩恵をもたらしてくれるのであろう。

Chapter 4

The 'Age- and Dementia-Friendly Cities' Movement: Intergenerational Omissions and Intergenerative Opportunities

Daniel R. George

1. Introduction

Concepts of aging are historically situated, with cultural, economic, political, and other social forces serving to inform our understanding of what it means to age, and what responsibilities society has to care for its elderly. In the early 21st century, trends in population aging, urbanization, and global economic instability have caused confrontation with the reality that, over the next several decades, an unprecedented number of elders, some of whom will invariably be affected by physical and mental decrements, will be living in cities, and not all will have access to institutional care. This has, in turn, engendered much discussion about how cities can adapt to become 'age-' and 'dementia-friendly', and thereby accommodate expanding aging populations. Within the emerging discourse of these movements, one might reasonably expect to find a focus on the essential role intergenerational relationships will play in cities that succeed in becoming more age/dementia-friendly; however, examination of the literature reveals that neither movement features intergenerational themes as a major point of emphasis. Therefore, the goal of this chapter is to critically examine the conceptual foundations of both the age- and dementia-friendly cities movements, and imagine how an intergenerational ethos might help transform theory and practice. In doing so, an emerging concept – intergenerativity – can be a tool that helps proponents of each movement open new repertoires for thinking and acting from

48

an intergenerational perspective in age/dementia-friendly cities.

2. Examining the age- and dementia-friendly cities movements

The very need for a concept of "age/dementia-friendly cities" is in some sense an indictment of current societal biases towards aging, as it implies an underlying "unfriendliness" towards those who are aged or affected by memory loss that requires remediation. Indeed, the past several decades have seen much scholarship critiquing the "ageist" tendencies of Western cultures and their potential to marginalize older persons to the point of engendering 'social death'[1] . Both the age/dementia-friendly movements push back against these social forces with ideologies drawn from the "active and successful aging" literature. These concepts have arisen in recent decades as a counterpoint to disengagement theory – the leading perspective on activity in the lives of older individuals in the mid-20th century,[2] which held that aging was a natural process through which older individuals would relinquish their claims to valued social roles as they aged, thus disengaging from society. Whereas proponents of disengagement theory believed that society would reciprocate in disengaging from aging individuals and transfer their responsibilities and roles to younger individuals, generally assuming that disengagement was positive for both older persons and society,[3] critics assailed its tendency to detract value from individuals once they lost their economic productivity. In fact, American geriatrician Robert Butler coined the term, "ageism" to refer to a prejudice against older persons that was analogous to "racism" or "fascism" in its exclusionary potential. In contrast, theories of active and successful aging hold that elderly people who remain productive and maintain or create new social networks and roles that stabilize selfhood and sense of purpose will generally experience better health outcomes than those who disengage from society and social commitments. Proponents believe that life events, aging, and environments interact with the biology of the body/brain to precipitate neurological and behavioral transformations that are pathological – a viewpoint referred to as "entanglement theory".[4]

Conceptually, the age-friendly cities movement, initially launched by the World Health Organization in the early 2000s, strongly reflects these aforementioned ideologies. While the movement defines "age-friendly" without making its sole focus the elderly – thereby allowing for a more cross-generational scope than the dementia-friendly movement – it nevertheless appears predominately concerned with identifying how cities can best accommodate and engage older citizens who will increasingly populate urban areas in coming decades. This balancing act can be observed in the WHO's definition of an age-friendly city as a place that, "enables *people of all ages* to actively participate in community activities and treats *everyone* with respect, regardless of their age...[and] makes it easy for *older people* to stay connected to people that are important to them ... and stay healthy and active even at the oldest ages and provide appropriate support to those who can no longer look after themselves to live with dignity and enjoyment" (my italics).[5]

In order to identify the characteristics of age-friendly cities, the WHO has held focus groups with older, city-dwelling adults from 33 worldwide cities, and produced a guidebook summarizing their findings.[6] Chapters in the guidebook cover a variety of themes – outdoor spaces and buildings, transportation, housing, social and civic participation, respect and social inclusion, communication and information, and community support and health services – with the findings in each domain reflecting the elder-centric approach employed in focus groups. Perhaps surprisingly, within the 82-page document "intergenerational" themes are mentioned only six times. The WHO also

50

maintains a global database of innovative programs in cities and communities worldwide that demonstrate adaptations to the needs of aging populations, and, presently, only six of the 40 programs are explicitly intergenerational in their orientation.[7]

While sharing conceptual DNA with the 'age-friendly' movement, dementia-friendly cities are unambiguously focused on improving inclusion and quality of life for people living with dementia, 60% of whom reside in their own community homes, and 1 in 7 who live alone. The call for more dementia-friendly communities takes its cue, in part, from disability studies, which has long challenged negative stereotypes of disabilities while developing strategies for the inclusion and participation of people with disabilities.[8] Although conceptual models for dementia-friendly cities vary across cultural contexts, most have been organized around some combination of the following attributes:

1) Increased community awareness about dementia and more humane attitudes towards those affected

2) Provision of supportive resources/opportunities/trainings for caregivers and families (e.g. dementia support, advance planning, etc.)

3) Dementia support training for citizens of all ages

4) Promotion of opportunities for meaningful participation in community life through dementia-friendly services, activities, and supports

5) Modifications in physical environments/infrastructure to ensure safety and inclusion (e.g. housing, transport, neighborhood design, etc.)

6) Increased dementia-friendly business and financial practices and reduced opportunities for fraud and abuse

7) Increased screening detection/diagnosis/specialized services for memory loss

8) Reduction of stigma and acknowledgment of the potential retained by persons with dementia

9) Promotion of independent living

10) Emergency preparedness

In the UK, the Alzheimer's Society has been a global leader in the movement, promoting an understanding of dementia-friendly cities as places where "people with dementia are empowered to have high aspirations and feel confident, knowing they can contribute and participate in activities that are meaningful to them."[9] In the US, the Dementia Friendly America initiative[10] aspires to foster cities equipped to support people with dementia and their family and friend caregivers, and seeks to establish 16 model cities by 2016.

When one examines the literature underlying these movements, there emerge several conceptual tensions. For instance, the movement valorizes individualism, independence, and autonomy while also emphasizing our fundamental interdependence as human communities. Further, it simultaneously calls for reducing stigma around dementia while explicitly advocating for early diagnosis that potentially extends stigmatizing labels to more of the population. There is also a clear attempt to lean on social services provided by the state while expecting private enterprise to play a role in supporting persons with dementia and their families. One also notices that the movement focuses much attention on physical/built environment with minimal acknowledgment of larger environmental concerns (i.e. climate change, natural disasters, which have been shown to disproportionately affect the elderly).[11] Lastly, and most conspicuously, while both aforementioned organizations have visions that seem reliant on an intergenerational ethos, the concept receives short shrift in their literature. For instance, in the Alzheimer's Soci-

52

ety's robust 95-page report *Building dementia-friendly communities: A priority for everyone*[9] the word "intergenerational" appears only 3 times; similarly, the website for the US Dementia Friendly America initiative contains no mention of "intergenerational" themes. Given that an increase in intergenerational relationships would seem to be the inevitable outcome of cities that succeed in becoming more age/dementia-friendly there is an opportunity for both movements to more explicitly embrace activities, programs, and services that bring the generations together.

3. 'Intergenerativity' in age/dementia-friendly cities

In recent years, the concept of "intergenerativity" has gained traction as a catchall term for the mutually beneficial effects observed when age-segregated (and other) barriers are removed and generations are brought together.[12] Colloquially, the notion of "generativity" is characterized by the creation of new internal ideas and behaviors. It has also been proposed as the seventh stage of Erik Erikson's Stages of Psychosocial Development as a struggle against stagnation that ascends during adulthood.[13] In a psychosocial sense, then, generativity refers to the concern for establishing and guiding the next generation. By adding the prefix "inter" to create the neologism "intergenerativity," the concept makes explicit reference to the generative nature of intergenerational relationships and the benefits that they confer.

Indeed, existing research demonstrates that older adults in intergenerational programs have experienced a range of bio-psychosocial benefits, including: gains in executive function and in the activity of prefrontal cortical regions in older adults at elevated risk for cognitive impairment[14] ; increased engagement and interactions[15], improvements in health status and well-being,[16] generational closeness, comfort, and empathy,[17] increased activity,

Chapter 4 The 'Age- and Dementia-Friendly Cities' Movement: Intergenerational Omissions and Intergenerative Opportunities   53

strength, and cognitive ability,[18] mutually supportive interactions and the creation of meaningful relationships,[19] positive affect, confidence, and enhanced self-esteem supporting personhood,[20] lower levels of negative forms of engagement,[21] increased social capital,[22] better psychological functioning,[23] improvements in subjective health, social support and network, consciousness of loving community and some aspects of physical performance,[24] and reduced stress,[25] just to name a few. There is also strong evidence that children who participate in intergenerational programs may benefit both socially and cognitively from interactions with elders,[17] be more likely to rate their health as 'good',[22] and demonstrate gains in the knowledge of dementia and more positive perceptions of older persons.[22,23,26] In short, bringing the young (with their energy, vigor, and openness to novelty) together with the old (with their rich experiences, long-term perspective, and desire for purposeful contribution) appears to engender life-affirming, intergenerative effects across the age spectrum. This dynamic holds up across cultures.[27]

Certainly, a greater emphasis on intergenerational relationships seems warranted in the age/dementia-friendly cities literature. Simply by invoking and explaining the concept of intergenerativity, proponents of both movements could stimulate thinking about the identification and removal of arbitrary age-barriers for programs, activities, and services, and thereby create myriad opportunities for intergenerative relationships/partnerships to form at the community level. For instance, as described elsewhere in this volume (Peter Whitehouse's chapter), the early 21st century has witnessed the fascinating trend of intergenerational schools, which open their doors to learners of all ages, and this model is spreading to other countries. The Intergenerational School in Cleveland, OH (USA) is an internationally-respected institution where elders – including persons with dementia who live in the community and in residential care – volunteer as "mentors" for elementary school children. For 15-years, the school has achieved sustained success for children, while demonstrating psychosocial benefits for the elders who volunteer there daily as respected members of the community.[28] Similar educational models, such as Providence Mount St. Vincent in Seattle, have established successful outcomes by hosting preschools in assisted living facilities.[29] Because of the established value of learning across the lifespan, educational institutions (primary, secondary, and higher) that are encouraged to embrace intergenerativity would seem poised to take a leadership role in creating opportunities for elders in cities aspiring to become age/dementia-friendly.

Other sectors, such as housing, would seem similarly primed for 'intergenerative' action. For instance, in recent years intergenerational living models have been established in several countries, particularly those bringing together elders and college-aged students. In the Dutch city of Deventer, a retirement facility in has offered college students free housing in exchange for volunteer work.[30] Similarly, in Cleveland (OH), USA, a retirement facility provides housing for students from the Cleveland Institute of Music in exchange for performances at each of the retirement community's campuses. Certainly, the same university housing partnership model could be brought to bear with elders living alone in cities, particularly in partnership with students pursuing training in the health professions. Recreational facilities also appear to have a role to play, and there have been recent calls[31] to transform current senior centers into intergenerational community centers where, rather than segregating elderly cohorts, people from different generations come together and nurture trust and empathy through interaction. An intergenerational ethos can stimulate inventive thinking about sharing resources and infrastructure, and foster unique partnerships. For instance, libraries and schools can connect struggling young readers with mentors in community residential care homes who find joy and purpose in teaching this skill to children.[32] Museums have begun opening their doors to groups of people in dementia-care homes, enabling elders normally excluded from such public spaces to enjoy social interaction and share in aesthetic experiences. Community spaces such as farmers markets, community gardens, and parks also have great potential to support intergenerational exchanges in urban environments. In each instance, the concept of 'intergenerativity' can provide a theoretical base to challenge the status quo and open new avenues for thinking and acting in cities that are truly becoming more age/dementia-friendly.

4. Conclusion

Ultimately, the age/dementia-friendly cities movements represent a positive worldwide trend towards providing more humane environments for aging persons. Both movements do seem to miss opportunities to emphasize the key role intergenerational partnerships/relationships can and should play in cities of the future, and this chapter has identified conceptual omissions while suggesting a new concept – intergenerativity – that can help break down the ideological and physical barriers of age-segregation that define many of our social environments, and lead to a powerful confluence of ideas, emotions, and actions in local communities. As proponents of the age/dementia-friendly cities continue to develop the conceptual and practical foundation of their respective (and overlapping) movements, an intergenerational ethic can only serve to enable the types of partnerships and relationships that can sustain the movements and bring about their visions for more humane cities of the future.

56

References

1 George DR. (2010). Overcoming the social death of dementia through language. *The Lancet* 376: 586-587.

2 Cumming, E. Henry, W. (1961). *Growing Old: The Process of Disengagement.* New York: Basic Books.

3 Hinterlong, JE. Williamson, A. (2007). The Effects of Civic Engagement of Current and Future Cohorts of Older Adults. *Generations* 30(4): 10-17.

4 Lock M. (2013). *The Alzheimer Conundrum.* Princeton University Press: Princeton NJ.

5 https://extranet.who.int/agefriendlyworld/

6 World Health Organization. 2007. *Global Age-Friendly Cities: A Guide.* Available at: https://www.google.com/url?sa=t&rct=j&q=&esrc=s&source=web&cd=1&cad=rja&ua ct=8&ved=0CB4QFjAAahUKEwis8oHQv5XJAhVC3mMKHQxwAO0&url=http%3A%2F %2Fwww.who.int%2Fageing%2Fpublications%2FGlobal_age_friendly_cities_Guide_English.pdf&usg=AFQjCNGnPXPixl5aLoQ7mk3Bpq2GE9Y0Mg&sig2=0HUG64W_cstoxT9ct-VQBow

7 See: http://apps.who.int/datacol/custom_view_report.asp?survey_id=600&view_id=653&display_filter=1

8 Popularizing Dementia Public Expressions and Representations of Forgetfulness. Aagje Swinnen, Mark Schweda (eds.), Transcript: Seitin. p.12.

9 Alzheimer's Society. 2013. *Building dementia friendly communities: A priority for everyone* - Executive Summary. Available at: https://www.alzheimers.org.uk/site/scripts/download_info.php?fileID=1918

10 See: http://www.dfamerica.org/

11 Whitehouse PJ, Sykes K, George DR. (2014). Ecological change and aging: A need to think deeply and act quickly. *International Journal of Aging & Human Development* 80(1): 3-9.

12 George DR, Whitehouse PJ, Whitehouse C. (2011). "Intergenerativity" in action: How intergenerational programs are rising to 21st century challenges. *Journal of Intergenerational Relationships* 9(4): 389-404.

13 Slater CL. (2003). Generativity versus stagnation: An elaboration of Erikson's adult stage of human development. J Adult Dev;10:53-65.

14 Carlson, MC. et al. (2009). Evidence for Neurocognitive Plasticity in At-Risk Older Adults: The Experience Corps Program. *The Journals of Gerontology Series A: Biological Sciences and Medical Sciences* 64A(12):1275-1282.

15 Camp, CJ. Orsulic-Jeras, S. Lee, MM. Judge, KS. (1997). Effects of a Montessori-based intergenerational program on engagement and affect for adult day care clients with dementia. In: Wykle ML, Whitehouse PJ, Morris DL, eds. *Successful Aging Through the*

Life Span: Intergenerational Issues in Health. New York: Springer: 159-176.

16 DeSouza, EM. (2003). Intergenerational interaction in health promotion: A qualitative study in Brazil. *Revista de Sau ́ de Publica* 37(4): 463–469.

17 Hayes, C. (2003). An observational study in developing an intergenerational shared site program: Challenges and insights. *Journal of Intergenerational Relationships* 1(1): 113–132.

18 Fried, L. Carlson, MC. Freedman, M. Frick, KD. Glass, TA. Hill, J. McGill, S. Rebok, GW. Seeman, T. Tielsch, J. Wasik, BA. Zeger, S. (2004). A social model for health promotion for an ageing population: Initial evidence on the experience corps model. *Journal of Urban Health* 81(1): 64-78.

19 Gigliotti, C. Morris, M. Smock, S. Jarrott, SE. Graham, B. (2005). An Intergenerational Summer Programme Involving Persons with Dementia and Preschool Children. *Educational Gerontology* 31: 425–441.

20 Jarrott, SE. Bruno, KA. (2003). Intergenerational activities involving persons with dementia: An observational assessment. *American Journal of Alzheimer's and Related Diseases* 18: 31–38.

21 Lee, MM. Camp, CJ. Malone, ML. (2007). Effects of intergenerational Montessori-based activities programming on engagement of nursing home residents with dementia. *Clin Interv Aging* 2(3):477-83.

22 DeSouza, EM. Grundy, E. (2007). Intergenerational interaction, social capital and health: Results from a randomised controlled trial in Brazil. *Social Science & Medicine* 65(7): 1397-1409.

23 Chung, JCC. (2008). An intergenerational reminiscence programme for older adults with early dementia and youth volunteers: values and challenges. *Scandinavian Journal of Caring Sciences* 23(2): 259-264.

24 Fujiwara, Y. et al. 2006. Research of Productivity by Intergenerational Sympathy. *Nippon Koshu Eisei Zasshi* 53(9):702-14.

25 George DR, Singer M. (2011). Intergenerational volunteering and quality of life for persons with mild to moderate dementia: Results from a 5-month intervention study in the United States. *American Journal of Geriatric Psychiatry* 19(4): 392-396.

26 Schwalbach, E. Kiernan, S. (2002). Effects of an intergenerational friendly visit program on the attitudes of fourth graders toward elders. *Educational Gerontology* 28: 175–187.

27 Kaplan, M. Kusano, A. Ichiro, T. Hisamichi, S. (1998). *Intergenerational programs: Support for children, youth and elders in Japan.* New York: SUNY Press.

28 George DR. (2011). Intergenerational volunteering and quality of life: mixed methods evaluation of a randomized control trial involving persons with mild to moderate dementia. *Quality of Life Research* 20(7): 987-995.

29 See: https://www.youtube.com/watch?v=6K3H2VqQKcc

30　See: http://www.theatlantic.com/business/archive/2015/10/dutch-nursing-home-college-students/408976/

31　See: http://www.forbes.com/sites/nextavenue/2015/03/19/why-we-need-to-get-rid-of-senior-centers/

32　George DR, Wagler G. (2014). Social learning and innovation: Developing two shared site intergenerational reading programs in Hershey, PA. *Journal of Intergenerational Relationships* 12(1): 69-74.

第4章　高齢者・認知症にやさしい都市への運動：世代間交流の欠落と「世代間交流性的」機会

ダニエル・R・ジョージ

1．序論

　21世紀の初頭から人口の加齢化、都市居住化、全世界的な経済的不安定さによって、今後数十年、心身の機能の低下を抱えたかつてないほどの数の高齢者が、都市部に住み続け、そのすべてが必ずしも介護サービスを受けることができないであろうという現実に直面している。このことが都市がどのようにして加齢・認知症にやさしい状況を作り出していけるのか、それによって増え続ける高齢者人口にいかに対応していけるのかという様々な議論をうみだしている。この議論には、加齢・認知症にやさしい都市づくりに関して、世代間交流に焦点をしぼった意見があってもよいはずであるが、世代間交流を主要なテーマに掲げた論文はみあたらない。それ故、この論考では加齢・認知症にやさしい都市という運動の概念的基盤を批判的に精査し、世代間交流の思考・精神がいかにその概念の理論化・実践化を形成するのに役立つのかを明らかにすることを目標とする。その過程で紹介したいのが、新たに言い出されている「世代間交流性」という概念である。

2．加齢・認知症にやさしい都市運動に関する調査

　「加齢・認知症にやさしい都市」という概念の必要性はある意味で現代の高齢者に対する社会的偏見への告発にある。過去数十年、西洋文化の「年齢差別主義」の傾向や高齢者を軽んじ、「社会的な死」に追い込む潜在性への批判を問題にした論文は多くみられた。この加齢・認知症にやさしい都市という運動は、正反対の「離脱理論」への対局にある運動として最近数十年おこってきているものである。離脱理論というのは、20世紀半ば頃から年配者は社会的に重要な役を主張せずに譲り、社会から身を引くのが自然だという考え方である。実際、アメリカの老年学者のロバート・バトラーは「レイシズム」、「ファシズム」と同類の高齢者への偏見を「エイジズム」と言う語で表現した。新たな社会的ネットワークや役割をになっている高齢者は健康にも良い結果を生んでおり、このような立場を支持する理論を「(コミュニティとの)掛かり合い理論」とよぶ。

　概念的には、2000年代の初期に世界保健機関で先ず打ち上げられたこの高齢者にやさしい都市運動は前述した理論を強く反映している。この運動はこれからますます都会で増加を続ける年配者にどう対応し、どう興味づけるか最善の方法をつきとめることに係っている。世界保健機関は全世界の33都市の高齢居住者にしぼった調査をし、それをまとめたガイドブックを出版した。その82頁の報告書の様々な高齢者に係るプログラムのうち、「世代間交流」

60

というテーマは6回しか言及されていない。

　認知症患者にやさしい都市はこのような人と係り、価値ある生き方を共にするという一点にしぼられているが、認知症の人の60%は地域の施設で暮らし、一人住まいは7人に1人である。認知症の人に一層やさしいコミュニティ作りへの要望はそのヒントを身体障碍者への処方から得ている。そこでも身体障碍者と係り、共に参加するという方策を発展させている。認知症にやさしい都市の方策モデルは文化環境で様々であるが10のモデルにまとめられる。例えば① 認知症の人たちへの気づきや一層暖かい姿勢の促進、② 認知症の人を世話する人、家族を支える方策、機会、訓練の提供などである。英国ではアルツハイマー協会がこの運動のリーダー役を担ってきている。アメリカでは、アメリカ認知症友愛協会（the Dementia Friendly America）が認知症の人たち、その家族や友人の世話をする人を支えることを決意して、2016年までに16のモデルとなる都市を築くことを目指している。

　これらの運動のことを強調している文献をみると、いくつかの概念上の衝突がみられる。この運動は個人主義、独立、自治の価値を主張すると思えば、人間社会の基本的な相互依存を主張するといった具合である。更に、この運動は認知症にまつわる徴候を少なめに抑えようとする反面、認知症の徴候を早めに公表しようとする。また、このような人への社会的サービスは国、州が担うと良いとしているかとおもえば民間企業がその役割をすることを期待するというはっきりした試みもあるといった状況である。さらに注目することは気候変動や自然災害といった比較的広範な意味の環境を過少評価して施設と言った環境に多大な関心を示すという動きもあることである。

　最後に指摘したいのは上述した団体は世代間交流的な精神に依拠しても良いビジョンを持ちながら、この精神は文献上ではほんのわずかしか扱われていない。英国のアルツハイマー協会の95頁におよぶ報告書 Building dementia-friendly communities: A priority for everyone では、「世代間交流」という単語は3回しか出ていない。アメリカ認知症友愛協会のサイトでは「世代間交流」のテーマは全く取り上げられてない。世代間交流的な関係の増加が高齢者・認知症によりやさしくなることを達成した都市において当然の結果ならば、この2つの運動が世代を一つにする活動、プログラムサービスをもっと明確に取り入れる機会はあるだろう。

3．高齢者・認知症にやさしい都市における「世代間交流性」

　「世代間交流性」という概念は年齢別障壁が取り除かれ様々な世代が一緒になる時に見られる世代相互にとって利益になる効果をひとまとめにする新語として牽引力を発揮してきている。「世代性」はエリック・エリクソンの心理社会的発達段階の7番目として提案されている。この段階は成人期に生ずる停滞と世代性が対立する段階である。「世代間交流性」は世代性（generativity）に接頭辞（inter）をつけて作った造語で（intergenerativity）、世代間交流の関係性という世代間という性質をはっきりと明示するものである。

　実際に世代間交流プログラムにおける比較的年配層の人が広範囲な生物的心理社会的利益

第4章 高齢者・認知症にやさしい都市への運動：世代間交流の欠落と「世代性的」機会 61

を享受していることをいろいろな研究が明らかにしている。また子どもたちも年配者と交流
することで社会性や認知論的にも良い結果を受けている強い証拠もしめされている。手短に
言うと、若者と年配者とを一緒にすると年齢別を横断して人生肯定的な世代間交流性的効果
を醸し出すと思われる。

高齢者・認知症の人へやさしくあるべきだと提唱者はいろいろなプログラム、活動、サー
ビスでの恣意的な年齢障壁をみつけそれを取り除く考えを促せる。それによって、世代間交
流性的交流関係・パートナーシップのあまたの機会を創出して、地域レベルで形成されてき
ている。Peter Whitehouse 氏の論文によると21世紀の初頭からみられ、アメリカ、オハイ
オ州のクリーブランドでは、地元の認知症の人も含めた年配者が小学生のボランティア先生
として活動している。15年間この小学校は子どもにとっては継続的に実りがあり、ボランティ
アをした年配者にとっても良い効果があった。シアトルのプロヴィデンス・マウント・セイ
ント・ヴィンセントのプリスクールでも同じことが見られる。

世代間交流にかかわるほかの分野での実施例もある。高齢者と学生との共同住宅は、オラ
ンダのデヴェンダー市、アメリカのクリーブランド市である。図書館・図書室でも子どもと
高齢者との交流でお互いにプラスがある。美術館では、認知症施設の人たちに開放すること
で鑑賞体験を共有しあえる。さらに、青空市場、市民庭園・公園も潜在的に交流の場となり
得る。このように、「世代間交流性」という概念は一層高齢者・認知症の人々にやさしい都
市づくりを促し新しい方策づくりの理論的基盤となり得る。

4．結論

高齢者・認知症の人々にやさしい都市運動は高齢者に対する世界的広がりの前向きな運動
である。この運動の問題は「世代間交流性」的なパートナーシップ・関係性樹立という要の
役割を強調するという機会をとりそこなっているように思えることである。この「世代間交
流性」概念こそ将来の一層人間性豊かな都市づくりの展望をもたらすパートナーシップ・世
代間交流関係性樹立を可能にするものなのである。

Chapter 5

Cultivating Generational Empathy: A Strategy for Combatting Ageism and Strengthening Intergenerational Understanding

Nancy Z Henkin

Increased life expectancy, changing family structures, and technological advances raise important questions about the future of age relations. How will the longevity revolution impact expectations between generations, perceptions of aging, and the nature of social networks? Will families be able to address the needs of all their members? How will growing racial and ethnic diversity influence decisions about public investments? In order to address these issues, it is critical to re-imagine and revitalize the *social compact-* the obligations we have to each other over time.

Ageism is one of the greatest barriers to the social compact. It involves prejudicial attitudes, discriminatory practices, and policies/practices that perpetuate age-related stereotypes. Recent studies confirm that ageism is pervasive, negatively impacting all ages and depriving communities of the skills and talents of both young and old (Robbins,2015). It prevents us from seeing our common humanity and working collectively to address the complex challenges we face locally, nationally and globally.

This article focuses specifically on the interpersonal and intergroup aspects of ageism. It reviews research related to age- stereotyping, intergroup contact, and empathy in an effort to better understand ways in which intergenerational practice can be an effective tool for combatting age- bias and fostering intergenerational understanding.

1. Why NOW?

Major demographic trends and a recognition of the pernicious effects of ageism are among the factors driving a global focus on intergenerational solidarity. The number of older persons in the world is expected to more than double, exceeding the number of children for the first time by 2047 (United Nations, 2013). Increasing dependency ratios, particularly in more developed countries, are placing greater responsibility on young people to support older adults than in any previous generation. In the United States, an increasing racial generational gap suggests the possibility of serious social divisions and policy dilemmas over the competing agendas of an older white electorate and a younger population that is increasingly Latino, Asian and African-American (Pastor and Carter, 2012).

Although communities are becoming more age-diverse, non-kin social networks are primarily age-homogeneous. The separation of ages is considered "natural" in most developed countries. Hagestad and Uhlenberg, (2005) identify three main types of age segregation: *institutional* (work, school, housing), *spacial* (lack of face-to face contact) and *cultural* (generational differences in language, food, dress, etc.). Research suggests that age-segregation limits an individual's perspective and meaningful exchange between different age groups, increases loneliness and isolation for older people, and decreases protective factors for youth (Hagestad and Uhlenberg, 2005). It is cited as both a cause and consequence of *ageism*- prejudice or discrimination on the basis of a person's age (Hagestad and Uhlenberg, 2005; Vanderbeck, 2007).

Ageist attitudes are both *implicit* (unintentionally activated by the mere presence of an attitude object) and *explicit* (conscious, deliberate and controllable) (Turner, 2007). Ageism can involve patronizing or demeaning communication, physical and psychological distancing, and/or policies that promote perceptions of older people as individuals who should be pitied or ignored (North, 2012). Butler (1987) suggests that because ageism allows younger generations to see older people as different from themselves, they subtly cease to identify with elders as human beings. This concept of "othering"- viewing a person or group as intrinsically different from oneself- is important in understanding ageism. A number of researchers argue that "othering" lumps all older people into a single, inferior category (Phillips, 2010) and that it is a psychological defense against fear of death and frailty (Martens, 2005).

Although ageism is typically used to describe negative attitudes toward the elderly, it is also a measure of how older adults view younger generations (Christian, 2014). Youth often are portrayed in socially pejorative ways---as self-absorbed, lacking judgement, impulsive, and irresponsible. Like elders, they are shaped by historical and cultural events, impacted by race, ethnicity and socio-economic status, and are often perceived as problems to be solved rather than assets to be tapped. With minorities making up nearly half the children born in the United States, there is growing concern that older adults who don't see themselves reflected in the faces of the young will be less supportive of investments in education and workforce development (Pastor and Carter, 2012).

2. Intergroup Contact as a Strategy for Reducing Ageism

Intergroup contact involves face to face interaction between members of clearly defined groups. Intergroup contact theory suggests than when people have positive relationships across boundaries, there is a greater likelihood of cross-group understanding (Pettigrew and Tropp, 2006). Allport (1954) hypothesized that prejudice could be reduced through intergroup contact

Chapter 5 Cultivating Generational Empathy: A Strategy for Combatting Ageism and Strengthening Intergenerational Understanding   65

under the following facilitating conditions- equal status between groups, common goals, intergroup cooperation and support of institutions or authorities. Although there are conflicting conclusions regarding the generalizability of prejudice reduction to entire outgroups, Pettigrew and Tropp (2006) in their meta- analysis of 515 studies concluded that intergroup contact is associated with decreased prejudice and that Allport's conditions enhance the likelihood of positive outcomes.

A number of researchers have examined the impact of intergroup contact on implicit and explicit bias. Turner (2007) and Tam, Hewstone, Harwood (2006) suggest that *implicit*bias is influenced more directly by the *quantity* of contact people had with elderly. *Explicit* bias, on the other hand, is influenced by the *quality* (how close they feel to the other) of the contact (Pettigrew and Tropp,2006 and Schwartz and Simmons, 2001).

The identification of *mediating* mechanisms that facilitate the translation of intergroup contact into more positive attitudes and relations has contributed to a deeper level of understanding of this issue. Dovidio (2003) identifies the following as key mediators: fostering positive norms of cooperation and intergroup acceptance in structured group experiences, reducing anxiety and negative emotions, learning new information and increasing cultural sensitivity, personalizing communication, and transforming participants' representations of memberships from two to one group (Common Ingroup Theory). He proposes that developing a common ingroup identity does not require rejecting one's own identity. Rather it is possible to achieve a dual identity with" both superordinate and sub group identity simultaneously salient" (Dovido, 2003, p. 12). Hewstone and Brown (1986) developed a complementary theory that suggests that members of different groups have distinct but complementary roles to contribute toward common goals and maintain positive distinctiveness within a cooperative framework" (Dovido, 2003, p.12).

Much of the research on intergenerational contact has focused on the impact of family relationships on attitudes toward older adults. Harwood (2000) found that high quality contact with grandparents predicted greater perspective taking, less anxiety and more communicative accommodation which are associated with more positive attitudes toward older people and greater recognition of variability among the elderly. Silverstein (1997) suggests that the quality of a young person's relationship with grandparents influences support of policies intended to improve the well-being of older adults.

Examining a range of intergenerational interventions and their affect on prejudice, Christian (2014) suggests that mixed results may reflect a lack of emphasis on theory by practitioners designing interventions. She emphasizes the importance of developing close personal relationships between age groups over time rather than short term interventions. Similarly, Kite and Wagner (2002) suggest that building sustained familiarity with age-diverse people and fostering long term interaction in age-heterogeneous settings are the most effective strategies for breaking down prejudice and overcoming stigma.

3. Generational Empathy: a bridge to intergenerational understanding

Empathy- the ability to sense other people's emotions, coupled with the ability to imagine what someone else might be thinking or feeling" (Wikipedia) has been identified as a critical factor in all human relationships and an important mediator of attitudes and behavior. Batson (1997) suggests that empathy can reduce bias by leading people to feel more positively about others and influencing people's motivations to behave in supportive ways toward others whether or not they like them. Empathy is not synonymous with sympathy nor does it imply compassion or concern (Biggs, 2011).

Researchers suggest that empathy includes both affective and cognitive components. *Affective empathy* refers to the sensations and feelings we get in response to others' emotions. This can include mirroring what that person is feeling, or just feeling stressed when one detects another's fear or anxiety. *Cognitive empathy* refers to our ability to identify and understand other peoples' emotions. It involves imagining or projecting oneself into the place of another in order to understand what s/he is feeling (University of California-Berkeley).

Perspective taking and *self-disclosure* are two key aspects of empathy that can be cultivated. Perspective taking leads to a personalized approach to the other which can help reduce accessibility and expression of stereotypes. Galinsky and Moskowitz (2000) suggest that the perspective taking approach focuses attention outward toward the target individual and can lead to a reduction of mistrust and increase in interpersonal sensitivity and understanding. They found that taking the perspective of an older adult resulted in increased overlap in representations of the self and the older person as well as decreased ageist stereotyping.

Self-disclosure has been found to reduce anxiety and personalize intergroup interactions by promoting familiarity, perceived similarity, and better processing of individuating information about out group members (Aron, 2004, Dovidio, 2003, Harwood, 2005). When outgroup members are seen as like oneself, they are likely to have positive attributes like self. Empathizing with the outgroup may increase participants' perception that a common humanity and destiny is shared with the other group (Stephan and Finlay, 1999).

Generational empathy, putting oneself in the place of the generational other, is identified by Biggs (2011) as an important strategy for building sus-

68

tainable intergenerational relations and combatting ageism. He considers it a key component of generational intelligence, the ability to "act with awareness of one's generational circumstances while also taking the priorities of other groups into account" (Biggs, 2011, p. 41). Generational empathy involves recognizing separate but related frames of reference, acknowledging the thoughts and feelings of the age- other without eliminating the boundaries between self and other.

Biggs (2011, p.15) identifies four strategies for cultivating generational empathy and understanding:

1. *Promoting generational awareness* by understanding how one's immediate experience is affected by cohort, family and life course position. According to Biggs, it is not until one becomes aware of one's distinctive generational position that one can develop authentic relationships with other ages.

2. *Engaging in perspective taking* by examining the relationship between self and other and learning about the age other's priorities, desires, hopes and fears.

3. *Examining how power dynamics, ambivalence, and other assumptions* that underlie age relations can create challenges to empathy.

4. *Taking action* through the development of *stainable partnerships* and the creation of *intergenerational spaces* that facilitate reflection and negotiation.

Research on empathy across the life course is mixed. A four-wave longitudinal study spanning 12 years with participants ranging from 10-27 years, suggests that older cohorts report lower levels of empathy than younger ones (Gruhn, Rebucal, Diehl et al, 2009, Bailey and Henry, 2008). Another study from University of Michigan, however, found that self-reported empathy among college students between 1979 and 2009 dropped off by 40%, with

75 percent of students today rating themselves as less empathic than the average student 30 years ago (Zaki, 2011). Although more research is needed to better understand age differences, it is clear that strengthening empathy skills within and across all age groups would benefit individuals as well as intergenerational relations.

4. Implications for Intergenerational Practice

Over the past several decades, a wide variety of intergenerational programs and community initiatives have been developed to address specific community needs and facilitate cross-generational learning (Christian, 2014). Less attention, however, has been paid to understanding the relational aspects of intergenerational work. As Sanchez (2010) notes, building a culture of relationships must be a key aspect of intergenerational practice.

As discussed in this article, empathy is essential for the creation of sustainable cross-age relationships and the reduction of ageism. Based on the research presented, the following are a set of conditions under which intergenerational interventions could effectively cultivate empathy and deepen cross-age understanding:

- *Long term versus short term experiences that promote sustained contact over time.*
- *Welcoming intergenerational spaces in which people from diverse ages and backgrounds can build mutual respect.*
- *Explicit focus on relationship building, not just service provision.*
- *Use of strengths-based approaches that recognize how different generations can contribute to common goals.*
- *Interventions designed to raise generational consciousness, foster self-disclosure and perspective taking, and promote cooperative learning (e.g. intergen-*

70

erational dialogue, role reversal, storytelling, joint tasks, reflection).

• *Exposure to diverse populations (age, race, ethnicity, ability) in order to diminish stereotyping.*

Achieving these conditions will require that practitioners identify the cultivation of empathic relationships and the reduction of stereotypes as EXPLICIT goals of intergenerational work and design activities that are aligned with these goals. In addition, more research is needed regarding cultural norms/ beliefs related to age relations, empathy across the life course, attitudes of older adults toward youth, and the intersection of race/ethnicity and age. In these challenging and complex times, enhancing generational empathy is an important step in helping different age groups recognize their shared fate and engage in collective efforts that address inequalities and improve the quality of life for all.

References

Abrams, D., Eller, A. and Bryant, J. (2006). "An age apart: The effects of intergenerational contact and stereotype threat on performance and intergroup bias." Psychology and Aging, 4,691-702.

Aron, A., Aron, E.N., and Nelson, G. (2004). "Close relationships as including the other in the self". Journal of Personality and Social Psychology, 60, 241-253.

Bailey, P. and Henry, J. (2008). "Growing Less Empathic With Age: Disinhibition of the Self-Perspective." Journal of Gerontology. 63B (4), 219-226.

Batson, C.D., Polycarpou, M. et. al. (1997) "Empathy and attitudes: Can feeling for a member of a stigmatized group improve feelings toward the group?." Journal of Personality and Social Psychology, 72, 105-118.

Biggs, S. and Carr, S. (2015). "Age- and Child- Friendly Cities and the Promise of Intergenerational Space." Journal of Social Work Practice, 29 (1), 99-112.

Biggs, S. and Lowenstein, A. (2011) Generational Intelligence: A Critical Approach to Age Relations. London: Routledge.

Butler, R. (1987). Ageism. In G.I Maddox and R.C. Atchley (eds), The Encyclopedia of Aging (pp.22-23). New York: Springer.

Chasteen, A.,Schwartz, N. and Park, D. (2002). "The Activation of Aging Stereotypes in

Younger and Older Adults." Journal of Gerontology Series B, 57 (6), 540-547.

Christian, J. Turner, R., Holt, N. et.al. (2014). "Does Intergenerational Contact Reduce Ageism? When and How Contact Interventions Actually Work?" Journal of Arts and Humanities, 3 (1), 1-14.

Cruz- Saco, M. and Zelenev, S. (2010) Intergenerational Solidarity: Strengthening Economic and Social Ties New York. Palgrave Macmillan.

Cuddy, A., Norton, M. and Fiske, S. (2005) This Old Stereotype: The Pervasiveness and Persistence of the Elderly Stereotype." Journal of Social Issues, 61 (2), 265-283.

Dovidio, J., Gaertner, S., and Kawakami, K. (2003). "Intergroup contact: The Past, Present, and Future." Group Processes & Intergroup Relations 6 (1), 5-21.

Finlay, K. and Stephan, W.G. (2000). "Reducing prejudice: The effects of empathy on intergroup attitudes." Journal of Applied Social Psychology, 30, 1720-1737.

Gaertner, S.L. and Dovidio, J.F. (2000)."Reducing intergroup bias: The Common Ingroup Identity Model". Philadelphia, PA: Psychology Press.

Galinsky. A. and Moskowitz, G. (2000) "Perspective Taking: Decreasing Stereotype Expression, Stereotype Accessibility, and In-Group Favoritism". Journal of Personality and Social Psychology, 78 (4), 708-724.

Gruhn, D., Rebucal, K., Diehl. et al. (2008). "Empathy Across the Adult Lifespan: Longitudinal and Experience- Sampling Findings." Dec. 2008, Emotion, 8 (6), 753-765.

Hagestad, G. and Uhlenberg, P.(2005) "The social separation of old and young: A root of agcism." Journal of social issues 61, no. 2 (2005): 343-360.

Harwood, J. (2000). "Communicative predictors of solidarity in the grandparent-grandchild relationship". Journal of Social and Personal Relationships, 17, 743-766.

Hewstone, M. and Brown, R.J. (1986). "Contact is not enough: An Intergroup perspective on the Contact Hypothesis." In M. Hewstone and R. Brown (eds.) Contact and conflict in intergroup encounters. Osford: Basil Blackwell.

Kite, M., Stockdale, G. Whitley, B. et al. (2005) "Attitudes toward younger and older adults. Journal of Social Issues, 61, 241-266.

Kite ME, Wagner LS. (2002). "Attitudes toward older adults". In: Nelson TD, editor. Ageism: Stereotyping and prejudice against older persons. Cambridge, MA: MIT Press, pp. 129-161.

Kuehne, V. (ed.) (1999). Intergenerational Programs: Understanding What We Have Learned. New York: The Haworth Press, Inc.

Martens, A, Goldenberg, J.A., and Greeenberg, J. (2005) "A terror management perspective on ageism." Journal of Social Issues, 61(2), 223-39.

Miller, N. (2002) Personalization and the Promise of Contact Theory". Journal of social Issues, 58, 387-410.

North, M. and Fiske, S. (2012) "An Inconvenienced Youth? Ageism and its Potential Inter-generational Roots." Psychological Bulletin, 138 (5).

Pastor, Manuel, & Carter, Vanessa. (2012). Reshaping the Social Contract: Demographic Distance and Our Fiscal Future. Poverty and Race, 21 (1), 1-6.

Pettigrew, T.F., and Tropp, L.R. (2006). "A Meta-Analytic Test of Intergroup Contact Theory". Journal of Personality and Social Psychology, 90 (5), 751-783.

Phillips, J., Ajrouch, K. and Hillcoat, S. (2010). Key Concepts in Social Gerontology. London: Sage.

Roberts, S. (2007) "New Demographic Racial Gap Emerges." New York Times, May 17. Retrieved from: http://www.nytimes.com/2007/05/17/us/17census.html.

Robbins, L. (ed.) (2015) "The Pernicious Problem of Ageism." Generations. Journal of the American Society on Aging.

Sanchez, Mariano, Saez, J. and Pinazo, S. (2010). Intergenerational Solidarity: Programs and Policy Development. In Cruz- Saco,. M. and Zelenev, S. (eds). Intergenerational Solidarity: Strengthening Economic and Social Ties, 129-146. New York. Palgrave Macmillan.

Schwartz, L.K. and J.P. Simmons (2001). "Contact Quality and Attitudes toward the Elderly." Educational Gerontology 27: 127–137.

Silverstein, M. and Parrot, T. (1997). "Attitudes toward public support of the elderly: Does early involvement with grandparents moderate generational tensions". Research on Aging, 19, 108-132.

Stephan, W.G. and Finlay, K. (1999) "The role of empathy in improving intergroup relations." Journal of Social Issues, 55, 729-743.

Tam, T, Hewstone, M., Harwood, J. et al. "Intergroup Contact and Grandparent-Grandchild Communication: The Effects of Self-Disclosure on Implicit and Explicit Biases Against Older People." (2006), 9 (3), 413-429.

Tavernise, Sabrina. (2011). "Numbers of children of whites falling fast." The New York Times, 6.

Turner, R., Hewstone, M. and Voci, A. (2007). "Reducing Explicit and Implicit Outgroup Prejudice Via Direct and Extended Contact: The Mediating Role of Self-Disclosure and Intergroup Anxiety. " Journal of Personality and Social Psychology, 93 (3), 369-388.

United Nations, Department of Economic and Social Affairs, Population Division (2013). World Population Ageing 2013. /SER.A/348.

University of California- Berkeley, Greater Good Newsletter. "What is Empathy?" Retrieved from http://greatergood.berkeley.edu/topic/empathy.

Vanderbeck, Robert M. (2007). "Intergenerational Geographies: Age Relations, Segregation and Re‐engagements." Geography compass 1, no. 2, 200-221.

Wang, Y., Davidson, M., Yakushko, O. et al. (2003). "The Scale of Ethno-cultural Empathy:

Development, Validation, and Reliability. Journal of Counseling Psychology, 50 (2), 221-234.

Zaki, J.(2011). "What, me care? Young are Less Empathetic." Retrieved from http://www.scientificamerican.com/article/what-me-care/

第5章　世代間の共感を醸成する：エイジズムを克服し、世代間理解を強化するための戦略

ナンシー・Z・ヘンケン

　エイジズムは社会契約に対する最も大きな障害の一つである。エイジズムには害を与えようとする態度や差別的な言行、年齢に基づくステレオタイプに基づく考え方や言行が含まれる。近年の研究からはエイジズムが広く蔓延していることが示されており、それがすべての世代にネガティブな影響を与えているほか、コミュニティにおける若者と高齢者の両者から技術や才覚を奪っている（Robbins,2015）。

　本稿では特に個人およびグループ間のエイジズムという概念に焦点を当て、年齢に関するステレオタイプ、グループ内でのやりとり、また年齢によるバイアスを退け世代間理解を促進するための効果的な方略としての共感のあり方に関する研究をレビューする。

1．なぜ今、世代間交流なのか

　エイジズムがもたらすネガティブな影響に対する認識の高まりが、世代間のつながりに対する世界的な関心を高めている要因の一つである。特に先進諸国において従属人口指数は上昇しており、今の現役世代はこれまでのどの世代よりも高齢者を支えることに対して大きな責任を担っている。コミュニティは多様な年齢構成となっているが、非親類による社会ネットワークは、ほとんどが均一の年齢層によって構成されている。世代間の分離は大部分の先進諸国において「自然なこと」であるとみなされている。

　Hagestad と Uhlenberg（2005）は、主に「職場や学校、住まいなどの組織」、「面と向かった接触の不足という空間」、そして「世代間の言語や食べ物、服装といった違いという文化」の3つにおいて世代間の分離があると述べている。世代間分離は、異なる世代との接触を通じた自身の将来展望や有意義なやりとりを制限し、高齢者の孤独と孤立を深め、子どもを保護する要因を減らすことが示唆されている。

　エイジズムは内在的でありかつ顕在的である。すなわち「意図せずに対象物がそこにあるだけで生起される」ものでありながら「意識的、作為的であり、かつ制御可能である」という性質を持っている（Turner, 2007）。エイジズムには恩着せや屈辱を与えるようなコミュニケーション、身体的あるいは心理的に距離を置くこと、あるいは高齢者を憐れまれるべき、または無視されるべき存在として認識することを奨める信念が含まれる（North, 2012）。Butler（1987）は、エイジズムは若い世代が高齢者を自分達とは異なるものであるとみなすことで生じるものであるとしている。

　この「othering（他人化）」、すなわち個人やグループを自分とは本質的に異なるものとして捉えるという概念は、エイジズムを理解するうえで重要である。他人化によって全ての高

第5章　世代間の共感を醸成する：エイジズムを克服し、世代間理解を強化するための戦略　75

齢者が同一であるとみなすようになる（Phillips, 2010）、あるいは他人化は死や衰弱の恐怖に対抗するための精神的な防衛機構である（Martens, 2005）と主張する研究者もいる。

　エイジズムは典型的に高齢者に対するネガティブな態度を表すものとして用いられるが、高齢者がどのように若い世代を捉えているかという指標としても用いられる（Christian, 2014）。若者はしばしば自己中心的、判断力を欠く、衝動的である、あるいは無責任であるといったような存在として描写される。高齢者と同様に、若者は社会的あるいは文化的な事物によって形作られ、人種や民族、そして社会経済的な地位によって影響を受ける。また若者はしばしば利用されるべき資産というよりもむしろ、解決すべき問題の主体として扱われている。

２．エイジズムを低減させるための戦略としてのグループ間の接触

　Allport（1954）は、偏見は「グループ間での対等な立場」で「共通の達成すべき課題」を持ち、「グループ間の協力と専門家や機関による支援がある」という促進的条件下での接触によって減少させることが可能であるという仮説を立てた。Pettigrew と Tropp（2006）は515の研究のメタ分析によって、グループ間での接触が偏見の低減に関係があるとし、Allport を支持した。

　グループ間接触が内在的および顕在的バイアスに与える影響について、Turner ら（2007）や Schwartz ら（2001）は、内在的バイアスは高齢者との接触によってより直接的な影響を受けることを示唆している。一方で顕在的バイアスは接触の質、すなわちどれほどお互いを近しいと感じたかによって影響されているとしている。世代間接触に関する研究の多くは、老親への態度が家族関係に与える影響に焦点が当てられてきた。Harwood（2000）は祖父母との良質な接触が、広い展望的視野の獲得や不安の低減、高齢者への肯定的な態度に関連付けられるコミュニケーション、加齢等の高齢者の変動性への理解をもたらし得ることを示した。

　世代間介入の範囲とそれが偏見にもたらす影響について検討した結果として、Christian（2014）は偏見を解消することを目指す介入デザインの作成者に共感についての理論の欠落を示唆するとともに、短い期間での介入よりもむしろ、異なる世代による大きな時間枠での緊密な関係性の構築の重要性を強調している。同様に、Kite and Wagner（2002）は多様な年代の人と親交を持つ機会を作ってそれを継続し、世代間の長い期間での関係構築を促進させることが、偏見を克服し、スティグマを封じ込める最も効果的な戦略であると示唆している。

３．世代の感情移入：世代間の理解への掛け橋

　共感はすべての人間関係における重要な要素であり、かつ態度や行動の重要な媒介物（メディエーター）であるとみなされてきた。研究者らは、共感が情動と認知の両者の成分を含

むことを示唆している。展望的視野の獲得と自己開示は、共感を育む上で重要となる2つの側面である。展望的視野の獲得は、他者への人間的なアプローチを導き、ステレオタイプの発現や利用を低減させる。また自己開示は親しみやすさを高めることや類似性を感じさせることで、不安感を低減させる。

世代間への共感、すなわち他の世代の立場に自分を置いて考えることは、持続可能な世代間関係を構築し、エイジズムと戦うための重要な戦略である（Biggs, 2011）とされている。彼は世代間の共感を世代知の重要な要素であるとみなし、「自分の世代の事情も考慮しながら、他のグループを優先する意識を持って行動する」能力であるとしている（Biggs, 2011）。世代間の共感は、自己と他者との間にある境界を排除することなく、世代の持つ考え方や感情を、別々ではあるが関連している認知の枠組みを認識し、認めることを含んでいる。

10歳から27歳までの参加者による12年間の縦断的研究では、年長者のコホートが若いコホートよりも低い水準の共感的意識を示していることが示唆されている（Gruhn, Rebucal, Diehl et al, 2009, Bailey and Henry, 2008）。しかしながら、ミシガン大学での別の研究では、今日の75%の大学生が、30年前の学生の平均よりも自分自身を共感的でないと評価した（Zaki, 2011）。

4．世代間における実践に対する示唆

ここまでで述べた通り、共感は持続可能な世代間関係の構築とエイジズムの低減に必要不可欠である。先行研究に基づけば、世代間介入を通じて効果的に共感をはぐくみ、世代間理解を深めるための条件として、以下が挙げられる。
1. 短期的であるよりも長期的な経験が、継続的な接触を促進する。
2. 多様な年齢や背景を持つ人々がお互いを尊重する意識を構築する上では、世代間で交流する場が求められる。
3. サービスの提供だけでなく、関係づくりのための明確な焦点化が必要である。
4. どのようにして異なる世代同士が共通の目的に向かって貢献できるかを認識した上で、強みに基づいたアプローチを使用する。
5. 世代の意識、自己開示と展望獲得、協調学習を促進するために設計された介入をデザインする。
6. ステレオタイプを低減させるため、多様な集団に触れる。

これらの条件を達成するためには、介入者が共感的な関係の成熟を認識することや、これらの目標と整合している「明確な」目標として、ステレオタイプの低減を目指そうとすることが求められる。世代間の共感を高めることが、人々の生活の質を高める上での重要なステップであるといえよう。

Chapter 6

Intergenerational-ESL Activities: Lessons Learned and Corresponding Actions

Alan Lai

1. Abstract

This chapter reports lessons learned from an intergenerational program conducted in Hong Kong. The program is oriented towards Hong Kong's unprecedented growth of the older population as well as the issue of secondary school children in the region who lack opportunities outside the classroom to practice English as a second language (ESL). With this, the program planner structured the program with six activities, all of which were de facto a series of predetermined object-oriented procedures involving retired citizens in secondary schoolchildren's ESL education. Before implementing them, a process that systematically solicited a group of students, teachers and retired citizens for comments and then fed them back to the design protocol was adopted. Discussion hints on issues encountered while conducting the program at a secondary school in Hong Kong. The web of experiences then elicits corresponding actions to redress the issues. Understanding in a wider context for both practice and theory is also considered.

Keywords: Intergenerational activities, English as a second language education, retired citizens, secondary schoolchildren

2. Introduction

This chapter attempts to report lessons learned from an after-school program, "Intergenerational-English as a second language" or "IG-ESL", conducted at a secondary school in Hong Kong. First, it introduces the program as a direct response to two needs of Hong Kong: i.e., (1) the need of providing opportunities for secondary schoolchildren of Hong Kong to practice English outside the classroom, and (2) the need of providing another active aging or civic engagement vehicle for retired citizens.

Next, it outlines the design procedures that helped create six IG-ESL activities for the program, all of which involved retired citizens to offer schoolchildren opportunities to practice English outside the classroom. Focus is then switched to issues encountered while conducting the program. Finally, it solicits actions that aim to address the issues, thereby optimizing the experience of running the program. Further understanding by practice and theory in a wider context is also considered as concluding remarks.

3. The Need to Create Opportunities for Schoolchildren

Conceptually, IG-ESL represents a response to the growing concern that Hong Kong's secondary schoolchildren are facing an adverse situation for English language learning. In the classroom, Liu & Littlewood (1997, p. 371) describe the situation as no more than "listening to teacher". Coniam (2014) reports that ESL learning in class is mostly catering to the overwhelming liking of passing exams. To illustrate, Photo 1 shows a booklist of a secondary school in Hong Kong that requires students to purchase exam preparation exercises as textbooks for their English language subject.

van Lier (2007) criticizes that such an exam-oriented education hardly supports learning since exam-based memory tends not to last long.

Outside class, To, Chan, Lam, & Tsang (2011) reports that many secondary schoolchildren in Hong Kong have no opportunities to practice English, let alone expecting them to adopt active speech roles with English as a daily life vehicle of communication. Even opportunities are available for students of EMI (English as the medium of instructions) schools outside the classroom, there are just a few of them (Luk, 2010). Clearly, this situation is a mismatch to one of Hong Kong Education Bureau's mandates (2001):

"... teachers are encouraged to provide greater opportunities for learners to use English for purposeful communication both inside and outside the classroom" (p. 36).

In this light, there appears a need to transform the way how English is practiced by secondary schoolchildren (Liu & Littlewood, 1997). In other words, exploring ways to offer opportunities for school children to experience the use of English inside and/or outside class is viewed essential.

4. The Need to Create Opportunities for Retired Citizens

According to the Hong Kong Census and Statistics Department (2013) and the Research Office of the Legislative Council Secretariat (2014), there were around 1.15 million retired citizens in 2013, and this number is likely to rise to 3 million in the next thirty years of Hong Kong. The fact that the population of the retirement sector in Hong Kong keeps increasing does not have to be considered as an issue. Rather, it could be seen as a valuable resource since older adults who choose to serve the community could offer a long-term supply of assistance for people in need.

Photo 1

As such, what seems to matter is the need of strategically offering volunteer opportunities for the retirement sector to become a support system of some sort. In Hong Kong, there are groups and organizations that provide retirees with some civic engagement and volunteer opportunities; however, considering the challenge and the rapidly growing size of the older adult population, more needs to be done in this area.

5. Intergenerational-ESL Activities

5-1 Aims and Strategies

In light of the two-pronged need, the approach that gets retirees involved in ESL education takes off as an intergenerational framework (see Lai & Kaplan, 2013). On the one hand, it revolves around a program-wise strategy to spawn opportunities for schoolchildren to practice English outside the classroom. On the other hand, it represents a way of providing retirees with opportunities to engage younger generations.

The rationale to get retirees involved is four-fold:

1) Retirees represent an abundant resource that accumulates lifetime stories. To quote Druin (2008), "Stories can be a reason to collaborate; they can be a reason to be social; stories can be what engages reluctant learners; stories can enable creative expression and communication" (p. 43).

2) Retirees are alongside a greater locus of control on availability. What children need for practicing English is an encounter available for them.

3) According to Erikson's (1959) psychosocial development theory, the more an individual accomplishes a lifetime career, the more they stand ready to contributing to the younger generations. Children who

Chapter 6 Intergenerational-ESL Activities: Lessons Learned and Corresponding Actions 81

are interested in practicing English need to have a friend who feels ready to help.

4) Research shows that an enhanced capability to forgive is conducive to health when one ages (Silton, Flannelly, & Lutjen, 2013). This aspect of aging can be a reason as considering that forgiveness is what most children in Hong Kong need as they are prone to have the fear of making mistakes when practicing English (see Tsui, 1996).

Following the rationales, the program set off to recruit retired citizens who were interested in providing schoolchildren with opportunities to practice ESL outside the classroom.

5-2 Activity Design

To design the IG-ESL activities, I invited eight secondary schoolchildren (at Forms 3 and 4 levels), six schoolteachers (including an English language panel head, four English language teachers, and a school activity specialist), and eight local retired citizens to be the design informants. Guha et al. (2013) indicate that getting different generations of stakeholders involved could bring in more voices, thoughts, and insights, thereby more possibly giving a creative edge to the design.

The entire design process lasted for six months. To jumpstart it, I created six protocol activities. Each week, I held a meeting to take turn seeing each informant. During the meeting, I introduced what had been designed, and I solicited feedback from them. Using an audio recorder, I recorded their inputs and later fed their comments back to the design protocol for improvement. The final stage of the design process was reached when all informants felt satisfied with all the changes.

To organize the comments systematically, I employed Corbin and Strauss's (2008) thematic analysis to sort them through theme by theme. As a result, insights gained to refine the activities were that students preferred opportunities to spawn through add-on enrichment (e.g., staying behind after lesson to engage older adults more) and partnership (e.g., demanding that each production outcome would be done with an older adult partner); teachers preferred in-depth engagement (e.g., adding a mission that requires students to interview an older adult); and older adults preferred technological supports (e.g., expecting all the WIFI, computers, the Internet, and technicians to stand prepared).

5-3 Activity Contents and Intended Outcomes

Through the design process, the IG-ESL model was materialized into six object-oriented activities, each of which involved both generations in role plays, writing a letter, sharing jokes, podcasting a talk show, and creating an e-learning video. The activity contents were qualitatively different, but they shared the same purpose of providing students with opportunities to practice written and spoken English outside the classroom. In this context, all the objectives could stay focused on friendship to foster, real-life stories to exchange with fun (e.g., older adults' childhood stories, toys or games), and either local issues or family-related topics to work with. Table 1 shows the titles, contents, and intended outcomes of each activity.

5-4 Implementation [Strategies, Site and Participants]

The co-shared site was located in a secondary school in Hong Kong. The school is government-subsidized and famed with many graduates who have achieved top positions across industries. According to the school principal, many of them like offering voluntary services to the schoolchildren particularly through the school's alumni association.

The school was selected due to the convenience of an adult member's

Chapter 6 Intergenerational-ESL Activities: Lessons Learned and Corresponding Actions　83

Activities	Core Activity Titles	Contents	Objectives
Activity 1	Time Machine	With guidance provided by an older adult partner, each IG group creates a drama based on older adults' childhood.	• To establish a relaxed and non-judgmental setting that encourages participants to express themselves in English. • To appreciate older adults' personal histories. • To feel excited about what old-time families look like. • To gain confidence in presenting in front of an audience.
Activity 2	I Love This Ad	In this activity, each IG group searches for a TV advert with a theme about family and then composes a reflective essay (200 to 300 words) about a family-related topic.	• To appreciate the importance of family relationships in their lives and in the lives of others. • To strengthen students' writing skills, speaking confidence, and sense of camaraderie with participating older adults.
Activity 3	I Love This Jokes	Each IG pair takes a turn telling an English language joke about family. Before telling, the group finds a group to challenge. The joke-telling group wins if the joke-listening group breaks into laughter.	•To acknowledge that family is a source of fun. • To realize that older adults can be funny as well as fun partners. • To speak in a creative way.
Activity 4	Your Voices in Press	Each IG group co-authors a letter about creating a positive environment in the family.	• To stimulate interest in creating a better family environment. • To obtain an enriched intergenerational partnership. • To practice English in real-world contexts.
Activity 5	Podcast Your Voices	Each IG group creates a podcast program based on Activity 4.	• To build confidence and coherence in conversation. • To demonstrate 'power of persuasive skills' and share it with families. • To extend intergenerational partnership to public discourse.
Activity 6	iG-ESL Academy	IG partners create a one-minute video with an educational topic and upload it to Youtube.com for sharing.	• To demonstrate creative discourses when different generations work together interactively.

Table 1

direct recommendation to the school principal. After an introduction meeting, the school principal considered this program worth a try and immediately arranged two English teachers and the school's panel head of English department to follow up.

Selection of students began with the teachers' decision to offer the program for their Form 3 (i.e., Grade 9) students. To recruit them, a letter with a brief introduction of the program and a reply slip was given to the students' parents. The teachers considered that asking parents to make the sign-up decision directly would receive more replies. Within two weeks, the teachers informed me that a total of 40 students enrolled in the program.

For recruiting retired citizens, I conducted a seminar with help offered by the Institute of Active Aging (IAA). Two weeks before the seminar, IAA sent out an email through their LISTSERV to their members. At this level of promotion, 20 retired adults attended the recruitment seminar. After a 30 minutes presentation, all of them signed up, which was quite a surprise.

Besides IAA, the adult member who recommended the program to the school also helped recruit three more retired members. All of them came from the school's alumni association. Supposedly, 23 retirees signed up, but before the program began, three of them decided not to join due to private reasons.

In this case, the program began with 20 adult members and 40 schoolchildren. In average, each adult member formed a group with two schoolchildren.

The six activities were implemented throughout a period of 12 weeks during the summer holidays. Each week, the adult members engaged the students for two hours. Their involvements included partnering up with the students as friends (rather than tutors) and co-sharing the responsibility of finishing each activity. To enrich the involvement process, the adult members were required to attend a one-hour session every week. During the time, they were introduced the activities as well as some theories about education and second language development.

In a pre-determined way, each activity's intended outcomes were fixed (e.g., performing a drama, producing a video clip, co-authoring a letter, etc.). To facilitate the implementation process, all groups were required to participate in the same activities in order. But after the first activity, the participants were encouraged to determine their own schedules (e.g., when to start the next activity). This flexibility was offered due to the fact that some groups perceived pressure when they progressed very differently from each other.

6. Issues Encountered and Corresponding Actions

During the twelve weeks, I encountered a series of issues. In this section, they are summarized and presented as four lessons. Actions that aim to redress the issues are proposed lesson by lesson.

6-1 Lesson 1: Overzealous Supporters

The program encountered a few overzealous senior supporters whose contributions were appreciative but overwhelming. Almost every week, I was told of the possibility of falling behind from schedule. The pressure remained even though the flexibility of scheduling by them had been introduced and recapped.

At times, I also received comments concerning students' exam skills, suggesting that the program should adopt more traditional learning methods, such as doing mechanical exercises, in order to boost exam performances.

Another overwhelming experience was encountered in the last two weeks when an adult member wanted to advocate some adventure-based games. The member was very passionate about them, believing that the games could bring the program up to the next level. In one lesson, the member brought all materials to the lesson and wanted everyone try. Since I learned that one of them had resulted in serious injuries in an adventure-based program before, I nipped that attempt in the bud.

6-2 Corresponding Action for Lesson 1: Starbucks Approach

Overzealous supporters are supporters. As such, ways to strengthening cooperation between them and the program staff are worth exploring. An action suggested to take is to invite adult members to a coffee shop, say Starbucks, and have a cup of coffee together. This will be a small group setting in which an adult member or two could join me in a relaxing environment. Although it seems informal, the contact could still be of courtesy, respect and commitment, thereby increasing the likelihood of building mutual understanding. If possible, new ideas or justifications behind plans that might otherwise be misunderstood could be exchanged.

6-3 Lesson 2: Unmotivated Students

Besides overzealous supporters, we also encountered a few student members who appeared unmotivated. They skipped lessons, easily wandered off to non-program matters, and even quit. The following feedback from one of them perceived the issue as a result of his parent's parenting style:

"I don't want to come. This is supposed to be summer holiday, but my parents forced me to join so many programs. I want a holiday. I want to do what I want."

After hearing what the student said, his adult partner suggested running the program beyond the summer time:

Chapter 6 Intergenerational-ESL Activities: Lessons Learned and Corresponding Actions   87

"We are giving students too much. No wonder he doesn't want to come. Do we have to do this program in the summer holiday? If it is activity to pursue intrinsically. That said, letting go of the power by giving participants opportunities to exercise the capacity to select seems to be an attempt worth considering.

6-4 Corresponding Action for Lesson 2: Seminar Approach

Students' lack of motivation may not have to be a result of parenting, be it authoritarian or not. Running the program beyond holidays may help boost the attendance rate, but if it is nothing more than chasing students around, exploring further strategies is necessary.

One action that seems worth taking is to recruit student members through seminar. In this approach, proposed strategies include introducing the program to students with introductory slides, anticipating their needs, emphasizing the non-punitive nature of the program (e.g., unlike traditional learning that emphasizes on high-stakes exam), probing questions for immediate feedback, clearing doubts, and clarifying the sign-up procedures.

Besides the strategies, the approach also needs to hinge on some pre-seminar preparations. For example, there is a need for some school staff to make corresponding arrangements such as giving out a promotional notice to students, organizing the seminar as an add-on event, determining all the sign-up criteria, etc.

Ultimately, these strategies and preparations, when weaved together, should serve the purpose of letting students, rather than their parents, decide whether they want to join or not.

6-5 Lesson 3: Unwanted Lectures

To recap, a one-hour training was provided for the adult members before having them engage the schoolchildren. At the beginning, almost all adult members attended it, but the attendance rate dramatically dropped after a few sessions. One day, I received a call from an adult member. He told me that most of the adult members found the professional development sessions unwanted since they perceived them either too long or too much of academic talk (e.g., having too many lectures). To my relief though, the member reported to me that most of them found the training necessary since it could give them a sense of preparation and teamwork. The issue was by and large a matter of duration and conducting mode.

6-6 Corresponding Action for Lesson 3: Discussion Approach

To address the issue, a review committee that included two older adult members was formed. They agreed that the professional development session should be reduced to 30 minutes. However, they advised that the first two sessions should still remain one hour in order to create a greater sense of preparation and teamwork from the beginning.

To deal with the issue of the lecturing mode, key materials for professional development could be kept minimal. Next, adult members are encouraged to select particular materials and discuss in a small group setting. In this discussion approach, they are the ones to initiate a topic based on needs or issues, thereby wanting to stay more possibly.

6-7 Lesson 4: Rigid Activities

Rigidity appears to influence the program at the activity level. As each activity was predetermined in order, it inevitably contributed to having a sense of falling behind when different groups compared with each other. Another derived issue is that participants were not given the opportunities to select right from the beginning which activity to pursue intrinsically. That

Chapter 6 Intergenerational-ESL Activities: Lessons Learned and Corresponding Actions 89

said, letting go of the power by giving participants opportunities to exercise the capacity to select seems to be an attempt worth considering.

6-8 Corresponding Action for Lesson 4: Toolbox Approach

To facilitate the idea of letting participants select what they would like to do, a toolbox or a case in which a variety of activity cards are kept inside will be created. By practice, participants will be encouraged to interact and negotiate with their group members not only which particular activities to select but also what outcomes to intend, what goals to set, and what actions to take.

By theory, it is to run with the rationale that learners who are given opportunities to explore, encounter, select and then exercise the capacity to act (or agency) tend to learn in a more intrinsic way (van Lier, 2004). As such, the issue about unmotivated students might also be addressed in this way.

In essence, the toolbox is to create a stimulating milieu, or a learning environment based on the premise that "an organism learns and grows so long as it actively engages in and with its environment" (van Lier, 2008, p. 602). From a linguistic point of view, a stimulating milieu is viewed essential since it is where semiotic (or meaning-making) affordances for ESL learners to practice English meaningfully might become possible (van Lier, 2004). Of note, promoting one's agency requires perceivable opportunities (or affordances) to engage with (van Lier, 2007).

7. Concluding Remarks

In this chapter, I have reported lessons learned from issues encountered. Upon this groundwork, a number of actions that aim to optimize the implementation process of the program have also been presented.

90

As a remark, the actions share a common ground: i.e., to weave the ecology of interconnecting and interacting generations into the program. For instance, the Starbucks approach is to create a comfort zone, whereby the program staff and participants may feel more interconnected to each other if each other' s preferences, backgrounds, beliefs, intentions, difficulties, etc. are shared and understood; the seminar approach is to interact with potential students before recruiting them, thereby incubating a sense of interconnection between them and the program; the discussion approach is to let adult members find their niche by exploring topics either pertaining to them or conducive to intergenerational partnership; and the toolbox approach is to connect all generations and build friendship as they share experiences and negotiate meanings in a stimulating milieu.

The ecological projection, when further looked at, may also underlie an "organic" implication. During a recent visit (organized by Generations United in July, 2015) to an organic farm in Hawaii, the farm manager said, "We don't feed the plants. We don't feed the animals. We feed the environment. In this way, the plants and animals will explore and select their own food. That's how they tend to grow differently from those produced in production farmhouses." In this wider context, the program is then meant to proceed with an organic vision: i.e., participants are not to follow suit; they are there to select; they are not there to receive instructions; they create them; they are not there to take orders; they take actions; they are not even there to produce outcomes; they advocate them.

To orient the program towards the vision, details are not just a group of minds planning in advance, but all the interconnected minds as a whole to unfold them dynamically in motion.

On this basis, hardly seen is just a bit of change here and there; more likely is a transformation of the way how the program gets optimized and

Chapter 6 Intergenerational-ESL Activities: Lessons Learned and Corresponding Actions   91

keeps sustaining.

References

Coniam, D. (2014). Private tutorial schools in Hong Kong: An examination of the perceptions of public examination re-takers. The Asia-Pacific Education Researcher, 23(3), 379-388.

Corbin, J., & Strauss, A. (2008). Basics of qualitative research: Techniques and procedures for developing grounded theory (3rd ed.). Los Angeles: Sage Publications.

Dora To, L. W., Phoebe Chan, Y. L., Lam, Y. K., & Tsang, S. K. Y. (2011). Reflections on a primary school teacher professional development programme on learning English through Process Drama. Research in Drama Education: The Journal of Applied Theatre and Performance, 16(4), 517-539.

Druin, A. (2008). LIFELONG INTERACTIONS Designing online interactions: what kids want and what designers know. Interactions, 15(3), 42-44.

Erikson, E. (1959). Identity and the life cycle. Psychological Issues, 1(1). New York: International Universities Press.

Guha, M. L., Druin, A., & Fails, J. A. (2013). Cooperative inquiry revisited: Reflections of the past and guidelines for the future of intergenerational co-design. International Journal of Child-Computer Interaction, 1(1), 14-23.

Hong Kong Census and Statistics Department (2013). Thematic Household Survey Report No. 52. Retrieved from http://www.digital21.gov.hk/eng/statistics/download/household-report2013_52.pdf

Hong Kong Education Bureau. (2001). Learning to Learn - The Way Forward in Curriculum. Retrieved from
http://www.edb.gov.hk/en/sch-admin/sch-registration/about-sch-registration/ index.html

Lai, A; Kaplan, M. (2013). Intergenerational strategies for enriching the ESL education platform, 11(4), 425-439.

Liu, N. F., & Littlewood, W. (1997). Why do many students appear reluctant to participate in classroom learning discourse?. System, 25(3), 371-384.

Luk, J. (2010). Talking to score: Impression management in L2 oral assessment and the co-construction of a test discourse genre. Language Assessment Quarterly, 7(1), 25-53.

Silton, N. R., Flannelly, K. J., & Lutjen, L. J. (2013). It pays to forgive! Aging, forgiveness, hostility, and health. Journal of Adult Development, 20(4), 222-231.

Research Office of the Legislative Council Secretariat (2014). Preparing for population ageing. Research Brief, 1, 1-14.

To, L. W., Chan, Y. L., Lam, Y. K., & Tsang, S. K. Y. (2011). Reflections on a primary school teacher professional development programme on learning English through Process Drama. Research in Drama Education: The Journal of Applied Theatre and Performance, 16(4), 517-539.

Tsui, A. B. (1996). Reticence and anxiety in second language learning. Voices from the language classroom, 145-167.

van Lier, L. (2004). The ecology and semiotics of language learning: A sociocultural perspective (Vol. 3). Springer Science & Business Media.

Van Lier, L. (2007). Action-based teaching, autonomy and identity. International Journal of Innovation in Language Learning and Teaching, 1(1), 46-65.

第6章　世代間 ESL 活動：教訓とそれに対応する活動

アラン・レイ

本章は、香港の中等学校で行われた"第二外国語としての世代間英語""IG-ESL"という、ある放課後のプログラムから学んだレッスンを報告する。

香港の二つのニーズは、（1）香港の中等学校の生徒への教室外での英語の練習の機会を与えること、（2）定年退職した市民へ、他の雇用手段を与えることである。これを受けて、プログラム作成に向けて6つの IG-ESL 活動を作りだす手順と4つのレッスンを述べる。

教室において、Liu & Littlewood（1997,p.371）は、その状況を"listening to teacher"に過ぎないとした。Coniam（2014）は、教室内における ESL 学習が主に試験に合格することに全般的に直結していると報告している。写真1は、香港の中等学校のブックリストで、生徒たちに英語のテキストとして試験準備用問題集を購入することを求めている。（写真1本書 p.79）

van Lier（2007）は、このような試験向けの教育では、試験基盤の記憶が長く持たないため、学習としてほとんど役立たないと批評する。

To, Chan, Lam, & Tsang（2011）は、教室の外では、多くの香港の中等学校の生徒は、英語に積極的なコミュニケーションの手段としての役割を期待しているにもかかわらず、英語を練習する機会がないと報告している。EMI（English as the medium of instructions）の学校の生徒たちには機会はあるが、ほんの一部である（Luk, 2010）。明らかに、この状況は Hong Kong Education Bureau's mandates（2001）とは合致していない。この観点においては、中等学校の生徒が英語を練習する方法を転換することの必要性を主張している（Liu & Littlewood, 1997）。

香港では 2013 年には約 115 万人の定年退職者がいて、この数は今後 30 年で 300 万人にまで増加しそうなのである。重要なのは、退職者層が何らかの支援システムとなるためのボランティアの機会を戦略的に提供することの必要性である。香港では、定年退職者に市民参加やボランティアの機会を提供する団体や組織がある。2方向に照らして、世代間 ESL 活動のねらいと戦略、ESL 教育に定年退職者を獲得するアプローチは、世代間の枠組みとして出発している（Lai & Kaplan, 2013 参照）。

定年退職者を獲得する理論的根拠は4つに分類される。

1. 定年退職者は人生の物語を積み上げてきたという豊かな人材を象徴する（Druin　2008, p.43）。
2. 定年退職者はよりよい可能性の根源である。子どもたちが英語を練習するのに必要なことは彼らとの出会いである。
3. Erikson（1959）の心理発達理論によると、個人が人生のキャリアを達成するほど、彼らより若い世代に貢献する準備ができている。英語の練習に興味をもっている子どもた

94

ちは助ける心構えのできている友人が必要なのだ。

4．研究によれば、人を許す能力の向上は、年齢が高くなると健康に有益であることが示されている（Silton, Flannelly, & Lutjen, 2013）。生徒は間違えることを恐れる傾向にあることから、許すことは必要である（Tsui, 1996 参照）。

IG-ESL モデルは、2 世代のロールプレイング、手紙を書くこと、冗談を言い合うこと、トークショーをポッドキャストすること、そして e-learning ビデオを作ることを取り込んでいる。活動内容は性質上異なっているが、それらは生徒たちに教室外で英語を書いたり話したりする練習の機会を与えるという同じ目的を分かち合っている。この背景においては、目的のすべてが、育成するためのフレンドシップ、楽しみを交換する実生活の物語（例えば、高齢者の子どもの頃の話、おもちゃ、ゲーム）、そして共に考える地域の問題や家族関係の話題に照準を当てることだった。図 1 は題名、内容、それぞれの活動の意図された成果を示している。

プログラムは 20 人の大人と 40 人の生徒で始まった。それぞれの大人のメンバーは 2 人の生徒と一緒にグループを作った。6 つの活動は夏休み期間中の 12 週間を通して実行された。各週、大人のメンバーは 2 時間生徒と従事する。彼らの参加は友人として（チューターよりむしろ）生徒と提携することと協同で共有する各活動の完了の責任を含んでいた。参加の過程を豊かにするために、大人のメンバーは毎週 1 時間のセッションに出席することを求められた。その間、彼らは教育理論や第二言語の発達理論などと同様に活動を紹介された。

実行の過程を容易にするために、すべてのグループが順番に同じ活動に参加することを要求されたが、最初の活動後、参加者は彼らのスケジュールを決めることを奨励された（例えば、次の活動をいつ始めるか）。この柔軟な対応はグループの進行が異なったときにプレッシャーを感じるという事実から提供された。次に、この 12 週間で直面した問題と活動の調整について述べる。

Lesson 1（熱心すぎるサポーター）：このプログラムはごく数名の貢献が評価されるも圧倒的な熱心すぎるシニアサポーターに直面した。毎週ほとんどわたしはスケジュールから遅れることの可能性を伝えられた。プレッシャーはたとえ彼らによるスケジュールの柔軟性が提供され繰り返されても、残った。また、わたしは生徒のテストへの技術に関して、テストの出来を高めるためにこのプログラムは機械的な練習のような伝統的な学習方法をもっと採用するべきだというコメントを受け取った。ほかには最後の 2 週間で、大人のメンバーがアドベンチャゲームをしたいと言ってきたときだった。そのメンバーはとても情熱的で、そのゲームがプログラムを次のレベルに持ち上げると信じていた。1 つのレッスンで、メンバーはすべての材料をもってきて、全員に挑戦するよう求めた。しかし、過去のけがを負った結果を知っていたので、その試みの芽は摘んだ。

Lesson 1への対応（スターバックス　アプローチ）：熱心なサポーターはサポーターだ。それ自体、彼らとプログラムのスタッフ間の協力を強くする方法は、探究する価値がある。支持された行動は、大人のメンバーをスターバックスのようなコーヒーショップに招待し、

第6章　世代間 ESL 活動：教訓とそれに対応する活動　95

活動	中心活動題目	内　容	目　的
活動1	タイムマシーン	高齢者パートナーが提供するガイダンスで、各 IG グループは高齢者の幼児期に基づいてドラマを制作。	• 参加者が英語で自分自身を表現できるように、リラックスした非批判的な環境を確立する。 • 高齢者の個人史を理解する。 • 昔の家族のように見えることに興奮を感じる。 • 聴衆の前でのプレゼンテーションに自信を得る。
活動2	私はこの広告を気に入っています	各 IG グループは家族についてのテーマを持つテレビ広告を検索し、家族関連のトピックについて省察的エッセイ（200 〜 300 語）を作成。	• 自分の人生と他者の生活における家族関係の重要性を理解する。 • 参加する高齢者と一緒に、学生のライティングスキル、話す自信、友情感を強化する。
活動3	私はこのジョークが好きです	各 IG のペアは、家族についての英語のジョークを語る。事前にグループは挑戦するグループを見つける。ジョークを聞くグループが笑ったら、笑わせたグループの勝ち。	• 家族が楽しいものであることを認める。 • 高齢者が面白いだけでなく楽しいパートナーでもあることを理解する。 • 創造的な方法で話す。
活動4	手紙の中のあなたの声	各 IG グループは、家族の中で肯定的な環境を創造するという手紙を共著する。	• より良い家族環境を作り出すことへの関心を刺激する。 • 豊かな世代間パートナーシップを得る。 • 現実世界で英語を練習する。
活動5	Podcast ボイス	各 IG グループは、活動4に基づいてポッドキャストプログラムを作成。	• 会話に信頼と一貫性を構築する。 • 「説得力のある力」を実証し、家族と共有する。 • 世代間のパートナーシップを公的談話に広げる。
活動6	iG-ESL Academy	IG パートナーは、教育トピックを含む1分間のビデオを作成し、それを Youtube.com にアップロードして共有。	• 異なる世代が対話的に協力して創造的な談話を実演する。

図1　活動の内容

ともにコーヒーをたしなむことだ。これはリラックスした環境で大人のメンバー1人あるいは2人がわたしを参加させる小さなグループセッティングになるだろう。けれども、これはくだけたように見えるがコンタクトはまだ礼儀正しく、敬意的で、ひたむきであり、それによって相互の理解を構築していく可能性が増加する。もしできれば、計画の裏にある、さもなければ誤解されるような新しい考えや事実が、交換できるかもしれない。

　　Lesson 2（やる気のない生徒）：情熱的なサポーターに加えて、わたしたちはまた、数名のやる気の無さが表出した生徒に直面した。彼らはレッスンをすっ飛ばし、プログラムでない問題に簡単にのがれ、静かなのだ。彼らのうちのひとりからのフィードバックで、彼の両親の子育ての方法に問題があるのが分かった。つまり、「ぼくの両親は強制的にこんなにたくさんのプログラムに参加させた。休みが欲しい。自分のやりたいことをしたい。」であった。生徒の言葉を聞いた後、彼の大人のパートナーは、夏休みを越えてこのプログラムをすることを提案した。

　　わたしたちは生徒たちに与えすぎた。彼が来たがらないのも無理はない。参加者の許容範囲を選択させる機会を与えることで出席が価値のあるものになると考えられる。

　　Lesson 2への対応（セミナーアプローチ）：生徒のモチベーションの欠如は、権威主義かどうかにかかわらず、育児の結果にはあたらない。休みを越えてプログラムを実行することは出席率を上げるのに役立つかもしれないが、それが学生を追いかけるだけなら、さらなる戦略の模索が必要である。

　　取り上げる価値があるように思われる1つのアクションは、セミナーを通じて学生会員を募集することである。このアプローチでは、導入スライドを使ってプログラムを学生に紹介し、ニーズを予期し、プログラムの非懲罰的性質を強調する（例えば、ハイステークス試験に重点を置く伝統的な学習とは異なる）、即時フィードバックによる質問の解答、疑惑の解消、申い込み手続きの明確化などが含まれる。

　　戦略に加えて、アプローチはセミナー前の準備にもヒンジを付ける必要があります。例えば、一部の学校スタッフは、学生に宣伝通知を出したり、アドオンイベントとしてセミナーを開催したり、申し込み基準をすべて決定するなど、対応する取り決めを行う必要がある。

　　最終的に、これらの戦略と準備が織り成されたとき、参加・不参加について両親よりも生徒が決定するという目的に役立つ。

　　Lesson 3（望ましくない講義）：要約すると、1時間のトレーニングは成人メンバーに提供されてから、彼らは学生に従事させる。当初、ほとんどすべての成人会員が参加したが、出席率は数セッション後に急激に低下した。

　　ある日、大人のメンバーから電話があった。彼は大人のメンバーの大部分が、講義が長すぎたり、多すぎたりして（例えば、講義が多すぎる）、専門性の向上セッションが望ましくないことを知ったと教えてくれた。私のなぐさめに、メンバーは準備とチームワークの感覚

第6章　世代間 ESL 活動：教訓とそれに対応する活動　97

を与えることができたので、彼らの大部分が必要なトレーニングを見つけたと私に報告した。これは、継続時間と運用方法の問題が大きかった。

Lesson 3への対応（ディスカッションプローチ）：この問題に対処するために、二人の高齢者会員を含む審査委員会が結成された。彼らは専門性向上セッションを 30 分に短縮することに同意した。しかし、初めの 2 セッションは、初めから準備とチームワークの意識を高めるために、1 時間のままでなければならないとアドバイスした。

　講義方法の問題に対処するために、専門性向上のための重要な資料を最小限に抑えた。次に、成人会員は特定の教材を選択し、小グループで話し合うことを勧めている。このディスカッションのアプローチでは、それらは、ニーズや問題に基づくトピックを開始するもので、それによって滞まる可能性を高めている。

Lesson 4（堅い活動）：堅さは、活動レベルでプログラムに影響が現れる。各活動は順番にあらかじめ決められているため、異なるグループが互いに比較したときに後ろ向きの感覚になった。もう一つの派生的な問題は、当初から本質的に追求する活動を選ぶ機会が与えられていないことである。つまり、参加者に選択の余地を与えることで権力を失うことが、検討に値する試みのようである。

Lesson 4への対応（ツールボックスアプローチ）：参加者に、やりたいことを選択させるという考えを容易にするために、なかにいろいろな種類の活動が書かれたカードが入ったツールボックスもしくは入れ物が作られる。実践によって、参加者はグループのメンバーとともに特定の活動を選ぶだけでなく、どんな成果が意図されるか、どんなゴールが設定されているか、どんな行動をとるかを、交流したり協議したりすることを奨励されるだろう。

　理論的には、探索、遭遇、選択、行動能力の行使の機会を与えられた学習者が、より本質的な方法で学習する傾向にあるという根拠に基づいて行われている（van Lier, 2004）。それ自体、やる気の無い生徒についての問題もまたこの方法で取り組まれた。

　大事なことは、ツールボックスが刺激のある環境や、「有機的組織体は、長く学び、育つ。それがその環境で活動的に取り組む間」（van Lier, 2008, p. 602）という仮定に基づいた学習環境を作りだすことである。言語学の視点から、刺激のある環境は、ESL 学習者が意味のある英語を練習するための記号的（もしくは意味をなす）アフォーダンスが可能になるかもしれないということから、重要であると捉えられる（van Lier, 2004）。注目すべきは、エージェンシーを促進するには知覚する機会（アフォーダンス）必要である（van Lier, 2007）。

　結論として、世代を相互に結びつけ、相互作用する生態系をプログラムに組み込むことであるといえる。例えば、スターバックスのアプローチは、お互いの好み、背景、信念、意図、困難などが共有され、理解されている場合、プログラムのスタッフと参加者がお互いにつながっていると感じる快適ゾーンを作成することである。セミナーのアプローチは、それらを

募集する前に潜在的な学生と交流することによって、彼らとプログラムの間の相互関係の感覚を生み出す（incubate）することである。ディスカッションのアプローチは、成人会員が、彼らに関係するトピックまたは世代間パートナーシップに役立つトピックを探求することによって、特定分野（miche）を見つけることです。ツールボックスのアプローチは、すべての世代を結び付け、経験を共有し、刺激的な環境で意味を交渉することで友情を築くことである。

Chapter 7

Disrupting Inequality in the United States: A Personal Essay

Maeona Mendelson

"Disrupting" has become a useful term across many disciplines to describe a precipitous change in a behavior or activity made possible by the introduction of a new technology or model.

What does it mean to be disruptive? As articulated by Richard Buckminster Fuller, "You never change things by fighting the existing reality. To change something, build a new model that makes the old model obsolete". This quote defines disruptive technology, a term created by Clayton M. Christianson in 1997 to describe one type of technological change.

For example, innovations such as email, smartphones, cloud computing, and social networks have changed communication - its speed and accessibility - forever. Tomorrow, something new, maybe in robotics, will disrupt how work is accomplished.

In her recent book, Disrupt Aging, Jo Ann Jenkins, CEO of AARP, describes four freedoms (to choose, to earn, to learn and to pursue happiness) that would change aging and help older adults live healthier, productive and financially secure lives. As America's largest and most influential membership organization, it would be possible for this new perception of aging to influence the lives of 37,000 individuals over 50 years of age (Jenkins, 2016).

This essay proposes that the best approaches to improving life in the United States in the 21st century will be disruptive and not incremental.

The American public, although polarized on how to achieve this change, has demonstrated readiness for it.

Today, the United States is challenged by an economic, educational and social perception and reality that undermine our basic belief in opportunity. We have historically believed in "The American Dream" - that through hard work and education, anyone can earn a living that supports themselves and their families.

Instead, the reality today is a dwindling middle class with more wealth held by the upper 1% and a growing population of poor including the working poor. Causes have been attributed to 1) lower educational attainment of young Americans who are not keeping pace with their counterparts in Canada, Australia, Japan and other nations, 2) the distribution of smaller shares of company profits to workers while top management in American companies are making more than their international counterparts, 3) weaker labor unions and 4) lower minimum wages. (Leonhardt & Quealy, The New York Times, April 22, 2014).

It has been proposed that the loss of manufacturing jobs through outsourcing is another example of why the American labor force is losing ground. However, even when manufacturing returns, wages are often low and basic needs such as housing are unattainable because of its high cost.

At the Intergenerational conference held by Generations United in Hawaii in July 2015, Dr. Robert Putnam spoke to the issue of the diminishing opportunities for children born into poverty. Lack of social mobility has turned America into an increasingly rigid class system. Putnam offered a

Chapter 7 Disrupting Inequality in the United States: A Personal Essay   101

number of potential solutions to closing the opportunity gap. Many were related to school reform (Putnam, 2015).

So where does this leave Americans? What is being done to address these concerns of growing income and opportunity inequality? On the federal level, two policies - controversial and with mixed results to date are truly bold and disruptive in their conception. Given time and with some changes in implementation, they can make a difference. Both models could be at risk with a change in national leadership in the United States.

The first federal policy is the Patient Protection and Care Act, known as Obamacare, which is a major overhaul of regulations directing physicians, hospitals and health insurance systems. The purpose is to bring affordable and accessible health care to a large number of Americans who do not have health care coverage.

Unlike most of the countries with advanced economies, the United States did not offer its citizens universal health care through the government and private sectors. About 49 million Americans were without health insurance in 2010. In 2015, a Rand corporation study cited that about 20 million Americans had been newly insured due to the Patient Protection and Care Act.Obamacare is projected to continue to increase coverage to the formerly uninsured and reduce costs.

The second effort at reform has been to the public education system. Known as the Common Core, the new curriculum addresses student competency through a set of standards that would prepare all students for entry level careers, college and the workforce. The focus on integrating knowledge across fields and teaching skills like critical thinking, problem solving and analysis would prepare students to utilize new knowledge as it emerged. States can adopt, modify or reject the Common Core. Several states have opted not to use the Common Core; instead, returning students to fact based education with multiple choice tests as measures of competency.

In the community, there is strength in a model where institutions such as museums are assisting schools to achieve their Common Core goals. Today public school students in Hawaii use tools like "slow art" in which they analyze one painting for 20 minutes; or they discuss the role of science or math in art creation and interpretation. Visits to the museum last from 90 minutes to 3 hours. Students return to the classroom with workbooks to continue to apply their art based education to achieving academic goals.

The Common Core is also designed to meet the challenges of the workplace. Changes at work are requiring new skills. As individuals begin their careers or as older workers return to work, some will encounter human resource managers who are placing more emphasis on the soft skills such as teamwork, communication, conflict management, and the ability to work within a group's diversity by age, ethnicity, gender, and ability.

In turn, employees entering the workforce want to integrate work and family life. Today most workers cannot and should not expect a lifetime career or a pension. In return, employees may articulate a desire for a flexible work schedule and recognition of a personal and family life outside the workplace. All of this change is happening in a company or start up that extends its reach across the globe -often working online, and requiring management to lead an unprecedented four generations of workers in new fields like the

Chapter 7 Disrupting Inequality in the United States: A Personal Essay   103

green economy.

The phenomenal growth of the sharing economy has allowed people online access to using and providing services, equipment, rental space, and skills both on demand and often cheaper than commercial services. One international model of the shared economy is UBER (a mobile car sharing application).

Retired elders can often be seen behind the wheel as an UBER driver. Older adults like both the additional income and appreciate the social connection to customers. For an elder rider, UBER can offer security. The passenger has use of the GPS to track a driver's route, know who he is and what he drives and eventually evaluate his performance.

As exciting and challenging as these changes might be, they have not addressed growing income and opportunity inequality in the United States.

Change will require the type of disruptive public policy cited earlier. Americans need the support of policy in health care, education and housing access and affordability as well as in tax reform and income generation. This is not social welfare as designed in the 20th century, but a new approach that is unprecedented in design and implementation.

References and Resources in Presentation Order:

Jenkins, Jo Ann with Boe Workman, *Disrupt Aging, a Bold New Path to Living Your Best Life at Every Age. Public Affairs, New York, 2016.*

Richard Buckminster Fuller quote from chapter 8, page 181 in Disrupt Aging.

Whatls.com for information on disruptive technology.

Leonhardt, David and Kevin Quealy, Middle Class is No Longer the World's Richest. The New York Times, 22, April 2014.

Putnam, Robert D. Our Kids, the American Dream in Crisis. Simon & Schuster, New York, 2015.

Rand Corporation, rand.org. A research organization that develops solutions for public policy challenges.

core standards.org for information on U.S. public schools initiative.

I have been a docent at the Honolulu Museum of Arts since 1977 and have seen dramatic improvements in how we educate our children and youth in art appreciation as we continue to integrate our curriculum with the school standards.

MacKay, Carleen. The Career Playbook, Second Half Plays for Boomer & Beyond. Produced with Jan Hively and Dorian Mintzer. Carleen is an emergent workforce expert and can be reached at 916-316-0143 or LinkedIn.com or ask Mae.

"Sharing Economy Brings Risks with Opportunities". The Japan Times, December 20,2015.

Additional notes:

President Franklin Delano Roosevelt created Social Security in August 14, 1935. and Lyndon Baines Johnson created Medicare and Medicaid in July 30, 1965. Originally Social Security was a retirement benefit that was enlarged by adding benefits for widows and orphans and the disabled of any age. Medicare is health insurance for individuals over 65 and Medicare provides health insurance to the poor. Obamacare expanded coverage for people with pre-existing conditions, small business owners, the previously uninsured and dependents up to age 26.

第7章　米国の格差を破壊する：パーソナルエッセイ

メイ・メンダーソン

「破壊（ディスラプト）」は多くの学問で、新しい技術やモデルの導入による活動や行動の大変化を意味する有用な言葉である。

破壊的とはどういう意味だろうか？リチャードー・バクマイスター・フラーいわく、「現状と戦うことは変化をもたらさない。変化をもたらすには、旧モデルが無用になるような新モデルを作ることだ」としている。これは、1997年にクレイトン・M.クリスチャンソンが「破壊的技術」と呼んだものでもある。例えば、電子メール、スマホ、クラウド、SNSといった技術革新はコミュニケーション - その速さやアクセシビリティを - 永久に変えてしまった。明日、ロボット産業の何か新しい出来事が、働き方を破壊するかもしれない。

AARP（全米退職者協会）の会長であるジョアン・ジェンキンスが彼女の近著である「エイジング破壊」のなかで、エイジングを変え、高齢者がより健康で、生産的、経済的に安定した生活を送るようにしてくれる4つの自由について語っている（選ぶ自由、稼ぐ自由、学ぶ自由、幸せを追求する自由）。アメリカの最大かつ最も影響力のある会員制組織として、このエイジングに対する新しい見方が、50歳以上の3万7千人へ影響することは可能であるとしている（Jenkins 2016）。

本エッセイは、21世紀のアメリカの暮らしをよくする最良の方法は漸次的なものではなく、破壊的なものであると提言する。アメリカ国民は、どのように達成するかの方法論は二極化しているが、そういう変化を待っているに違いないと考える。

今日、アメリカは「機会の平等」への確信を揺るがすような経済的、教育的、社会的な現状や見方に対処しなければならない。我々は「アメリカンドリーム」を歴史的に信じてきた。それは、勤労と教育により、だれでも自分と家族を養うことができると信じることである。

しかし、中産階級が減り、トップ1％の人たちの富が増し、貧しい人（ワーキングプアを含む）の人口が増加している現状がある。原因として、1）カナダ人・オーストラリア人・日本人など他国の若者に比べ、アメリカの同年代の若者の教育レベルの低いこと、2）アメリカの企業のトップの給料は他国のトップより高く、社員の給料は低いこと、3）労働組合の弱体化、4）最低賃金の低さが挙げられる（Leonhardt & Quealy, The New York Times, April 22, 2014）。

生産業の海外移転や発注によるアメリカ労働者への影響は大きく議論されているが、生産業の仕事がアメリカに戻ってきたとしても国内の賃金は低く、住居などが高すぎて生活ができないだろう。

ハワイで開催された2015年7月のGenerations United主催の国際会議において、ロバート・パットナム博士が貧困層に生まれる子どもの様々な機会の減少について語った。社会的流動性がなくなり、アメリカが徐々に固定化された階級社会になりつつある。パットナム博

士が格差をなくすいくつかの解決策を提案したが、その多くは教育改革に関係するもので
あった（Putnam 2015）。

　では、アメリカ人はどうすればよいのか。格差社会、機会の不平等さに取り組むために何
かされているだろうか？連邦レベルでは、今日まで物議を醸し、複雑な結果を出している二
つの政策がその概念においては、大胆であり破壊的である。時間をかけ、修正すれば、変化
をもたらしうるが、二つの政策は、政権交代で、危機にさらされる可能性もある。

　その一つ目は、医療保険制度改革法（通称オバマケア）であり、医師、病院、保険会社に
関連する法令の抜本改革であった。この制度改革の目的は、健康保険のない多くのアメリカ
人に、安価で入手しやすい健康保険を提供することが目的である。

　ほとんどの先進国と違い、アメリカは政府や民間保険会社によるユニバーサルヘルスケア
はなかった。2010年に、４千９百万人のアメリカ人は健康保険を持っておらず、2015年の
ランド・コーポレーションの研究によると、医療保険制度改革法のおかげで２千万人のアメ
リカ人が新しく保険に加入したとされている。オバマケアの影響で保険のなかった人の加入
の増加、コストの削減が予想されている。

　二つ目の政策は、公的教育に関する改革である。各州共通基礎スタンダードと呼ばれる新
制度は、生徒の能力基準を設け、その達成によりエントリーレベルの仕事・大学・就職の準
備を図ろうとするものである。分析力、問題解決能力、論理的思考力、教科間のつながりを
把握することを重要視し、新しい知識をすぐに自分のものにできる生徒の育成を目指してい
る。各州共通基礎スタンダードを、それぞれの州は採用するか、修正するか、採用しないか
を決めることができる。各州共通基礎スタンダードを使用せず、知識ベースの選択問題を使っ
た試験で生徒の能力を測ろうとしているいくつかの州もある。

　地域社会では、博物館・美術館などが学校と連携を図り、各州共通基礎スタンダードの基
準を満たすことに協力している有力なモデルがある。ハワイの公立学校の生徒が20分をか
けて一つの美術作品を分析する「スローアート」というプログラムに参加したり、理科や数
学の美術作品への影響を議論したりする。博物館・美術館への訪問は90分から３時間続き、
生徒は、学校にワークブックを持って帰り、他教科の取り組みに美術ベースの考え方を応用
し続ける。

　各州共通基礎スタンダードは職場のニーズにもこたえるようデザインされている。職場の
変化は新しい技術・スキルを必要とする。初めて仕事に就く人も、高齢者で再び働き始める
人も、チームワーク、コミュニケーション、コンフリクト・マネージメント、多様（年齢・
人種・性別・能力）なグループの中で働くことができるというような、いわゆるソフト能力
を求める人事担当者に出会うことになるだろう。

　一方、働く人たちは仕事と家庭を両立させたいと考えている。今日、ほとんどの働く人は
終身雇用や退職金を期待できない（しないほうがいい）。その分、働く人は融通が利くスケ
ジュールを求め、家庭の存在を認識してほしいと考えている。このような変化は、グリーン
経済などの新しい分野の企業や、創業したばかりの会社において既に起きている。それらの
企業は世界規模で事業を展開したり、オンラインでの働き方を導入したり、または前例のな

い4世代の社員を率いたりする経営を進めているのである。

　シェアリングエコノミーの飛躍的成長は、オンラインアクセスのある人にサービス・備品・レンタルスペース、技術を利用・提供することを可能にした。そうした国際的なモデルの一つが、UBER というカーシェアリングアプリである。

　定年退職後の高齢者は、UBER のドライバーとしてよく出会うことがある。高齢ドライバーは追加の収入も、お客との出会いに喜びを感じている。お年寄りの利用者に対しても、UBER は安全を提供できる。乗客は、GPS 機能でドライバーが使っているルートを確認でき、ドライバーのプロフィールにアクセスしたり何の車を運転しているのかもわかり、最終的に運転が良かったかどうか評価ができるからである。

　これらの変化はワクワク感じさせてくれても、アメリカの格差や機会の不平等の問題にまで影響を及ぼしてはいない。本当に変化するには、前述のような破壊的な政策が必要である。アメリカ国民は医療・教育・住居が容易に手に入るような政策を必要とし、税制の改革、所得を増やす政策も必要であろう。これは２０世紀に設計された社会福祉的なもので達成できるのではなく、全く前例のないデザインや実施の方法を必要とするものである。

108

Chapter 8

The Challenge posed by Intergenerational Relationships Today

Pablo Galindo-Calvo

Mariano Sánchez-Martínez

1. Introduction

In June of 2008 the King Baudouin Foundation, based in Belgium, published a report entitled *Une société pour tous les âges. Le défi des relations intergénérationnelles* (De Mets & Vassart, 2008). After extensive field work consisting of multigenerational group discussions on the topic, which took place over the period of a year and all over the country, one of the fundamental conclusions was this:

The subject of intergenerationality involves taking a new look at our lives together. It is not about giving specific [intergenerational] responses to certain problems but rather using a framework that combines various different spheres: public spaces, work, care giving, housing... In each of these spheres, our actions must be permeated by an intergenerational dimension (p. 15).

At least for the authors of the Belgian report, this is where the challenge of intergenerational relationships lies: transversally incorporating the intergenerational dimension into our shared life. We agree: talking about intergenerational relationships means talking about ourselves as relational beings, and it points to the fact that, when considering ourselves as persons, *we-are-in-relation-to-others*. As Raimon Panikkar (1993) put it in his day:

Every person is a knot in the net of relationships [...] reaching out to the

Chapter 8 The Challenge posed by Intergenerational Relationships Today   109

very antipodes of the real. An isolated individual is incomprehensible and un-viable. Man is only Man with the sky above, the earth below and surrounded by his fellow beings (p. 75).

It would be hard to say it more clearly or more emphatically.

We have before us a multi-faceted and provocative challenge, a difficulty we must face with decision: to recover and recreate shared life, which is not only relational but also intergenerational. We are talking about lives with chronologies that, in general, have lengthened. Therefore, the idea is not only to find out how to live a better shared life but how to do it together, and for longer.

As our Belgian colleagues said in their study, the challenge behind inter-generationality is really just one question –and a very old one at that: *how to organize things in such a way that we can live a better and longer shared life together.* To put it differently, at this time, in this corner of the planet in which we are writing, there is a growing clamor to shift from a 'me' culture to a culture of relations. This is the main idea put forward in these pages.

We have selected three contemporary social thinkers who, in distinct yet complementary ways, seem to have heard the clamor and made refer-ence to it, each in their own manner. Their analyses can provide some clues that will help us better understand the challenges posed by intergenerational relations and practices at this time.

2．Bauman: more experiences and fewer boundaries

The Polish sociologist Zygmunt Bauman has devoted much of his life to thinking about our postmodern societies. Bauman believes that in a liquid modern setting such as the one in which we live, the current rebirth of the generation category has to do with a crisis in collective identities (Bauman,

2007, p. 118-119). Bauman is essentially telling us that discontinuity surrounds us and that, as a result, we are forced to move around "blindly"; it is as if – in allusion to Hannah Arendt's metaphor on thinking without a banister– the section of the banister that we have been using for support as we walk suddenly disappears; and now we are trying to find out, in the dark, where the next section we can hold onto is.

In this situation, says Bauman, we feel a strong temptation to look behind us, in search of guidance. This could be one of the reasons explaining the current interest in the generations that came before us: How did they do it back in their times? What security and solidity did they use for support? What did they do to avoid being left hanging, without a banister? And when it did happen, how did they get out of it?

Our modern world, more liquid than solid, "is in a state of ongoing revolution" (p. 126), Bauman believes. That is, "changes are constant and ubiquitous and therefore, in this context, the particular condensations of changes dense enough to justify the drawing of new generational frontiers seem either to be an almost daily phenomenon, or to come closer together than ever" (p. 125). And herein arises an interesting paradox: since our collective identities –in connection with our family, friends, professional position, cultural goods, socialization, nationality....– are always slipping through our fingers, we try to find new identities, new identity banisters to grasp, but, at the same time, since we are surrounded by constant change, our new handles become liquid again before we expect them to and so we must once again start out on a new search. So we find ourselves, exhausted, going through the same process over and over again.

In a situation like this, is it possible for a feeling of belonging to a specific generation to take hold inside us? Bauman believes it is unlikely:

The pace of change tends, perhaps, to be too fast and the speed with

Chapter 8 The Challenge posed by Intergenerational Relationships Today 111

which new phenomena burst into public awareness, grow old, die and disappear again, is too dizzying for the experience to have time to become established, solidify and crystallize into lasting attitudes or models of behavior, and into valuable syndromes and world views that are apt to be recorded as lasting features of the 'spirit of the times' and considered the unique and permanent characteristics of the generation (p. 125).

Viewed from this perspective, the current inclination to pay attention to intergenerational relations is linked, on the one hand, to our search for opportunities that give us back that feeling of being connected, that we are holding on to some type of relational banister, and that we form part of some kind of us (a feeling that can appear only if we expose ourselves to the gaze of the other, of others); and, secondly, to our desire that each of these opportunities will reconnect us with a past experience of community that has largely vanished today.

Bauman gives us some basic clues for understanding how to think about the delimitation of the different generations in times like these:

Boundaries are not usually drawn because of differences. The opposite is true in fact: differences are noticed and even become a 'social and cultural entity' because of having previously drawn boundaries. First a boundary is drawn and then a twisted search begins for distinctive, even incompatible, features of the individuals situated on the other side, so that the legitimacy and the essential nature of the boundary can be justified beyond any reasonable doubt (p. 112).

Here we find another explanation as to why the generational theme is knocking so insistently on our door: as we have advanced in our geography toward the construction of boundaries between the generations –for example, between parents, children and grandchildren; between kids, youth and adults; between baby-boomers, members of Generation X and those who were part of the generation of '68-, we have also been occupied producing each of these generations as something different. This naturally has paved the way for observing the mutual relationships between them.

The discontinuity of our feeling of inter-connectedness with other generations is not a mere accident; the 'me' culture has acted as a seedbed for that feeling of discontinuity. How is it that now we complain nostalgically about a past that seems to have been better –filled with cooperation and intergenerational solidarity, some would have us believe– while at the same time we promote the construction of boundaries which, according to Bauman, do nothing but accentuate differences in place of commonality?

3. M.C. Bateson: increasing trust

Mary Catherine Bateson, besides being the daughter of two great figures in 20th century thinking –Gregory Bateson and Margaret Mead–, is a well-known anthropologist in her own right. A disciple of Erikson, she has developed an original hypothesis to explain the consequences of the longevity explosion that we have been witnessing over the past century. In her view, what has happened is not just that we have added years to life but also that we have inaugurated a new space/section in the life cycle; the second adulthood. This section precedes old age and Bateson describes it as a period of "active wisdom."

For Professor Bateson, what we have before us is really much more profound than the fact that our life expectancy has increased. In her opinion, we have changed the form and meaning of our lifetime in a manner that we do not yet fully understand and "we are evolving into a rather different species, inhabiting a new niche and challenged to adapt in new ways" (Bateson, 2010, p. 10).

Chapter 8 The Challenge posed by Intergenerational Relationships Today   113

In July of 2011, Bateson gave the keynote speech at the international conference that takes place every two years in Washington, D.C. and is organized by *Generations United*, the organization leading work in the intergenerational field in the United States. Bateson's reflections revolved around the following idea: given the evident erosion in intergenerational trust in our society, how can we manage to teach children who they can trust and, at the same time, make them capable of trusting?

Bateson believes that we can only achieve this if we, those of us who are no longer children, offer young people examples of trustworthiness. In other words, if we are capable of trusting others and of putting this trust into practice. In contrast with those who foster mistrust among the generations, this anthropologist says there is an idea that must be acknowledged: all of us face during our lives moments in which we have no choice but to trust someone –one of those moments is childhood– and, what is more, there will be moments in which someone else will have no choice but to trust us.

Taking this as our point of departure, it becomes necessary to create the conditions that will enable us, when we make a choice, to opt for trust rather than mistrust, something not often the case. Bateson believes that we must view ourselves as trustees of the future. In this respect, our task consists not only of taking care of the present so as to ensure a good future for upcoming generations but also in developing the capacity for different generations to work together, trusting one another. To do so, we must take the time to reflect on how this goal can be achieved, because creating trust is not automatic, it takes time and it requires intentionality; trust is something that we must pursue, something we make possible.

VanderVen and Schneider-Munoz (2012) have concluded that mistrust represents one of the dangers to social relations but that this can be modified through intergenerational relationships. In this regard we can think that the current interest in and challenge around these relationships may also have something to do with the potential that such relationships hold inas much as they are instruments for the development and support of a sense of trust, in times such as these, in which trust and social capital are eroding at a rapid rate.

4. K. Lüscher: personality and difference

Fascinated by the growing number of activities taking place under the label of intergenerational programs or dialogue between generations, I wonder about the reason for the great appeal of these activities. Could it be the result of the demographic changes taking place and of growing concern about the social context? Are they perhaps a substitute for family relationships? My answer [...] is the following: The appeal of intergenerational programs is due to the desire to experience the self, to develop one's own personality (Lüscher, 2012: 32).

With these words the sociology professor Kürt Lüscher begins an article, one of the many he has dedicated to analyzing intergenerational relationships and, within them, the issue that constitutes his main area of interest: ambivalence. Lüscher says that while some people believe the growing interest in intergenerational programs can be explained by demographic evolution, by the risks that social cohesion now faces or by the need for more "solidarity," he wonders if it really is these ideas and abstract contexts that motivate active participation in opportunities to relate to other generations. It is obvious, for Lüscher, that opportunities for intergenerational contact – especially those that arise outside of the family– are not totally new; what is new, in his mind, is the special and express attention being paid to the generational factor and, more specifically, to intergenerational relationships that

Chapter 8 The Challenge posed by Intergenerational Relationships Today   115

arise in the framework of all the projects, programs and policies that, with the *intergenerational* label, are becoming increasingly widespread. And he asks himself: Do intergenerational relationships have specific and particularly relevant characteristics and potentialities in today's social circumstances? Do they involve factors that we should be noticing in the light of new reflections and research? His answer is basically this:

Intergenerational relationships are closely linked to the practices of all those people involved in processes of learning and personality development. Therein lies an important aspect of the appeal (...) that these intergenerational projects have in terms of practice, research and policy (Lüscher, 2012: 33-34).

Since intergenerational programs are oriented around personal encounters and collaboration, for Lüscher it is interesting to notice what happens at the very moment in which we perceive, characterize and realize ourselves as members of a specific generation. So exactly what is it that happens? In his opinion, we mutually attribute certain identity features to one another. In other words: belonging to a generation is an aspect of personality. In brief, what happens when we gain generational awareness? Lüscher says that the first thing is the attribution of identity traits. And it is through this process that we come to the question of personality development, understanding personality as a set of thoughts, feelings, desires, acts, ways of living and life trajectories of individuals and collective actors. For Lüscher, therefore, the first key lies in the idea of *identity relevance*: intergenerational relationships are important because they help us answer the question of who we are. But, at the same time –we would add– in order to find an answer to this question we will necessarily have to compare ourselves to others, with respect to whom we will coincide (then we will say that we are of the same generation) and we will also be different (therefore, we will acknowledge belonging to different generations).

And, in fact, the question of how we experience and respond to difference is at the root of the second way that Lüscher responds to his question. He believes that while the difference factor is present in all types of relationships, in the case of intergenerational relationships it is especially intense. Furthermore, this difference permeates all levels of the specific activity taking place and of the intergenerational relationship, and it is based on the multiple and varied experiences of the different generations. For example, in the case of only children, grandparents, with their personal dedication and affection, can offer the youngsters an important experience of difference –by contrasting with the relation these children have with their parents– which will be very useful in their later life which, as it will probably be a long one, will likely give them the opportunity to live with people of other generations for more time. And in the other direction, grandparents, through their relationship with their grandchildren, can gain an appreciation of difference when, for example, they see themselves treating their grandchildren differently from how they treated their own children when they were younger. In line with Lüscher, we believe that intergenerational relationships are especially suited for marking differences, and therefore it is through them that we are being challenged to experience that which is different. But as this occurs, a certain similarity is also necessary, because we are talking about relationships between generations: the generated (a new generation) and the generator (the previous generation that engendered the new generation) are both similar and distinct. Nowadays we must learn to live more and better amongst differences. And in this regard *generative socialization* has gained importance: there are more and more processes of intergenerational learning through which we acquire facets of our social identity.

In times such as these, the experiences of difference, contradiction and

Chapter 8 The Challenge posed by Intergenerational Relationships Today 117

rejection, that is, experiences of ambivalence, are very present. Intergenerational relationships are human spaces characterized by ambivalence; that is the reason (as well as the challenge) for the importance and the appeal of the opportunities for learning, socialization and personality development provided by participation in intergenerational relationships.

5. A challenge rediscovered

Intergenerational relationships have always been around, true, but we are rediscovering them. However, it is not just a matter of rediscovering something that has remained unaltered, but rather of rediscovering something that is no longer the way it used to be. And it no longer is the way it used to be because, as we have tried to convey, the substrate in which many intergenerational processes take place today has been transformed: our experiences are more discontinuous, our collective identity is slippery, trust has eroded and differences stand out everywhere, differences beyond those that are necessary for the development of our personality.

The challenge we face is not to do away with intergenerationality; that cannot be done. It is rather to observe it with new eyes; intergenerational relationships are a gateway to finding out how we can live a longer life in common, us-with-others and us-among-others. This change in perspective is only a symptom of the weariness that comes from living in a culture that favors me over us.

The true challenge goes beyond the necessary acceptance and non-discrimination of persons belonging to other generations and enters the realm of shaping our sensibility, to help us understand how much some generations owe other generations, a debt that, if we see it and understand it responsibly, leads to obligation and improvement: it obliges us to pay attention to each other, to take care of each other, to trust and to improve ourselves because this is what enables us to create a better life in common, and at the same time a more enjoyable experience of difference (as in "Wow, other generations are so different!") and of belonging (as in "We are part of an essential multi- and inter-generational sequence!").

References

Bateson, M.C. (2010). *Composing a Further Life. The Age of Active Wisdom*. New York: Knopf.

Bauman, Z. (2007). Entre nosotros, las generaciones. In J. Larrosa (Ed.), *Entre nosotros. Sobre la convivencia entre generaciones* (pp. 101-127). Barcelona: Fundació Viure i Conviure.

De Mets, J. & Vassart, C. (2008). Une société pour tous les âges. Le défi des relations intergénérationnelles. Bruxelles: Foundation Roi Baudouin. Retrieved from https://goo.gl/ZCi8Vf

Lüscher, K. (2012). Generationenprojekte – Generationendialoge als Bildung. Eine These zum Gespräch zwischen Praxis und Theorie. In *Jahresbericht 2012 Projektebüro Dialog der Generationen* (pp. 32-45). Berlin: Projektebüro Dialog der Generationen. Retrieved from http://goo.gl/eJHHap

Panikkar, R. (1993). *The Cosmotheandric Experience. Emerging Religious Consciousness*. New York, NY: Orbis Books.

VanderVen, K. & Schneider-Munoz, J. (2012). As the World Ages: Attaining a Harmonious Future World Through Intergenerational Connections. *Journal of Intergenerational Relationships, 10*(2), 115-130. doi: 10.1080/15350770.2012.673972

第8章　世代間交流がもたらす今日的課題とは

パブロ・ガリンド・カルボ
マリアーノ・サンチェス・マルティネス

　2008年6月、ベルギーに拠点を置くキングボードウィン財団は、「世代間交流の挑戦−全ての世代が関わり合う社会へ−（"Une societe pour tous les ages. Le defi des relations intergenerationnelles"）」（De Mets & Vassart, 2008）と題した報告書を公表した。我々は、ベルギー全国で1年間に渡って、この報告書に関する多世代のグループディスカッションによる大規模なフィールドワークを実施し、一つの基本的な結論を発表した。その一つが以下である。

　　　世代間という主題は、異世代と共にする我々の生活を新たな視点から捉えることを含んでいる。これは、ある問題に対する特定の「世代間的」な反応を示すのではなく、むしろ、公共空間、仕事、介護、在宅といった多様な領域を組み合わせたフレームワークを使用することである。これらの領域のそれぞれにおいて、我々の行動は、世代間という次元によって浸透しなければならない（p.15）。

　少なくとも、このベルギーの報告書の執筆者にとって、世代間交流における課題がどこに存在するのかといえば、世代間という次元を横方向に我々の共有生活に組み込んでいくことであろう。世代間交流について言及することは、我々自身が関係の中にある人間であることを意味しており、個人として我々自身を捉える時、"我々は、他者との関係の中にある"という事実を示していることに同意する。ライモン・パニッカル（1993）は、生前、以下のように述べている。

　　　すべての人は、関係という網に存在する一つの結び目であり（中略）、現実とは正反対のことに手を伸ばそうとしている。孤立した個人など理解できないし、生存不可能である。人は、空が上に、地面が下に存在し、仲間に囲まれているときにのみ人と言える（p.75）。

　この事柄について、さらに明確に、かつ強調して表現することは難しいだろう。

　我々の目の前には、多面的で挑発的な課題が存在している。それは困難な課題であり、決定を迫られるものである。すなわち、人間関係だけでなく、世代間交流が共有生活を復活させ、再度創り上げていくことも含んでいる。我々は、一般的に長くなった寿命のことについて述べているのである。そのため、より良い共有生活をどのように営むかということだけでなく、それをどうやって共に行うか、それもどのように長期間に渡って行うのか、そうしたことの方法を探り当てることとしたい。

　我々のベルギーの同僚の研究によると、世代間交流の背後にある課題に関しては、ただ一つの問いしかない。それは、「我々が共により良く、長期間に渡って共有生活を営めるようにするには、どのように物事を整理すればよいのか」という非常に古典的な問いである。換

言すれば、現在、我々が執筆しているこの片隅で、「自分」重視の風潮から「関係」重視の風潮に移行しようとする叫びが大きくなりつつあるということであり、これが、これらのページにおいて表現したい主要な考えとなる。

我々は、明確ながら補完的な方法で、3人の現代における社会思想家を取り上げている。彼らは、それぞれの方法でこの叫びに耳を傾け、言及してきたように思われる。彼らの分析は、我々が、現時点での世代間交流や慣行によってもたらされる課題に対し、より一層理解を深めるための手助けになるいくつかの手がかりを提供している。

バウマン：より多くの体験と少ない境界線

ポーランドの社会学者であるジグムント・バウマンは、ポストモダン社会について考えることに人生の大半を捧げてきた。バウマンは、我々が住んでいるような流動的な現代という場面において、世代間カテゴリーの復活は、集団的アイデンティティーの危機と関係していると確信している（Bauman, 2007, p. 118-119）。バウマンは、本質的に、不連続なものが我々を取り囲み、結果として、我々は「盲目的に」動き回ることを余儀なくされていると述べている。それは、まるでハンナ・アーレントの手すりのない思想の隠喩をほのめかすように、我々が歩くときに補助として使ってきた手すりの一部分が突然消え、そして今、我々は掴まることができる次の手すりを暗闇の中で探そうとしているのである。

バウマンは、「このような状況では、我々は、後ろを振り返って指導を求めたい強い誘惑にかられるものである」と述べている。これは、現在、我々以前の世代に対する関心を説明する理由の一つかもしれない。彼らの時代はどうであったのか、彼らは補助としてどのような安全装置を使ったのか、彼らは手すりなしで、宙づり状態で取り残されないために何をしたのか、それが起こった時、どのようにそこから抜け出したのか。

バウマンは、我々の現代社会は、固定的というよりもむしろ流動的であり、「継続的に変革している状態である」と述べている（p. 126）。つまり、「変化は絶え間なく起こり、同時にどこでも存在し、この文脈では、新時代の新境地を描くことを正当化するのに十分な濃い変化が凝結するには、日常的な現象に等しい、または、以前よりも身近なことのように思える」（p.125）そして、その中に興味深いパラドックスが生じている。我々の家族、友人、社会的地位、文化、社会、国籍等に関連する我々の集団的アイデンティティーは、常に我々の指をすり抜けてしまい、我々は新たなアイデンティティー、つかまることのできる新しいアイデンティティーという「手すり」を見つけようとしている。

しかし、それと同時に、我々は絶え間のない変化に囲まれており、新たに見つけた手すりは、我々が予想するよりも早く流動化してしまうことから、我々は、再び新たなアイデンティティーを探し始める必要がある。このように、我々は、何度も何度も同じプロセスを繰り返し、疲れ果ててしまう。このような状況において、特定の世代への帰属意識が、我々の内部で根付くことは可能であると言えるのだろうか。バウマンは、その可能性が低いと考えている。

第8章　世代間交流がもたらす今日的課題とは　121

　おそらく、変化のペースが速すぎる傾向があり、変化という新たな現象が国民の意識の中に訪れ、老い、死んで、再び消滅してしまう速度には、目まいを感じざるを得ない。体験が確立され、定着し、持続的な態度や行為の見本へ、かつ「その時代の精神」という持続した特徴として記録されやすい貴重な一連の現象や世界観へと結晶化され、その世代が持つ独特で恒久的な特長としてみなされるには、十分な時間がないのである (p. 125)。

　この観点から捉えると、世代間交流に注視するという現在の傾向は、以下につながる。

　第一に、つながっているという感覚を得られる機会を我々が模索していること、我々が関係という手すりにつかまっていること、ある種の「われわれ」の一部を形成すること（我々が相手や他者の視線に自分自身をさらす場合にのみ表れる感情）、そして第二に、これらの機会が我々を今日ではほとんど消滅してしまったコミュニティの過去の経験と再びつなげてくれるだろうという望みである。このような、時代によって異なる世代の境界線をどのように考えるか、その方法を理解するための基本的な手掛かりをバウマンは我々に与えている。

　通常、境界線は相違に基づいて引かれているわけではない。実際には、その反対である。相違は認識され、以前に描かれた境界線が存在するために「社会的、文化的な実体」となる。まず、境界線が描かれ、その後、反対側に位置する個人の独特な、さらには、正反対の特長を探すという歪んだ探索が開始される。そうすることで、境界線の正当性と本質的な性質を、あらゆる合理的な疑いを超えて正当化することができるのである (p. 112)。

　ここでは、なぜ、世代に関するテーマが、我々にしつこく訴えかけてくるのかについて、別の説明も探りたい。たとえば、両親、子どもと孫との間、子どもたち、若者と大人の間、団塊世代、X世代、1968年世代の一部などの世代間の境界線の構築に向けて、我々は地理学ともいうべきものを発展させてきた。その際、我々は、これらの世代のそれぞれを何か異なるものとして作り上げることにも専念してきた。これは、当然、彼らの間の相互関係を観察するための道を開いた。他の世代との相互関係への我々の感情が途絶えたのは、単なる偶然ではない。個人主義の風潮は、この感情が途絶える苗床として作用した。現在、我々は世代間の連帯と協力にあふれていた（一部の者から、そう確信させられていた）、より良い時代に見えた過去を懐かしがり、不満を漏らしているのである。その一方で、バウマンによると、共通点を強調することとは違う方法で、違いを強調する以外は何もしないで、境界線の確立を促進しているということは、一体、どういったことであろうか。

M.C. ベイトソン：信頼を深める

　メアリー・キャサリン・ベイトソンは、グレゴリー・ベイトソンとマーガレット・メッドという2人の偉大な人物として名を知られている20世紀の思想家の娘であることに加え、生まれながらに能力を備えた有名な人類学者である。エリクソンの弟子である彼女は、我々が過去の一世紀にわたって実際に目にしてきた爆発的な長寿化が与える影響を説明した独自の仮説を立てている。彼女の意見では、実際に起こっているのは単に人生に何年かが追加されたということだけではなく、ライフサイクルにおける新たな空間・場所、すなわち第二の

人生も授けられたということである。ここでは、ベイトソンが「活発な知恵」の期間として
表現する老齢について述べる。ベイトソン教授にとって、我々の前にあるのは、我々の寿命
が延びているという事実よりも、実際にはより深い問題であるとしている。彼女の意見では、
我々は、我々自身が理解していない方法で、一生涯の形と意味を変えてしまい、そして、そ
れは「我々は、異なる種に進化し、新たな隙間に生息し、新しい方法に適応するために挑戦
している」という (Bateson, 2010, p. 10)。

　2011 年 7 月に、ベイトソンは、ワシントン D.C. で 2 年に一度行われる Generations United 主催の国際会議で基調講演を行った。Generations United とは、世代間の分野で研究を先
導している組織である。ベイトソンの省察は、以下の意見を中心に展開された。我々の社会
における世代間の信頼が明らかに減少していることから、子どもたちに誰を信頼できるかを
教えると同時に、人を信頼することができるようにさせるにはどうすればよいのかである。

　ベイトソンは、もはや子どもではない我々が、信用や信頼の見本を若者に提供するなら、
これを達成できると確信している。言い換えれば、大人が他者を信頼することができ、この
信頼を実行に移すことができるなら、それは可能であるという。世代間の不信を身に着けた
者とは対照的に、この人類学者は、認識されるべき見解があるという。すなわち、我々全て
が人生のいくつかの時点において、誰かを信頼せざるを得ない瞬間に直面するということで
ある。その瞬間とは、子ども時代である。さらに、他の誰かが我々を信頼せざるを得ない瞬
間もあるといえる。

　これを出発点として捉え、不信よりも、むしろ信頼を選択する（それはよくあることでは
ない）という決定を下す時、それを可能にする条件を整えることが必要になる。ベイトソン
は、将来を託せる者として、自分たち自身を見出さなければならないと考えている。この点
において、我々の任務は、今後の世代の良い未来を確保するために現在を世話するだけでな
く、異なる世代が互いを信頼しながら共に協力しうる能力を開発することであるとしている。
そのためには、時間をかけて、この目標をいかに達成することができるのか省察する必要が
ある。すなわち、信頼を築くことは自動的ではなく、時間と意志を要することであり、信頼
とは我々が追求しなければならないものであり、我々がそれを可能にすべきものである。

　ファン・デ・ヴェンとシュナイダー・ムニョス（2012）は、不信感は、社会的関係へ危険
を提示するが、これは世代間の交流によって変えることができると結論付けている。我々は、
これらの関係をめぐる現在の関心と課題、また、信頼と社会関係資本が急速に侵食されてい
くような時代において、関係が信頼感の確立と支援のための手段である限りは、このような
関係が有する潜在的可能性と何か関係がある場合がある、と考えることができる。

K. リュッシャー：個性と違い

　世代間交流プログラムや世代間の対話という名のもとで行われている活動の増加に魅せら
れ、私はこれらの活動が持つ大きな魅力の理由について考えたい。それは、人口構造の変化
の結果であるのか、社会的な状況について膨らむ懸念の結果であろうか。これらの活動は、

第8章　世代間交流がもたらす今日的課題とは　123

おそらく家族関係にとって代わるものなのかである。私の考えは、以下の通りである。世代間交流プログラムが持つ魅力とは、自己を体験したいという願望や自分の人間性を育成したいという願望に起因する。(Luscher, 2012: 32).

　社会学のカート・リュッシャー教授は、彼が世代間関係の分析に貢献した作品の一つに、これらの言葉で記事を書き始めている。彼の主な関心分野には、アンビバレンスが含まれる。リュッシャーは、世代間交流プログラムへの関心の高まりは、人口統計学の進化や社会的結束が直面している危機、あるいはより強い「団結」の必要性によって説明できると確信する者がいる一方で、他の世代と関わる機会への積極的な参加を動機付けるのは、本当にこれらの見解や抽象的な状況であるかは疑問であるという。リュッシャーにとって、世代間の接触の機会、特に家族の外で発生するものは、まったく新しいものではないということは明らかである。彼の考えでは、世代的要因、より具体的には、世代間という名目で行われる全てのプロジェクト、プログラムや政策の枠組みの中で発生する世代間の関係に配慮されている特別な、かつ明白なる注目が新しいものであり、それがますます世界に広がってきている。そして、彼は、自身に尋ねる。世代間の関係は、今日の社会状況に固有な、特に関連のある特性および潜在的可能性を持っているのかである。彼の答えは、基本的には以下の通りである。

　世代間の関係は、学習と人格的発達のプロセスに関与する全ての人々の実践に密接につながるものである。ここに、これらの世代間プロジェクトが実践や研究、政策において有している魅力の重要な一つの側面が存在する (Luscher, 2012: 33-34)。

　リュッシャーは、世代間交流プログラムは個人的出会いとコラボレーションを重視しているので、我々が自分自身を特定の世代の一員として感じ、特徴づけ、認識するその瞬間に何が起こるのかということに気づくことは興味深いことであるとしている。それでは、正確には何か起こるのだろうか。彼の意見では、我々は特定のアイデンティティーの特長に互いに帰属しており、ある世代に属するということは人格の一態様であるとしている。すなわち、我々が世代意識を得るとどうなるのかということである。リュッシャーは、最初に、アイデンティティーの特徴の帰属が起こると述べ、我々が個人と集団の思考、感情、望み、行為、ライフスタイル、人生の軌跡をひとまとめとした人格形成の問いや人格への理解は、このプロセスを介して達せられる。したがって、リュッシャーにとって、最初の鍵は、アイデンティティーの関連性という考えである。世代間の関係は、我々が何者であるかという問いに答えるための重要な手助けとなると同時に、この問いへの答えを見つけるためには、我々は誰と一致する人なのか（それに対して我々は「我々は同じ世代である」と言うだろう）、そしてまた誰と違うのか（この場合、「我々は世代が違う」と認めるであろう）という点で、他者と自分自身を比較する必要に迫られるであろう。

　そして、実際には、いかに我々が違いを体験し、どのように対応するのかという問いは、リュッシャーが彼自身の問いに応答する第二の方法の根底にある。彼は、相違の要因は、あらゆる種類の関係に存在するものの、世代間の関係の場合には、それが特に顕著であると確信している。更に、この違いは、実施されているすべてのレベルでの特定の活動および世代間の関係に浸透し、それは、異なる世代の複数かつ多様な経験に基づいたものである。例え

ば、子ども達だけの場合は、祖父母は個人的な献身と愛情で、これらの子ども達と両親との関係を比較することによって違いという重要な体験を提供することができる。これは子ども達のその後の人生で非常に有用になると考えられる。そして、それはおそらく長期間にわたり持続すると考えられ、より長く他の世代の人たちと共に生きるための機会を提供することになるだろう。そして、もう一方では、祖父母は、孫との関係を通じて、例えば、彼らが若い頃、自分自身の子どもに接した方法とは異なる方法で孫に接していることに気付く時など、違いの価値に感謝することができるのである。リュッシャーの意見に基づいて、我々は、世代間交流が違いを明確にすることに特に適しており、それらを通して我々は何が違うのかを体験することを試されていると確信する。しかし、これが起こった際には、特定の類似性も必要である。というのは、我々は、世代間の関係について話しているからである。作られた世代（新世代）と作った世代（新世代を生み出した前世代）は、類似しているし、また、はっきりした違いもある。今日、我々は違いの中で、より良く生きることを学ぶ必要がある。そして、この点で、「世代的社会性」が重要性を増していると言えよう。世代間の学習にはますます多くのプロセスがあり、それを通して我々は社会的アイデンティティーのいろいろな面を理解するのである。

　このような時代において、相違、矛盾および拒絶の体験、つまり、アンビバレンスの体験は、まさに存在している。世代間の関係とは、アンビバレンスによって特徴づけられる人の空間である。それが、世代間交流の参加によって提供される学習、社会性および人格形成の機会が重要性と魅力を持っている理由と課題である。

再発見された課題

　世代間の関係は、常に身近に存在しているが、我々はそれらを再発見しているのである。しかし、それは単に不変のままであったものを再発見するというのではなく、むしろ、もはやかつてそうであった方法ではなくなったものを再発見することである。多くの世代間のプロセスは、今日行われる環境自体が変化していったものであり、もはやかつてのやり方ではないのである。我々の体験は、より不連続になっており、集団的アイデンティティーはすり抜けやすく、信頼は侵食され、我々の人格の発展のために必要となる違いを超えた違いというものが、あちこちに目立ってきている。

　我々が直面している課題は、世代間の交流を止めないことである。これは止めるべきではない。むしろ新たな視点で観察すべきである。世代間の関係は、共同で、我々と他者で、そして、他者の間で、長い人生を生きる方法を見つけるための成功への道となる。この視点の切り替えは、「我々」より「自分」を優先する風潮で生活するということから生まれる疲労の症状にすぎないのである。

　真なる課題とは、他の世代に属する者の承認と非差別的なものを超え、我々の感性を形成するという領域に入ることである。どのくらい１つの世代が他の世代に借りがあるのかを理解する手助けとして、我々が責任を持ってそれに注視し理解するならば、そのような借りは

責務及び向上につながる。それは、互いに気を配り、互いを世話し、信頼し、我々自身を向上させる責務を我々に負わせる。それを行うことで、我々が共同でより良い生活を送ることを可能にし、それと同時に違い（「他の世代は全然違う！」）と帰属意識（「我々は重要な多世代、連続した世代の一員だ！」）の体験をより充実したものにするのである。

Chapter 9

Promoting Intergenerational Connection and the Creation of Intergenerational Contact Zone (ICZ)

Leng Leng THANG

1. Introduction

Intergenerational programs and activities have commonly been perceived as important ingredients promoting bonding between the old and the young. As the intergenerational field develops, we are seeing an expansion of the conceptual idea in bonding the generations to move beyond structured programming, and to include "cultural and communal practices for bringing the generations together" (Kaplan et.al. 2007:84). More recently, the increasing attention on building conducive intergenerational spaces has also extended the intergenerational field to consider the intergenerational approaches as contributing to social and community cohesiveness, and hence concerns with how to create intergenerational environment in public spaces and environmental design practices that will promote intergenerational connections (Kaplan et.al. 2007; Thang and Kaplan, 2013).

An emphasis on the intergenerational approach highlights the problems of age-segregation, known to have undesirable consequences for the individuals, neighborhoods and society, leading to age-discrimination, age-based conflicts, increased vulnerabilities, social isolation, among others (Kaplan 1993; Foner 2000). In urging for an intergenerational approach in the cities, Van Vliet (2011)'s article on "Intergenerational Cities" cited a tragedy in Tokyo where a man had died for three years without his neighbors noticing. This may have been a case of social isolation to the extreme, but such tragedies are not so inconceivable when socially segregated neighborhoods deprived of mutual support and interaction becomes the norm in a generational/age-segregated environment.

How to build intergenerational conducive space in the community? It should first be noted that beyond the widely known ideas of inclusive design or universal design where the physical and psychological needs of people of different ages and abilities are considered, here, intergenerational conducive space also emphasizes the "relational" aspect, where opportunities for meaningful engagement – communication and relationships building between members of different generations can take place (Thang and Kaplan, 2013). The co-located, shared-sites or age-integrated centers such as Kotoen in Tokyo where age and children settings are co-located are among the most researched intergenerational shared spaces (see for example Jarrot, Kaplan and Steinig eds., 2011; Thang, 2001). Beyond these purpose-built shared sites often complemented with programs and activities, the potential of building intergencrational environment in public spaces in promoting spontaneous interaction still remains little explored. This chapter is an attempt to advance discussion on this aspect in the hope to offer new insights to the potential of environment design in promoting spontaneous intergenerational interactions.

2. Intergenerational contact zone

In examining intergenerational interaction in public spaces and ways to promote environment design focusing on intergenerational connection, I propose that we consider the "intergenerational contact zone" (ICZ) framework to help us conceptualize relational space in place making. The ICZ concept is inspired by the concept of "contact zone" proposed by Pratt (1991) where examined from a classroom context, she brings attention to "contact zone" as a space for cultures to meet, clash, and grapple with each other (p. 34). In her example of a college class on multiculturalism as the contact zone, she observes chaos when students were confronted with cultures, ideas and values vastly different from their own. Nonetheless, she concludes that "along with rage, incomprehension, and pain, there were exhilarating moments of wonder and revelation, mutual understanding, and new wisdom – the joys of the contact zone." (p. 39). I contend that when generations meet in co-located public spaces, the meeting of different age groups with different ideas and values may similarly cause confrontations, but at the same time, also provide space for mutual understanding and generational connections.

3. Public recreational spaces as ICZ

What are the potential public spaces that the generations can gather and have opportunity to connect? In this chapter, I focus on public recreational spaces and briefly introduce the concept of 3-generation (3G) recreational facilities to examine its potential as ICZ. It is common to perceive recreational spaces to be age-segregated, with playgrounds for children, and fitness stations for senior wellness and so on. In Singapore, where close to 80% of its total population of over 5 million are living in high-rise, high density public housing, the Housing and Development Board (HDB) in charge of public housing – also concerned with new ways to bond the generations in the community – has introduced 3-Generation (3G) facilities which are now relatively common sites within the housing estates (Goh, Giam and Wan, 2012; The Straits Times, 2013).

3-Generation (3G) facilities refer to the co- or nearby location of recreational facilities for different generations, for example, the near-by location of playground, adult fitness corner and fitness corner for older people with exercise stations for wellness. Curious to whether the closeness of facilities for different generations could promote intergenerational connections, I have done a pilot investigation of a playground co-located next to a fitness corner for older people in a small HDB neighborhood (see Thang, 2015). The following section provides a summary of the observation (ibid.).

4. The potential and limits of co-located recreational spaces as ICZ

The site selected for the study has observed to be one of the most popular gathering spot for residents in the neighborhood. The site has a playground where a big combo colorful Little Tikes play system is erected. At two sides of the playground is a row of wooden bench. Next to the playground is a fitness corner for older people where six exercise stations are located. This is a typical open space in neighborhood planning, being clustered by four blocks of flats on three sides, with a parking lot on the remaining side. It is also situated next to a child care center, and at the nexus where there are link ways and other seating areas that attract human traffic.

On a typical evening, children and adults (mostly caregivers of the children) start to congregate at the site from 5:30pm onwards, and could swell to more than 30 people packed in a small area, usually small children using the slides and play equipment, while older children of 10 years old and above screaming and running around the playground. Children casually flow from the playground to the exercise stations and vice versa. Around 6 pm, some children who are from the childcare center just next to the playground can be seen joining in the play, as their fathers, mothers or grandparents look on, sitting at the side. Other adults around include the common caregivers of children: grandparents and live in foreign female domestic workers. The

130

busy sights and sounds slowly taper off when the sky turns dark close to 7 pm, where children and adults start to head home.

This is a site where intergenerational contact is evident, albeit within certain parameters. It should be noted although a co-located site, distinct notices are set up by town council on each facility to specify the users suitable for each. At one glance, age-integration is obvious at the site with cross-use and the presence of older people with children. However, they are characterized by familial interaction between grandparents with their young grandchildren, suggesting the significance of such a space in facilitating the play and contact between grandchildren and their grandparents, who are likely to be caregivers to their grandchildren when their parents are at work. Much less communication have been observed between community older people with the young unless the older people know the children. So far, parallel co-existence is most common, older people are expected presence at the co-located site vicinity, generally, they stay at a distance from the children and chatting to each other while looking onto the lively playground. Sometimes, they did a little exercise at the fitness corner, where children are also seen around playing at the exercise stations. Besides the parallel co-existence of older people and children, similar parallel patterns are also found between different ethnicities and cultures, between citizens and permanent residents. The daily gathering of people at the playground somewhat resembles a microcosm of multi-cultural Singapore society, including Chinese, Malays and Indians, foreigners from mainland China, South Asia and other countries who have settled into local society with young kids. The foreign domestic workers are a prominent group at the playground area, often outnumbering local mothers, especially during the weekdays. However, the adults usually gather and interact within their own groups. Occasionally, cross-cultural intergenerational interaction is evident when older local residents are seen chatting

Chapter 9 Promoting Intergenerational Connection and the Creation of Intergenerational Contact Zone (ICZ)   131

with the domestic workers sitting at the bench, with exchanges that can varied from local cooking to caring for children. Children, on the other hand, tend to integrate more naturally regardless of their race and ethnicity. The children also serve as help stimulate conversations between adults.

5. Concluding remarks

As a public space which comes alive every day for about one to two hours in the evening, the co-located site has provided a natural space which facilitates the gathering of different people in the community. On the one hand, this site plays the role of a contact zone - not only one for different generations, but also a manifestation of the larger multi-ethnic and multi-cultural make-up of the society.   However, the intensity of contacts differs; generally shown to be of parallel co-existence between different age groups and ethnic groups. Nonetheless, the parallel co-existence is dynamic, the encounters have at least turn total strangers into somewhat familiar faces in the neighborhood, and pave the way for more opportunities of spontaneous befriending.

The co-located case observed discovers exciting multiplicity of the locale which increases the potential for intergenerational encounters between different cultures and ethnicities, also at the same time suggests the limits of such co-located public spaces as a contact zone for the old and the young, although benefits for grandparents interacting with their grandchildren is observed. Despite the limitation, the existence of such a co-located space remains important for incidental meetings; implying the potential of its role as an intergenerational contact zone in promoting age-integration in the community. Finally, the case study suggests that more design efforts should be invested for a more conducive intergenerational environment. The creation

132

of intergenerational spaces should be more comprehensively incorporated into town planning and design from the initial stages so that co-located facilities in the public places could be seamlessly complemented and complementing with the surrounding activities and other spaces.

References

Foner, Anne. 2000. "Age Integration or Age Conflict as Society Ages?" *The Gerontologist* 40: 202-275.

Goh, Shi Ting, Sarah Giam and Wan Gek Teo. 2012.'The Changing Face of Playgrounds: Play Areas Today Feature Sophisticated Attractions and Cater to 3 Generations. *The Straits Times*, June 15.

Jarrott, Shannon E., Matthew S. Kaplan and Sheri Y. Steinig, eds. 2011."Special Issue: Shared Site Intergenerational Programs: Common Space, Common Ground." *Journal of Intergenerational Relationships* 9(4).

Kaplan, Matthew S. 1993. "Recruiting Senior Adult Volunteers for Intergenerational Programs: Working into Create a 'Jump on the Bandwagon'Effect." *Journal of Applied Gerontology* 12(1):71-82.

Kaplan, Matthew S, Jawaid Haider, Uriel Cohen and Dyke Turner. 2007. "Environmental Design Perspectives on Intergenerational Programs and Practices: An Emergent Conceptual Framework. "*Journal of Intergenerational Relationships* 5(2):81-110.

Pratt, Mary L. 1991. "Arts of the Contact Zone." *Profession*, 33-40.

Thang, Leng Leng and Matthew S. Kaplan. 2013. "IntergenerationalPathways for Building Relational Spaces and Places." In *Environmental Gerontology: Making Meaningful Places in Old Age*, edited by Graham D.

Rowles and Miriam Bernard, 225-250. New York: Springer Publishing Company LLC.

Thang, Leng Leng. 2001. *Generations in Touch: Linking the Old and Young in Tokyo Neighborhood*. Ithaca: Cornell University Press.

Thang, Leng Leng. 2015. "Creating an intergenerational contact zone: encounters in public spaces within Singapore's public housing neighbourhoods." In *Intergenerational Space*. Edited by Robert M.

Vanderbeck and Nancy Worth, London: Routledge. *The Straits Times*. 2013. Multi-generation facilities to cater to changing needs: HDB. June 18.

Van Vliet, Willem. 2011. "Intergenerational Cities: A Framework for Policies and Programs." *Journal of Intergenerational Relationships*, 9(4): 348-365.

第9章　世代間のつながりの促進と 世代間の接触空間（ICZ）の創造

リン・リン・タン

1. はじめに

　世代間交流プログラムは、一般に高齢者と子供を繋ぐことを促進する重要な材料であると受け止められてきた。さらに近年では、世代間交流を促進する場の構築に対する注目の高まりを通じて、社会やコミュニティの凝集性を高めるための世代間交流を行うフィールドも整備されつつある。どのようにして公共の場所に世代間交流の環境を作り出したり、そのような環境をデザインしたりするかということへの関心が、世代間交流を促進することにもつながっている。

　世代間交流の重要性は、世代間分離の問題や近所同士のトラブルといった社会問題、年齢による差別、世代間摩擦、コミュニティとしての脆弱性の増大、社会的孤立といった問題を解決しうることにある（Kaplan 1993; Foner 2000）。

　では、いかにしてコミュニティの中に世代間交流を促進する場を作るか？　予め注意すべきことは、異なる年齢や能力を持つ人々のニーズを考慮したユニバーサル・デザインという概念を越え（ここが重要なのだが）、意味のある世代間接触のための機会（例えば異なる世代によるコミュニケーションや関係構築の場）を提供する、「関係性」を重視した場を作ることに重点を置くことである。

　本章では、そのような環境デザインの可能性に新たな洞察を提供することを期待して議論を進めたい。

2. 世代間接触の領域

　公共スペースにおける世代間交流に焦点を当てた環境デザインの検討をする上で、場所づくりにおける「世代間の接触領域」(ICZ) の枠組みを用いることを提案したい。ICZ の概念は、Pratt（1991）によって示された「接触領域」という教室での文脈によって示された概念により生成されたものであり、「接触領域」の中でも異文化の出会いや衝突、融合に注意を置くべきであるとした。

　筆者は多世代が同じ空間で接触する際、様々な考えや価値観を持つ異なる年齢層が出会うことで対立が生じる可能性を指摘しているが、同時にその空間は、異なる世代同士の相互理解とつながりの場所を提供しているともいえよう。

3．ICZ としての公共のレクリエーションスペース

　多世代が集い接触する機会のある潜在的な公共スペースとは何か。この章では、公共の娯楽スペースに焦点を当て、ICZ としての可能性を調べるべく、3 世代が集うレクリエーション施設の概念について紹介する。

　一般的に ICZ は、世代別のレクリエーションスペースと子どものための遊び場、そして高齢者の健康増進のためのフィットネス施設などがあるものをいう。

　全人口の 80％近い 500 万人がマンションや住宅開発庁 (HDB) の提供する公営住宅に住んでいるシンガポールでも、コミュニティ内の世代を繋ぐ新しい方法に関心が向けられており、3 世代に対応する設備が導入されはじめている。3 世代に対応した設備としては、多様な世代のためのレクリエーション施設が挙げられる。例えば近隣の遊び場や大人のためのフィットネスコーナー、高齢者の健康増進のための運動施設などがこれにあたる。

　多世代のための施設に近いことが世代間交流を促進するかという点に興味を持ち、筆者は小さな公営住宅周辺の遊び場とそれに隣接する高齢者のためのフィットネスコーナーでパイロット調査を行った。次のセクションでは、調査の概略を述べたい。

4．世代間交流の場としてのレクリエーションスペースの持つ可能性と制限

　研究のために選んだ場所は、居住者にとって最も人気の集まる場所の一つである。その場所には、大きなシステム遊具が置かれている遊び場がある。遊び場の両サイドには木製のベンチがあり、遊び場の隣には 6 台の運動器具が置かれた高齢者向けのフィットネスコーナーがある。これは計画に基づいて整備されたオープンスペースであり、3 辺をブロックで、残り 1 辺を駐車場で区分けされた場所である。この場所は子ども養育センターと隣接しており、他の道や休憩場所とも繋がっていて、人通りの多い場所に位置している。

　そこに子どもと大人（ほとんどが子どもの世話人）が午後 5 時 30 分頃から集まり始める。通常、小さな子どもたちは滑り台や遊具を使って遊ぶ一方、10 歳以上の子どもたちは大きな声をあげて遊び場を走り回る。子どもたちは自由に遊び場から運動器具へ、あるいは運動器具から遊び場へと移動する。

　夕方 6 時ごろになると、子ども養育センターから遊び場へと移動して遊び始める子どもがおり、彼らの父親や母親、祖父母あるいは子供の面倒を見る外国人女性家事労働者は、その様子をベンチに座って眺める。その後、午後 7 時に近づくにつれ、広場は子どもたちや大人たちが家に戻ることで徐々に落ち着きをみせる。

　広場の利用状況や高齢者が子どもと一緒にいる様子から、異なる世代の交流が生じているのは明らかである。子どもたちは祖父母や親との間の家庭内でのやりとりによって陶冶されるのであり、孫と祖父母の間での遊びや交流を容易にするような空間は重要である。

　高齢者は一般に並列的な共存が普通であり、彼らは子どもから離れた場所にいながら、活

気のある遊び場を眺めつつおしゃべりすることを期待されている。時々、高齢者は運動コーナーでちょっとした運動をするが、子どもたちもその周囲にある運動器具で遊んでいる様子がみられる。同様の並列パターンは、異なる民族や文化の間、あるいは市民や永住者の間にも見いだされる。

　遊び場に日々人々が集まる様子は、中国人やマレー人、インド人、あるいは中国本土からやってくる南アジアやその他の国の人々が若い子どもたちと一緒に定住することで形成された、多文化が混在するシンガポール社会に似ている。特に平日は、外国人の家事労働者らはしばしば、地元に住んでいる母親以上に遊び場にいる様子が見られる。

　とはいえ、大人たちは通常自分たちのグループの中で集まったり交流したりする。時々、古くから地域に住んでいる人々が家事労働者とベンチに座っておしゃべりをしている様子がみられ、そこでなされた意見交換によって家事労働者は地元の料理や子どもの世話の在り方を理解するが、それが異文化間での世代間交流であることは明らかである。一方で子どもたちは、より自然な形で人種や民族に関係なく集まる傾向にある。子どもたちは大人同士の会話を促進するための手助けも提供する。

5．結論

　毎日、夕方の1〜2時間、活気を帯びる公共の場所として、レクリエーションスペースはコミュニティ内の様々な人々が集まるように働きかける自然な場所を提供してきた。一方で、この場所は接触空間の役割、すなわち、異なる世代だけでなく社会におけるより大きな枠組みとしての多民族、あるいは多文化間の交流を形成するための場としての役割を持っている。

　しかしながら、接触の強度は異なっている。例えば一般に、異なる年代グループや民族グループでは並列的な共存関係となることが示されている。それにもかかわらず、並列的な共存関係は動的であり、近所付き合いにおいて少なくとも出会う人を全くの他人から顔なじみへと変化させるとともに、自発的に親交を深めるより多くの機会を提供する道を開く。

　今回のケースでは、異なる文化や民族間の世代を超えた出会いの可能性を高める刺激的で多様な発見が観察されたと同時に、孫が祖父母と接触することによって得られる利益は観察されたものの、高齢者と若者のための接触空間として公共の場をそのように設置することへの限界も示唆された。それでも、そのような制限にもかかわらず、このような場所の存在は偶然的な出会いの場としてなお重要であることが示唆された。コミュニティにおける多世代間の統合を促進する上で、このようなコミュニケーションスペースは世代間の接触空間として重要な役割を担う可能性があることを示唆しているといえるだろう。

　今回のケーススタディから、世代間交流の環境をより良いものにするために、より多くの場づくりのための設計努力が費やされるべきであると考えられる。公共の場におけるコミュニケーションスペースがシームレスに周囲の活動や他の場所のもつ機能を補完することができることが示されたことから、世代間交流のための場の造成は、より包括的に初期段階からの都市計画と設計に組み込まれるべきであるといえよう。

Chapter 10

Age Friendly Communities:
A Strategic Approach to a Connected Intergenerational Society?

Alan Hatton-Yao

"It may have been well-meaning, but we now talk and think about maternal health, child health, old people's health, this artificial compartmentalization marginalises older people. By making us think about how we all link to each other, regardless of our age, age-friendly communities show us a different, more connected, future." (Beard ···quoted by Parry 2010).

The Author of this chapter has been involved in the strategic development of intergenerational work in the UK and internationally for 20 years. Throughout that time the greatest challenge has been how to move intergenerational work from an interesting approach, which is mainly about time limited projects, to a model of thinking and practice that is embedded in mainstream policy.

This can be illustrated through the development of intergenerational work in Wales. In 2003 the Welsh Government published their 'Older People' s Strategy' (2003). This was developed from a national consultation and made a commitment to develop intergenerational work. As a consequence the Beth Johnson Foundation was commissioned to develop this programme and this lead to the Welsh Government publishing their 'Strategy for Intergenerational Practice in Wales' (2008). Following on from this the Welsh Local Government Association (WLGA) published 'Bringing Generations Together in Wales Guidance' (2012).

Whilst this demonstrated a significant interest at all levels in intergenerational work in Wales and a massive amount went on it was uneven and largely project focused and so vulnerable to the changing priorities of funding. It also became increasingly clear that the government were not going to be able to make a long-term investment in intergenerational work. As a consequence work began in Wales to rethink how intergenerational work could be sustained particularly in the context of the plans for 2012 to be the European Year of Active Ageing and Intergenerational Solidarity.

Building on the World Health Organisation (WHO) programme to develop Age-friendly Cities and Communities (WHO 2007) the European Year for Active Ageing and Solidarity between Generations 2012 developed a vision for a European society for all ages (Age-Platform 2012). This has gained visibility with an increasing number of stakeholders now interested in this effort to achieve fair and sustainable solutions that promote the best use of financial and human resources to develop smart and innovative solutions to develop age-friendly environments.

AGE's Manifesto for an Age-Friendly European Union by 2020 (Age-Platform 2012) outlined a list of benefits from creating an age-friendly European Union. These include:

1. A positive attitude to ageing that recognises the value of all age groups' identities and contribution to society;
2. Goods and services that are adapted to the needs of all highlighting the need for solutions that are based on the concept of Design-for-All and Universal Design – essentially intervention for environments with the aim that

all ages can enjoy participating in the 'construction' of our society with equal access to use and understand their environment with as much independence as possible;

3. Accessible outdoor spaces, buildings and transport as well as adapted housing and physical activity facilities that promote participation in society for longer, while increasing opportunities for exchange within and across generations;

4. The opportunity to actively participate in volunteering, cultural, sport and recreational activities thus creating and/or maintaining their social networks, gaining new competences and contributing to their personal fulfilment and wellbeing.

According to WHO (2007), the physical and social environments are key determinants of whether people remain healthy and independent throughout the life course. Demographic change is a major challenge facing all EU countries. As such, promoting all age-friendly environments is an effective approach for responding to demographic change. Creating age-friendly environments means adapting our everyday living environment in order to empower people to promote social inclusion, active participation and maintain an autonomous and good quality of life. What is more, such a solution has the potential to help our society better cope with demographic ageing in a way that is fair for all generations.

The legacy of the 2012 European Year was the establishment of the AFE-innovet programme (www.afe-innovet.eu) with the vision to develop an all-age-friendly Europe by 2020. Wales used the learning emerging from 2012 to launch the national Ageing-Well programme (2014) that had the development of all-age-friendly communities as one of its core themes. The work

Chapter 10 Age Friendly Communities: A Strategic Approach to a Connected Intergenerational Society? 139

that had been undertaken to develop intergenerational practice across Wales was integrated into this age-friendly approach to ensure it became part of the national response to building communities for all ages.

The author's vision has always been to see intergenerational practice as one of the core approaches that can be used to build cohesive communities that mutually benefit all of the generations (Hatton-Yeo, 2008). As such we have always been looking for a way to write intergenerational work into policy to ensure its value is understood and that it becomes a sustainable element of national and international policy. By reframing intergenerational approaches as a core element of the move to develop both all age-friendly Europe and Wales we believe we have achieved this. Our aim was to move intergenerational work from project to system thinking and over the next 5 years we will continue to promote this approach.

December 7th will mark the launch of the European Union Covenant on Demographic Change (forthcoming). This will establish a Europe Wide network to promote the development of All Age-Friendly Europe, working across the life-course to create a good society for us all. We are confident that intergenerational thinking and approaches will be an underpinning pillar of this work.

References

AFE-INNOVNET (2015). "*What are Age-Friendly Environments? Why should European Cities & Regions become Age-Friendly?*"

Age-Platform Europe (2012) *Towards an Age-Friendly European Union by 2020*

Ageing Well in Wales (2014) "*Ageing Well in Wales 2014 -2015: Ensuring Wales is a good place for everyone to grow older*"

Hatton-Yeo, A. (2008). Programas intergeneracionales, solidaridad intergeneracional y cohesión social. In M. Sánchez (Ed.), *Hacia una sociedad para todas las edades. Lavía de los programas intergeneracionales.* Barcelona: Fundación La Caixa.

Welsh Assembly Government (2003) *'Older People's Strategy'*

Welsh Assembly Government (2008) *'Strategy for Intergenerational Practice in Wales'*

Welsh Local Government Association (2012) *'Bringing Generations Together in Wales Guidance'*

World Health Organisation (2007) *"WHO (2007). Global age-friendly cities: A Guide."*

第10章　年齢にやさしいコミュニティ：つながりが強い世代間交流社会への戦略的アプローチ

アラン・ハットン・ヤオ

「それは善意によるものだったかもしれないが、我々は今、母親の健康、子供の健康、老人たちの健康について語り且つ考えねばならない。この人為的分類は、超高齢者たちを除外することになる。我々全てが年齢に関わりなくいかに結合し合ってしているかを考えさせることによって、高齢者に友好的な社会は、異なった、より緊密な未来を示してくれる。」(Beard, Parry 引用、2010)

　この章の筆者は、20年間、英国連邦内と国際的な世代間研究の戦略的発展に関わってきた。その期間を通して最大の挑戦は、主に時間的に限定された課題として、政治の主流に組み込まれている思考や実践の規範への興味深いアプローチから、世代間交流の研究をいかに切り離すかということであった。

　このことはウエールズにおける世代間交流の研究を通して例証することが出来る。2003年ウエールズ政府は超高齢者戦略を公表した（2003）。これは国の協議会から発展して、世代間研究の発展を公約したものである。その結果、Beth Johnson 基金がこのプログラムを発展させる権限を与えられ、それによって、ウエールズ政府は「ウエールズにおける世代間交流実践戦略」を公表することになった（2008）。これに続いて、ウエールズ地方政府連合（WLGA）は「ウエールズ・ガイダンスにおいて複数世代を結合する」を公表した。

　これはウエールズでの世代間研究に対するあらゆるレベルでの大きな興味を示しており、興味の大きさは持続したが、それは不均一で、基金の優先権の変動に左右された。さらに、次第に明確になったことは、政府が世代間研究に長期的な投資をすることが出来なかったことだ。その結果、ウエールズにおいて研究が始まり、特に2012年を「活動的高齢化と世代間連帯意識のヨーロッパ年」とする計画に関連させて、いかに世代間研究が持続されうるかを再考することになった。

　世界保健機構（WHO）のプログラム「高齢者に友好的な都市と共同体」（WHO 2007）発展プログラムに基づいて、「活動的高齢化と世代間の結合 2012」は全世代のためのヨーロッパ社会（年齢綱領 2012）の指針へと発展した。この目に見える成果は、株保有者たちが、公正で持続可能な解決、すなわち、資金的・人的資源を最良に活用し、賢明で革新的な解決方法を進展させて、高齢者に友好的な環境を作り上げることに関心を示すようになったことである。

　2020年までに高齢者に友好的なEUを目指すAGE宣言は（年齢綱領 2012）は、高齢者に友好的EU創設によってもたらされる一連の利点を概略している。その中に含まれるものを列挙する。

1. 全世代集団の存在証明と社会貢献を認識する高齢化への積極的姿勢

2.「全てのためのデザイン」と「ユニバーサル・デザイン」という概念に基づいた解決方法の必要性を強調する必要性に合わせた商品やサービスを、全ての年齢層が可能な限り自主的に彼らの環境を利用し理解する同等な権利によって、我々の社会「構築」に参加できる喜びを目指す。

3. 適合した住宅と身体活動施設のみならず、戸外のスペース、建物と交通の利用を可能にし、長期に渡って社会参加を促進する中で、同一世代内や世代を超えて意見を交換する機会を増やす。

4. ボランティア活動、文化、スポーツ、リクレーション活動に積極的に参加する機会を得ることによって、社会ネットワークを構築し維持する新たな能力を獲得し、彼らの個人的達成感や幸福に貢献する。

WHO（2007）によれば、身体的・社会的環境は、人々が一生を通して健康で自立した状態を維持するかどうかの重要な決定要素である。人口統計的変動は、全てのEU諸国が直面する主要な挑戦である。しかるに、全ての高齢者に友好的な環境は人口統計の変動に対応する有効なアプローチである。高齢者に友好的な環境を作るのは、社会参加を通して、自立的で質の良い人生へ積極的に参加し、維持促進する能力を人々に与えるためである。更に、そのような解決は、全世代に公正な方法で、統計的高齢化に対して、社会がよりよく対処する可能性を有するということだ。

2012年におけるヨーロッパ年の遺産は、AFE（高齢者に友好的な環境）の刷新的プログラムを確立することであり、2020年までに全ての世代に友好的ヨーロパを進展させるビジョンを伴っていた。ウエールズは2012年を起点とする知識を用いて、「全ての世代に友好的共同体」を中心テーマとした高齢者福利プログラム（2014）に着手した。ウエールズ全地域で世代間慣習の発展に着手した研究は、この高齢者に友好的なアプローチに集約され、あらゆる世代のための共同体を作り上げる国家的対応の一部となった。

筆者が掲げたビジョンは、常に世代間慣習は全ての世代が相互に利するような結束した共同体を作り上げるのに役立つ主要なアプローチの一つであった。（Hatton-Yeo, 2008）。そのようなものとして、我々は常に世代間研究を執筆し、政策につなげ、その価値を理解し、そしてそれが国家的・国際的政策の持続可能な要素になる方法を模索している。世代間のアプローチを全世代に友好的なヨーロッパとへと移行させるよう組み直すことによって、我々は次の点を達成したと信じる。我々の目標は、体制的思考のプロジェクトから世代間研究を切り離すことであり、次の5年間に渡って、我々はこのアプローチを促進し続けて行くだろう。

12月7日は人口統計変動に関するEU規約に着手する記念となるだろう（今後の日程）こ

第10章　年齢にやさしいコミュニティ：つながりが強い世代間交流社会への戦略的アプローチ　143

れにより、全ヨーロパのネットワークにより、全世代に友好的なヨーロッパの発展が促進される。それは、我々全てにとって、生涯を通して良い社会を作り上げることになる。世代間交流の思考とアプローチは、この仕事の土台の柱の一本になると我々は信じている。

Chapter 11

Intergenerational Schools International: Sharing across the Ages

Peter Whitehouse
Yachneet Pushkarna
Qinghong Wei
Richard Owen Geer

1. The Global Challenge

Now is the time to seek wisdom in the old place, in the bonds between generations.

Human life faces a bewilderment of challenges including global climate change, income and social inequity, and spiritual/ethical/cultural conflicts. Unbridled capitalism allied with unskeptical scientism has created wealth for a few, poverty for many, and a threat to the survival of life itself.

As humans, our strengths are that we are generalists and that we learn better than other species. But to ensure flourishing, learning must be shared among generations. Therefore, our most important activity is multiage learning. (de Souza, & Grundy, E. ,2007; Fried, Carlson, Freedman, et al., 2004; Kaplan & Liu, 2004) The organization of schools, structure of universities, the roles of the arts, the very processes of knowledge creation and dissemination, and even innovation itself, all require renewal. The digital era creates new opportunities for sharing across time and space. Learning organizations need to become more glocally--focused on a future that encompasses diverse international perspectives, yet stays true to the values and needs of place, relationship, and the local community.

Chapter 11 Intergenerational Schools International: Sharing across the Ages   145

2. The Intergenerational Schools (TIS)

One organizational form for innovative learning is intergenerational education as practiced by The Intergenerational Schools (TIS) in Cleveland Ohio. (Whitehouse, Bendezu, FallCreek & Whitehouse, 2000). The original school has been in existence 15 years and has demonstrated its value to the elementary students who attend, the young adults and elders who volunteer, and the community at large. The fundamental pedagogical processes are developmentally appropriate experiences and socially constructed knowledge making (www.tisonline.org). Test scores have made the schools beacons of hope in the challenged landscape of public education. But we aim to produce more than successful test takers, we aim for spirited citizens. Published research, including both quantitative and qualitative methods, have demonstrated that volunteering in the school can enhance the cognitive/brain health of older individuals, even those with cognitive challenges, like dementia (Whitehouse & George, 2008; Whitehouse, 2010 George & Whitehouse, 2010; George & Whitehouse, 2011). The schools have received many local, national and international awards, including the 2014 Eisner prize for the best intergenerational program.

Our now three intergenerational schools fosters an educational community of excellence that provides skills and experiences for lifelong learning and spirited citizenship to learners of all ages. Its vision is to serve as a model to encourage and invigorate communities and to create new environments which empower learners of all ages as they contribute to a just society. Its pedagogy is based on two principles: (1) learning is a lifelong developmental process and (2) knowledge is socially constructed in the context of culture, experience and community. The goal of TIS is to infuse age-integrated concepts and relationships into all areas of curriculum through an intergenerational learning model. This model includes sharing of wisdom among the generations, creating a common narrative, infusing life-issues into curriculum, creating positive two-way relationships and reflecting real life in community. This approach begins with the sharing of life stories across the generations, the simplest and oldest vehicle for conveying wisdom and building relationship. Next, in the multi-age classrooms where every child is empowered to become both a teacher and a learner, elders serve as reading mentors sharing their rich intergenerational literature with the children. Students regularly visit long-term care facilities and form relationships and engage with elders in shared activities that support the social studies curriculum. The school has been successful not only at transforming and improving public education for children but also creating opportunities for reframing aging and improving the quality of life for elders, including those with cognitive impairment. Recent data demonstrate the value of volunteering at the school in reducing stress and improving the experience of aging George & Whitehouse, 2011). Ecological learning is a key aspect of the school's pedagogy and also of great relevance to addressing today's environmental challenges (Ingman, Benjamin, and Lusky, 1999; Okun, 1984; Stenig & Butts, 2010).

The inclusion of older adults and the sharing of stories are intentional design elements in the schools' model. On a daily basis through structured learning programs seniors and other community members share with TIS students their time, stories and enthusiasm for lifelong learning. Not only do all of these events directly support and enhance the academic curriculum, but the students gain experience which prepares them to interact successfully with others different from them. And, most importantly, they make friends across boundaries like age and class.

Chapter 11 Intergenerational Schools International: Sharing across the Ages 147

As we celebrate 15 years of model development and success, we are broadening our dissemination activities beyond the three schools in Cleveland. Recently we formed Intergenerational Schools International, (ISI), and are developing collaborations in India, China, Japan, the United Kingdom, Spain, and Canada.

3. Intergenerational Schools International (ISI)

ISI was formed in 2014 as a nonprofit organized in the state of Ohio. ISI promotes multiage learning through pedagogically and organizationally innovative approaches tailored to diverse communities around the world. Focusing on organizations, such as schools that attend to the needs of children, and programs and living arrangements that provide services for elders, ISI fosters intergenerative community development. ISI does its work as a decentralized organization in colorful and vibrant ways. By spending the time necessary for children and adults, and especially elders, to build relationships, ISI plays with ideas, actions, and engagements that contribute to the emergence of brain health, co-learning and community-based collective wisdom. ISI aims to inspire everyone to imagine a sustainable and flourishing future with respect for all living creatures and all cultures. And we begin by sharing stories. Through that intimate and trust-building process are formed the relationships that make possible everything which follows.

4. Structure

ISI is a decentralized organization which promotes certain organizational philosophies and processes. Its major focus is to help other organizations create intergenerational learning programs. The locus of activity can be a na-

148

tion, a state, a community, or an existing organization. Although we started with intergenerational public schools, we believe a variety of organizational forms are essential to move the ideas forward. Many country's school systems may be resistant to the creation of completely new schools, and add-ons or afterschool programs may be appropriate. Long-term care institutions may also house intergenerational learning programs. In fact, many existing programs are already intergenerational. However, to be truly intergenerational means to mark, celebrate and expand the opportunities associated with age diversity. In whatever organizational form, programs begin as people share their stories of life experience. Stories naturally relate participants to each other and the organizational mission of intergenerational co-learning and the co-creation of wisdom.

5. Process

ISI aspires to a certain level of organizational development itself, including the commitment to remaining a learning organization. New organizational forms are emerging that mimic living systems and contribute to the evolution of human consciousness. We aim to create ourselves as a Teal organization in the rubric of the book *Reinventing Organizations* (Laloux, 2014). We hold an open, participatory space in which a diversity of voices is respected and included in decision-making. We will operate with glocal and glozonal principles in mind, i.e. to strategize globally with a common set of cognitive frameworks and values but to operate in a regional or zonal fashion depending on the type and location (community, state or nation) of intervention.

6. Projects

ISI is leading The Intergenerativity Project (TIP), the first venture of the organization. The neologism, "intergenerativity," as in intergenerational (the prime example), interprofessional, interdisciplinary, interfaith, international, etc, captures the main quality of TIP. Intergenerativity celebrates the blending of positive sources of cultural change. TIP utilizes the Story Bridge methodology (storytelling across multiple platforms, developed by members of the ISI team; Geer, Corriere et. Al., 2012) to convene a national conversation around education and innovation. In Story Bridge, story sharing, theater, visual art, dance, music, and video games merge in a intergenerational transmedia project. Through storytelling and performance, TIP creates a co-learning laboratory for communications, creativity, tolerance, empathy, passion, self and collective presentation skills, and critical consciousness. Research has found that Story Bridge empowers individual participants as it positively transforms the community.

7. Partnerships

Creative partnerships are key to our success. Here we will illustrate with examples from India and China. National Federation of Indian American Associations, India

The National Federation of Indian Americans Associations (NFIA; http://www.nfia.net/) is based in the United States currently headquartered in Los Angeles with a rich 35 years history of celebrating diversity within the community here in America and supporting activities in both India and America. . The Indian American community in the United States is highly accomplished in the spheres of innovation, particularly information technology, healthcare and business entrepreneurship. NIFA is planning to provide funding and technical support for launching our 1st Intergenerational Knowledge Center in India (in a state called as Himachal Pradesh). NFIA's objective of 2015-16 is to develop projects in tune with Prime Minister Narendra Modi's Digital India initiative providing skill development by connecting the best of United States to the neediest of India.

8. pARTicipate, China

pARTicipate (http://www.participate-global.org/) is an award winning social enterprise which aims to engage and empower individuals and communities through art education. Its pedagogy is grounded in advanced research and years of practice in the fields of arts, community development, education, psychology, etc. It provides three lines of services – online art education, international leadership development, and creative community building. pARTicipate works at the grassroots with migrant and rural communities, and engages policy makers to advocate for educational innovation at the national level. pARTicipate became the partner of ISI in May 2015 and since then has integrated intergenerational learning into its programming to positively transform the lives of citizens and develop communities.

9. Curriculum

Individuals and organizations grow in response to internal and external forces; innovative curricula support healthy responses. ISI is developing two such curricula. The first helps individuals understand their own aging as an opportunity for learning and career and life development. The second sup-

Chapter 11 Intergenerational Schools International: Sharing across the Ages   151

ports organizations that wish to intensify the power of lifelong learning and collective wisdom for their own success. Both curricula are built around the premise that individual human beings thrive in organizations that welcome the whole person and attend to individual strengths and values. Organizations succeed when they take full advantage of external opportunities and the internal resources of their diverse members. The curricula lead to certificates for either individual or organization, or both, and signal that recipients are better prepared to take on today's economic, social, political, and environmental challenges, and contribute to a better future.

Each curriculum is designed around ten content areas. However, each is flexible and readily adaptable to the current status of the individual and/or the organization. The curricula succeed not by replication, but by adaptive innovation. Process is as important as content in the certificate programs. Participants are lifelong learners and social entrepreneurs committed to the sustainability and flourishing of the planet.

10. Conclusions

In this chapter we have presented the development of ISI against the background of global challenges and human evolution. We have emphasized that values and process, especially human relationships, are as, or even more, important than structure and rationality in the development of our educational products. The world is facing highly complex problems where deep reflection on the role of human beings on the planet both as individuals and a species is critical. We believe that intergenerative narrative in the form of shared personal and community stories is critical to systems thinking and to expanding our moral scope necessary to support human flourishing and survival.

Table 1 Certification Process- Individuals

- Self knowledge - purpose
- Learning skills - narrative
- Health - being in balance
- Aging -life course and legacy
- Social networks and IT

- Organizational life -collective
- Global context - natural and social
- Human creativity -innovation
- Wisdom - aspiration
- Quality of life - legacy

Table 2 Certification Process -Organizations

- Mission and vision
- Organizational - design & culture
- Learning principles
- Pedagogy and IT
- Programming -arts and science

- Human Resources
- Community context
- Planning and innovation
- Partnerships
- Outcomes - CQI

References

de Souza, E. M., & Grundy, E. (2007). Intergenerational interaction, social capital and health: Results from a randomised controlled trial in Brazil. *Social Science and Medicine, 65,* 1397–1409.

Fried, L. P., Carlson, M. C., Freedman, M., et al. (2004). A social model for health promotion for an aging population: Initial evidence on the experience corps model. *Journal of Urban Health, 81,* 64–78.

Geer, R.O., Corriere, J., et al. (2012). *Story Bridge: From Alienation to Community Action.* Denver: Community Performance Press.

George, D. R. & Singer, M. (2011). Intergenerational volunteering and quality of life for persons with mild to moderate dementia: results from a 5-month intervention study in the United States. *American Journal of Geriatric Psychiatry, 19*(4), 392–396.

George, D. R., & Whitehouse, P. J. (2010). Can intergenerational volunteering enhance quality of life for persons with mild to moderate dementia? Results from a 5-month mixed methods intervention study in the United States. *Journal of the American Geriatrics Society, 58,* 796.

Ingman, S., Benjamin, T., & Lusky, R. (1999). The environment: The quintessential intergenerational challenge. *Generations, 22,* 68–71.

Kaplan, M., & Liu, S. (2004). *Generations united for environmental awareness and action.* Washington, DC: G. United.

Laloux, Frederick *Reinventing organizations: A Guide to Creating Organizations inspired by the Next Stage of Human Consciousness* (2014) Brussels: Nelson Parker.

Okun, M. (1994). Earth in mind: On education, environment, and the human prospect. *Jour-*

Chapter 11 Intergenerational Schools International: Sharing across the Ages 153

nal of Applied Gerontology, 13, 115–126.

Stenig, S., & Butts, D. (2010). Generations going green: Intergenerational programs connecting young and old to improve our environment. *Generations, 33,* 64–69.

Whitehouse, P. (2010, Spring). Taking brain health to the next deeper and broader level. *Neurological Institute Journal,* 17–22.

Whitehouse, P. J., Bendezu, E., FallCreek, S., & Whitehouse, C. (2000). Intergenerational community schools: A new practice for a new time. *Educational Gerontology, 26,* 761–770.

Whitehouse, P., & George, D. R. (2008). *The myth of Alzheimer's: What you aren't being told about today's most dreaded diagnosis.* New York: St. Martin's Press.

第11章　国際的世代間交流学校

——年齢を超えた分かち合い

ピーター・ホワイトハウス、ヤクニー・パッシュカーナ
クインホン・ウエイ、リチャード・オーウェン・ギア

　人類繁栄を保証するために、学習は世代間で分け持たれなければならない。すなわち、私たちの最も重要な活動は、多世代学習（multiage learning）である。また、進みつつあるデジタル化の時代は、時間と空間を超えて分担するための新しい機会を作成する。学習組織はよりグローカルになる必要がある。

1．世代間交流学校（TIS）

　革新的な学習のための1つの組織的な形がクリーブランド・オハイオの世代間交流学校（TIS）により行われている世代間交流教育である（Whitehouse, Beudezu, FallCreek & Whitehouse, 2000）。

　この独創的な学校は15年存続し、小学生をはじめ、ボランティアとなっている若い大人と高齢者、そして大きな社会にその価値を示している。

　学校は、ベスト世代間交流プログラムであるアイスナー賞（2014年）を含む全国的かつ国際的な賞を受賞している。

　現在、私たちは、3つの世代間の学校が、すべての年代の学習者に、生涯学習と元気な公民権のためのスキルと経験を提供し、優秀な教育的コミュニティを養育している。そのビジョンは、コミュニティを促進し、力づけるモデルを提供することであり、正しい社会に寄与するようにすべての年齢の学習者を力づける新しい環境をつくることである。

　その教育学は2つの原則に基づく。

　（1）学びは生涯発達的なプロセスである。

　（2）知識は文化、経験とコミュニティの文脈において社会的に構成される。

　TISのゴールは、世代間交流学習モデルを通して、カリキュラムのすべてのエリアに、年齢の統合概念や関係を吹き込むことである。このモデルは、世代間での知恵の共有、共通物語の創作、カリキュラム上に生活問題を入れること、ポジティブな双方向の関係をつくること、およびコミュニティに実生活を反映させることを含む。

　学校は、子どものための公教育の変換と改善の機会をつくるだけでなく、認知的損傷を受けた高齢者も含め、高齢者にとっては老化を防ぎ、生活の質向上を図る機会をつくる。最近のデータでは、ストレスを減らし、老化の経験を改善する上で、学校でのボランティア活動の価値を述べている（George& Whitehouse 2011）。エコロジカルな学習は、学校の教育学

の重要な見地であり、また今日的な環境への挑戦に大きく関連性がある（Ingman, Benjamin, and Lusky1999；Okun 1984; Stenig & Butts 2010）。

私たちは 15 年のモデル開発とその成功を祝福するように、クリーブランドの 3 つの学校を越えて普及活動を展開している。最近、私たちは世代間交流学校の国際化（ISI）を形成し、インド、中国、日本、イギリス、スペイン、およびカナダとの協力関係を強めつつある。

2．世代間交流学校の国際化（ISI）

ISI は、オハイオ州の非営利団体として 2014 年に結成された。ISI は、世界中の多様なコミュニティに合うように調整された教育学的、組織的に革新的なアプローチを通して多世代学習（multiage learning）を促進する。子どものニーズに合わせる学校のように、また高齢者にサービスを提供するプログラムや生活適応のように組織に焦点付けながら、ISI は世代間交流コミュニティの発展に寄与している。

ISI がめざしていることは、誰もが、すべての生き物およびすべての文化への敬意によって持続可能で繁栄する未来を想像させようとすることである。

＜構造＞
ISI は、一定の組織的な哲学とプロセスを促進する分散化された組織である。その主要なフォーカスは、他の組織が世代間の学習プログラムを作成することを手助けすることである。活動の場所は、国家、州、コミュニティ、または既存の組織であることができる。私たちは世代間の公立学校で始めたけれども、私たちは、アイデアを前に動かすために、各種の組織的な形が必須であると思っている。多くの国の学校システムは完全に新しい学校の作成に抵抗力があるかもしれない。どのような組織的な形においても、プログラムは、人々が人生経験の物語を共有するとき始まる。物語は、自然に参加者同士を関係づけ、世代間交流の共同学習と知恵の共同作成という組織的任務と関係づける。

＜プロセス＞
ISI は、それ自身が学習組織であり続けることへの関与を含む組織的な開発の一定のレベルを切望している。

私たちは、意志決定において多様な声が尊重されかつ含められる、開かれた参加のスペースを保持する。すなわち、認識の枠組と価値の共通のセットによってグローバルに戦略を練るけれども、介入のタイプ、および位置（コミュニティ、州または国家）に依存している地域またはその地方の方式で動作する。

＜プロジェクト＞
ISI が最初のベンチャー組織であるインタージェネラティヴィティ・プロジェクト（TIP）を導いている。世代間（主要な例）、異業種間、学際的、異教徒間、国際などのように新語

「インタージェネラティヴィティ（intergenerativity）」は、TIP の本質をとらえている。TIP が利用するストーリーブリッジ法では、物語共有、劇場、ビジュアル・アート、ダンス、音楽、およびテレビゲームが世代間のメディア横断プロジェクトにおいてつながる。ストーリーテリングとパフォーマンスを通じて、TIP は、通信、創造性、寛容さ、共感、情熱、自身および集合的なプレゼンテーションスキル、および批評的意識のための共同学習研究所をつくる。

＜パートナーシップ＞

創造的なパートナーシップは私たちの成功にとって重要である。ここでは、インドと中国からの例を説明する。

インドアメリカ人協会全国同盟（NFIA；http://www.nfia.net/）は、現在ここアメリカ、ロサンゼルスに本部を置き、インドとアメリカのサポート活動とコミュニティ内で多様性を祝福する豊かな 35 年の歴史がある。NIFA が、私たちの第 1 番目のインタージェネレーショナル・ナレッジ・センターをインド（ヒマーシャル・プラデーシュ Himachal Pradesh 州）で展開させるための出資とテクニカル・サポートを提供することを計画している。

中国の pARTicipate（http://www.participate-global.org/）は、芸術教育を通じて個人とコミュニティを雇い、エンパワーメントすることをめざす社会的な企業を勝ち取っている賞である。その教育学は高度な研究と長年実施されてきた芸術、地域開発、教育、心理学などのフィールドに基づいている。pARTicipate は、2015 年 5 月に ISI のパートナーになり、それ以来、世代間交流学習を、市民生活の改善とコミュニティを開発するためのプログラミングに組み込んだ。

一般大衆でオンラインの芸術教育、国際的なリーダーシップ開発、および創造的な地域づくりである。pARTicipate は、2015 年 5 月に ISI のパートナーになり、それ以来、世代間交流学習を、市民生活の改善とコミュニティを開発するためのプログラミングに組み込んだ。

＜カリキュラム＞

ISI が 2 つのそのようなカリキュラムを開発している。最初のものは、彼ら自身が、学習とキャリアと生活向上のための機会として年老いることを理解していることを助ける。2 番目は、生涯学習のパワーおよび彼ら自身の成功のための集合的な知恵を強めることを望む組織をサポートする。

個々のカリキュラムは約 10 分野で内容がデザインされている。しかし、それぞれは柔軟で、すぐに個人および／または組織の現在のステータスに適応できる。カリキュラムは複製ではなく、順応的な革新によって成功する。

3．結論

私たちは、グローバルな挑戦および人類の発展の背景に対して ISI の開発を示した。私たちは、価値とプロセス、特に人間関係が私たちの教育的結果の発展における構造や合理性と

同様に、あるいはそれ以上に重要であることを強調する。

　私たちは、共有された個人と地域の物語のフォームにおける世代間交流の語りが、人類の繁栄と生存をサポートするために、必要組織を考えることや私たちのあたりまえの視野（normal scope）を広げることにクリティカルであることを信じている。

第２部

Part 2

世界へのメッセージ

Message to the World

第1章　現下の社会保障としての世代間交流
―― 「社会」をつくる「学び」の観点から

牧野　篤

1．教育と世代間交流

　私たちは社会を「分割」してとらえることに慣れている。その一つの形が、社会を個人のライフステージに分割することである。この観点では、個人の成長と発達が社会の発展、さらには経済発展と重ねられて理解される。それは、GDP の増大に対比されるような、経済規模の拡大や社会モデルの拡大再生産のアナロジーであるだけでなく、たとえば農業から工業さらに情報・金融への経済構造の質的転換が高度化と称されるように、個人の精神の質的な変化が、時間軸に沿って高まっていくと理解されることと重なっている。しかも、この時間軸に沿った人の変化には、衰退としての高年期が設定されている。それは、個人が社会の拡大に寄与できなくなった年齢であることを示している。私たちは社会を個体主義的にとらえることに慣れているといってもよいであろう。

　それゆえに、世代という観念も、年齢の違いを示すだけではなく、幼少年期（子ども）・青壮年期（生産年齢人口）・高年期（高齢者）と分けられ、明確に経済発展の観点と連動していると見ることができる。つまり、規律・訓練によって労働力として形成され、工場における生産労働に従事できる年齢が、統計的には 15 歳から 65 歳まで（以前は 55 歳や 60 歳）なのであり、それ以前の子どもとそれ以後の高齢者は、工場労働には適さない存在として定義されていることを示している。私たちが世代とくに世代間というとき、一般的にはこの幼少年期・青壮年期・高年期の 3 つの時期区分で観念している。

　さらにこれを人間の成長・発達を社会システムとして扱う教育制度に見てみると、それは端的に少年期に対応する義務教育、青年期に対応する高校・大学、そしてその後の生涯学習と分割されている。それはまた、人々の生活が、保護

され、教育・訓練される対象としての幼少年期と、生産労働に参加し、家計を維持する青壮年期、そして生産労働から引退し、いわば余生を送る高年期と分かれていることに対応している。それゆえに、学校教育の延長がすなわちモラトリアム、つまり就労の猶予と表現されたりもする。

この観点は、個人の生涯を時間軸に沿って分割し、かつ成長・発達を価値と見なして、未来を志向するものであり、子どもたちを発達可能態として価値づけようとするものでもある。それは裏返せば、超高齢社会の今日、高齢者を社会的な負担と見なし、世代間対立を煽ることへとつながっている。

それゆえに今日、世代間交流は次のように語られる。たとえば文部科学省「超高齢社会における生涯学習の在り方に関する検討会」の報告書 (2012 年 3 月) [1] では、人の一生を幼児・青少年期、成人期、高齢期に分割した上で、世代間交流の意義を次のように述べている。「世代間交流は、高齢者の生きがいを高めるだけでなく、青少年にとっても高齢者との交流を通して豊かな人間性や職業観、人生観等を学ぶことができ、人生の先輩として尊敬することにもつながる。[2]」

このように、世代間交流も個人を基礎として（個体主義的に）、個人の成長・発達に価値を措いて、社会を分割する観点から評価されてきたものだといえる。

2．子どもの貧困と社会の再生

しかし他方で、世代間交流に新たな観点を求める事態が進行しているのも事実である。その一例が、子どもの貧困率の急激な高まりである。2012 年現在、日本の子どもの貧困率は 16.3 パーセントで、主要国の中ではアメリカ・イタリアに次いで三番目に高い数字である。この事実を受けて、日本財団のレポート（2015 年 12 月）[3] では、子どもの貧困を社会福祉政策としてだけではなく、経済的・投資的な観点から検討して、次のような推計を試みている。

つまり、現在 15 歳の子ども約 18 万人を対象とし、子どもの貧困解決に有効な手段として教育機会の保障を取り上げ、貧困家庭の子どもの高校進学率が現

状のままである「現状シナリオ」と、高校進学率と高校中退率をそれぞれ非貧困家庭の子どもと同じにし、かつ大学進学率を 22 パーセント上昇させる「改善シナリオ」を設定し、現状シナリオと改善シナリオそれぞれの社会的損失を推計した。その結果、子どもの貧困を放置することで、所得総額が 2.9 兆円、税・社会保障の純負担額が 1.1 兆円それぞれ減少することが明らかになった[4]。

　この結果から、レポートは子どもの貧困を解決することは、1. 経済的・投資的な観点から見て十分に大きな効果が期待される施策であること、2. 労働力の確保の点からも大きな効果をもたらすものであること、を指摘する。つまり、現在の児童手当給付総額の年齢ごと給付額が、所得総額 2.9 兆円損失分の約 5 パーセント、税・社会保障純負担額減少分の約 10 パーセントにあたり、貧困問題解決の経済効果は高いものがあり、また将来の情報・金融社会は創意工夫のできる質の高い労働力を求めており、改善シナリオでは、正規社員が 1 割程度増え、無業者は 1 割程度減少することから、少子高齢社会における労働力確保の観点からも子どもの貧困対策は有効であるとされる[5]。

　このレポートは、個人の成長・発達の保障が経済的・投資的効果を高めるという観点にもとづいており、将来に価値を措くという点では従来の議論と変わらない。しかし、福祉政策的な意味における現金給付ではなく、投資的な意味における現物給付つまり教育機会の保障による貧困対策を提案する点において、福祉政策を個人単位（または家庭単位、個体主義的な文脈）で考えるのではなく、社会経済的な文脈（関係論的な文脈）で考えようとする議論とつながっている。

　社会の歴史は、経済を軸に次のように描くことができる[6]。人間が農業を営み、生活の糧を交換していた時代には、人々は家族を基本とした共同体における人間関係に生きており、それが人々の生活を安定させ、ともにあるという感覚を生み出していた。共同体を基本とする社会のあり方であった。その後、工業社会に移行するにつれて、共同体が解体し、人々は自由で孤独な労働力として、都市に集まり、生産労働に従事することとなる。そこでは、「われわれ」という意識をもたらす帰属が人々の存在の基本となる。この「われわれ」をよ

第1章　現下の社会保障としての世代間交流　163

り大規模な生産と交換の仕組みへと統合するために、政府が「生政治」（フーコー）を発動して、人々の「われわれ」を国家へと回収する装置、つまり福祉国家の形成が求められた。国家（政府）を基本とする社会のあり方だといってよい。

　さらに、この工業社会は大衆消費社会へと移行する。そこでは、経済活動の基礎は人々の承認欲求であり、その表象としてのマネーとなる。ここでは、人々の承認欲求はすべてマネーへと表象されて、相互性を失い、マネーの離合集散が人々の社会的な位置づけを与えるものへと移行する。そこで繰り返されるのはゼロサムのマネーゲームであり、承認欲求のコレクションである。それは、マネーのマーケットが支配する社会である。

　しかも、大衆消費社会の進展は、経済のグローバル化と軌を一にしており、それはそのまま福祉国家の機能不全を意味している。経済発展を背景とした潤沢な税収に支えられた現金給付による国民生活の平等な保障である福祉政策は、人々の市場への参加を促し、それがさらに経済発展を導く循環を形成していた。しかし、経済のグローバル化の時代には、資本は国境を飛び越えて移動し、税収が不安定となり、福祉国家の所得の再分配機能を脅かすことになる。国家が後景に退いて「生政治」が不全化し、福祉が後退することで、人々が孤立する時代、つまり国家の基盤である社会が解体する時代がやってくるのである。

　子どもの貧困問題は、このような社会の解体とマーケット（市場）の優位の中で生じているという側面がある。市場はすでに旧来のような「われわれ」意識を生み出し、人々の連帯と統合を促すものではなくなり、福祉による所得の再分配は、人々の社会統合と包摂に失敗し始めている。そのため、現金給付（個体主義的）ではなく、現物給付（関係論的）による福祉のあり方が模索される必要があり、それはまたマーケットに絡め取られない、新たな社会のあり方を構想するものでなければならない。それを神野直彦は、参加保証型福祉社会だという[7]。

3．現下の社会保障としての世代間交流

　参加保証型福祉社会の構想と深く切り結んでいるのが、2015年12月に中央教育審議会から出された「答申」である[8]。この「答申」を貫いているのは、昨今の日本社会に対する深い危機意識である。従来の経済発展モデルが無効化し、国家の基盤である社会が、雇用や家族のあり方を含めて、解体の度合いを深めている。その中で、学校そのものが子どもたちの成長・発達を保障する機能を失いつつあるのではないか。学校は、子どもの教育や成長・発達にかかわるだけでなく、学校区を基本とした住民自治制度一つを取ってみても、この国の社会基盤の根幹を成す基幹システムである。この社会はすでに学校中心主義とでもいうべき制度設計がなされている。学校を活用しつつ、新たな社会のあり方を検討すべきだ。これが、議論の出発点である。

　「答申」ではまず、学校を地域住民がその運営を協議する学校運営協議会を持つコミュニティスクールへと組み換えて、その上で「地域とともにある学校」へと切り換えることが提案される。「地域とともにある学校」を実質化するための基本的な考え方が、地域と学校の関係を「支援」から「連携・協働」へ、また「個別の活動」から「総合化・ネットワーク化」へと組み換えることである。その具体的な施策が、学校運営協議会とともに学校との連携・協働を進める「地域学校協働本部」を、小学校区を基本としたコミュニティに設置し、学校と地域の様々なアクターとを結びつける「地域コーディネーター」を地域学校協働本部に配置することである。従来住民が個別に対応してきた学校支援が、地域コーディネーターによってネットワーク化されて、子どもたちの成長を支えるために、学校と連携・協働する関係に組み換えられるのである。

　重要なのは、この構想では、子どもたちはもはや保護され、教育されるだけの存在ではなく、地域コミュニティをおとなたちとともに担うアクターとして位置づけられるということである。そのためにこそ、地域のおとなたちも、自らが学び続け、地域コミュニティを担うことが期待される。学校を核として、

第1章　現下の社会保障としての世代間交流　165

子どもの成長を軸に、地域総がかりで、地域コミュニティを担うこと、そのことを通して、地域コミュニティの持続可能性を高め、この社会を次の世代に確実に手渡していくこと、この方向性が明示されたのである。これはまた、教育が将来への投資であるとともに、現下の社会保障であることをも示している。

　この「答申」が指し示すのは、住民自身が、行政に対してサービスを要求するという意味での制約された自由を行使するのではなく、むしろ他者とのかかわりの中で、自分が新しい価値やサービスを創造することの自由を相互に認めあい、それを基盤として、コミュニティを創造し、組み換え、経営し、持続させていくという新たな社会の姿である。それを権利の側面からとらえれば、自分の生活を他者とともに営む権利を十全に行使すること、そういうことを行政的に保障するということである。そこでは、住民は常に「学び」続け、他者との関係を相互の承認関係へと組み換え続け、自分の住むコミュニティを常に新たなものへと変革し続けることが求められることになる。

　さらに、この「答申」が描く社会の姿は、世代間交流のあり方を、学校と地域コミュニティの連携・協働という方向性において提示したものだと見てよい。世代間交流とは、「学び」を世代間で組織し、人々総がかりで相互承認関係を構築し、ともに社会をつくりだし、改革し、経営する自由を認めあうこと、そのためにこそ人々が連携・協働すること、このことを意味しているのだといえないだろうか。そこでは、社会はすでに、個体主義的にとらえられ、分割されるものではなく、むしろ関係論的にとらえられ、分割できない総体的なものとして、すべての成員をフルメンバーとして受け入れつつ、社会をつくりだす自由を相互に認めあうことにおいて、その生活を保障しあうプラットフォームへと組み換えられている。参加保証型福祉社会とは、子どもも高齢者も含めてすべての住民自身が、地域コミュニティのフルメンバーとして、コミュニティの創造と経営に参画し、自らの生活を持続可能なものへと生成し続けることであるといってよい。それはまた社会をつくり続けることと同義である[9]。

　世代間交流とは、このような社会をつくる事業の一角を担う人々の営み、すなわち現下の社会保障の一環をなすものといってよいのではないだろうか。

引用・参考文献

1）文部科学省超高齢社会における生涯学習の在り方に関する検討会『長寿社会における生涯学習の在り方について～人生 100 年 いくつなっても 学ぶ幸せ「幸齢社会」～』（平成 24 年 3 月）。

2）同上報告書、p.16

3）日本財団・三菱 UFJ リサーチ & コンサルティング『子どもの貧困の社会的損失推計レポート』、2015 年 12 月

4）同上レポート、p.47

5）同上レポート、p.50

6）神野直彦『「人間国家」への改革―参加保証型の福祉社会をつくる―』、NHK 出版、2015 年など。

7）同上

8）中央教育審議会「新しい時代の教育や地方創生の実現に向けた学校と地域の連携・協働の在り方と今後の推進方策について（答申）」（平成 27 年 12 月 21 日）。

9）これらの具体的な実践には、筆者の研究室がかかわっている千葉県柏市高柳地区の「多世代交流型コミュニティ・地縁のたまご」プロジェクト、また長野県飯田 OIDE 長姫高校の「地域人教育」の実践、北海道庁の「小中高校 12 年間一貫「ふるさと」に心が向くキャリア教育」など、様々な取り組みを挙げることができる。

Chapter 1
Intergenerational Interaction as Current Social Security: From the Perspective of "Learning" that Builds "Society"

Atsushi Makino

We are used to understanding society by dividing it. One such form is dividing society into personal life stages. From this perspective intergenerational interaction can, for example, be explained as follows. In a report by the Ministry of Education, Culture, Sports, Science, and Technology (MEXT), an individual's life is divided into the stages of early childhood, adolescence, adulthood, and old age and it states the following: "Intergenerational interaction" does not only enhance the motivation of the elderly. For adolescents too, interaction with elderly enables them to acquire an enriched sense of humanity, career perspectives, and a view of life and also leads them to develop respect for the elderly as seniors in life.

On the other hand, in this society, as indicated in the aggravation of poverty of children, redistribution of income from welfare is beginning to fail in the social integration and inclusion of people. Rather than relying on taxes, the conception of a participatory welfare society by the residents themselves is being sought. Therefore, rather than considering children as the target of welfare it is required that the local community be positioned as responsible actors along with adults. We must conceive that by being responsible for the local community with all the residents in charge, it is possible to enhance sustainability and hand over this society to the next generation with certainty. The foundation of this is the "learning" that encourages the building of "society" by residents.

From this perspective, intergenerational interaction refers to the construction of mutually approved relationships and building of "society" together through "learning" among people, to the mutual acknowledgment of the freedom to reform and manage, and to the fact that it is precisely for this reason that people collaborate and cooperate. In this perspective, as an already indivisible collective entity, society continues to accept all members as full members and by mutual acknowledgment of the freedom to construct society, and it is being reclassified as a platform that ensures that life.

It can be said that intergenerational interaction is a part of the work of people who construct this kind of "society", in other words, a part of current social security.

第2章 世代間交流学とエリクソン及び ヴィゴツキーの概念
―― 「第9段階」及び「他者」概念の考察を通して

佐々木　剛

草野　篤子

1．はじめに

　世代間交流学では、人生の経験者である高齢者を「あらゆる世代の健全な人間発達とその地域作り（草野 2010）[1]に位置づけ、若年世代との結びつきを強化する。近年、この世代間の結びつきをエリクソン[2]の心理社会的発達論（GENERATIVITY 理論）や、ヴィゴツキーの「発達の最近接領域」論[3]にある社会文化的発達論の「他者」から考えようとする見方が出来てきた。そして、この両者の概念から得られる考えが、世代間交流プログラムの構成や世代間交流学の理論構築に新たな視座を提供している。

2．文献検討から得られる知見

(1) エリクソンの「第9段階」と世代間交流学

　エリクソンが心理社会的発達論として述べている GENERATIVITY 理論は、フロイトの発達論の影響を受けたエリクソンが人生を8段階に区切った発達概念として述べたものであった。近年、この概念はエリクソンとその妻エリクソン J.（1997）の著書『The Life Cycle Completed: Extended Version』により9段階に修正された。

　世代間交流学では、ジャコブソンとカプラン（2011）[4]が世代間交流学研究の理論的プログラムの一つとして、HAVIGHURST の活動理論に依拠するその考え方を述べている。また、ニューマン（2003）[5]は、幼児期と成年期

の比較・統合・活動論にその考えを述べている。しかし、GENERATIVITY
理論に関する多くの文献は従来の「8段階」により紹介されており「第9
段階」による論述は少ない。世代間交流研究では、田渕（2011）[6]がWell-
beingによる概念にその考えを取り入れたものや、大場ら（2013）[7]の日本語
による世代間交流プログラムの評価に向けた尺度開発に「第9段階」が使用さ
れている。また、概念としては日下（2008）[8]が「高齢者と若年世代の間の
他者との共存の考え方」により高齢者の適応を「第9段階」として述べている。

(2) ヴィゴツキーの「他者」概念と世代間交流学

　日本の教育では、「発達の最近接領域」論は、学習過程・教育課程論とし
てデューイ及びブルーナーの理論に取り上げられて来た。今井（2008）[9]は
これらの理論過程の説明で、ヴィゴツキーの概念がブルーナーの「足場かけ
（Scaffolding）」により評価されたと述べている。「足場かけ」とは教育におけ
る教師介入の課題を述べる考え方である。近年、この考えは「学びの共同」や
「協同」との考え方（佐藤1999）[10]にヴィゴツキーの「発達の最近接領域」に
ある自発的学習環境及び学習過程を認知発達概念から捉えた研究もある。
　世代間交流学の分野では、糸井（2012）[11]がヴィゴツキー概念にある「よ
り賢明なる他者（More Knowledgeable Others）」をもって世代間交流学上の
基礎理論が展開できると述べ「他者」概念を扱った。また、日本世代間交流
学会第3回全国大会講演で、折出（2012）[12]が哲学的な「アザーリング概念」
を述べ、そのなかで「他者を通して自己が豊かに蘇る」との考え方を示した。
すなわち、世代間交流学では、ヴィゴツキーの理論から導かれる「他者」の概
念が、子どもと高齢者の間の活動にある「相互互恵性」を高めるプログラムに
示唆を与えること、また、新たなプログラムの形成につながると考えられる。

3. 世代間交流研究の新たな視座

(1) 世代間交流学の課題に関する論点

藤原（2012）[13] は、老年学の視座から世代間交流の実践的研究の課題を「世代間の確執」と「世代間交流の必要性の希薄さ」、及び「世代間交流事業の企画・運営上の負担」と考え、世代間交流学の学術的エビデンスの不足を指摘している。この背景には「人や地域からの『絆』の重要性が再認識」されつつも、「万人から推奨される」具体的なプログラムの不足があると言える。

この課題に対応した研究の一つに、吉津（2012）[14] らが進める保育者養成課程在籍者の高齢者との交流事業や、安永（2012）[15] らが実践する小中学校の高齢者と児童生徒による世代間交流研究（REPRINTS）、田渕（2012）[16] らが進める高齢者と若者との間の「Well-being の関係」の検討等がある。特に、田渕はエリクソンの心理的発達課題である GENERATIVITY 概念をマカダンとオーブスの尺度の考察による「世代性行動と心理的 Well-being の関係」から追究している。また、竹内ら（2012）[17] は藤原らが進める研究（REPRINTS）の考え方に、文部科学省が推進する「学校支援地域本部事業」を取り上げ、学校と地域の結びつきの可能性を検討しているが、その検証は難しいと述べている。それは世代間交流学での定義の難しさと内容の関係性に起因する。教育の基本的な考え方である学習指導要領も 10 年を一つのサイクルに改訂される。そのため、実際の教育現場に浸透するには時間を要する。世代間交流プログラムが学校教育の場で実践されるようになったのは最近のことである。

(2) 世代間交流学と心理社会的発達論の関連性

心理社会的発達は 1997 年にエリクソンから彼の妻エリクソン J. との共著"The Life Cycle Completed : Extended Version"『ライフサイクル、その完結（増補版）：日本訳 2001』に引き継がれた。そのなかでエリクソン J. は TORNSTAM（1993）らが述べた「トランセンデンス（老年的超越）」を、エリクソ

ンが「トランセンダンス」と造語することにより、高齢者への尊厳を表現する「第9段階」を作ったと述べている。エリクソン J. (1997)[18] によると「第9段階における絶望」と8段階の「絶望」は「異にした経験を反映している」と言う。また多くの人が持ち続けた老年期の概念は「誤った老年期の概念」であると述べ、超高齢化の時代を経たエリクソンの新たな心境を伝えている（図1）。

その意味で、「第9段階」の概念は高齢者と他世代のつながりについて新たな視座を示す。例えば、草野（2010）[1] は「次の世代への命の連鎖」に言及し、金田 2010)[19] も「命の継続発展と世代間交流」、及び「地域づくりと間接的五世代共生時代の発達支援」の観点から、幼児と高齢者との関係を論じている。この考え方は「第9段階」が示す「全ての段階につながる基本的信頼感である」に通じる。すなわち金田が述べる「五世代共生の社会」とは、この世代と世代の信頼をつなぐ幼児期の「トランセンダンス」の具体例を示唆するものと考えられる。そして、その実践は高齢者への「基本的信頼感」につながる。また、「家族の絆」のきっかけを形成する（図1）。

(3) 世代間交流学と社会文化発達論の関連性

糸井（2012）は、ヴィゴツキー概念にある「より賢明なる他者（More Knowledgeable Others）」をもって、世代間交流学上の基礎理論が展開できると述べた。このことは、子どもの体験が子ども自身の他者との関係、すなわち人と人のつながりや役割、学ぶことの意味を世代間交流学が示すとの考えに立つ。

このブルーナーの「足場かけ」により一般化されたヴィゴツキーの「他者」概念は、世代間交流プログラムが子どもと高齢者との関係（高齢者は子どもにとっての他者に当たる）や学習への参加（活動の場）が基本的な信頼や尊厳、命の絆等の概念を獲得する過程を説明する（図2及び図3）。

ヴィゴツキーは「発達の最近接領域」論で学習をする子どもにとって必要な高次の学習が子どもの発達を促すことを述べた。この関係は、「ヴィゴツキーの三角形（茂呂 1999）」として説明される（図2）。ヴィゴツキーの考えによ

れば、A・Bは「刺激」、Xは心理的道具を示す（茂呂 1999）[20]。この場合、A・B・Xの間には、「A－B」が直接の連合的結合。「A－X」と「B－X」には、Xという心理的道具が介在する。

茂呂によれば、「人為的な記憶術的記銘X」により学習者は、「人間の精神過程に『新しいもの』が生じる」と言う。すなわち、Xは子どもの高次の体験、すなわち、学習効果を示す。このことを世代間交流プログラムで考えると、Xはプログラムに含まれる「他者」概念であり、世代間交流における「相互互恵性」は、この三角形に含まれる「媒介」部分に働く「活動の場」や「他者理解」となる交流体験の拡大を示す（図2）。このとき、体験の拡大は、世代間交流プログラムの展開において、図3に示すような相互互恵性もしくは命の絆へと螺旋的な変化（見方によっては「回転体としての独楽の働き」）をする。すなわち、計画的なプログラムという「他者」の働きが、子どもにとってより高次な「命の絆」という互恵的経験による広がりの場を形作る。世代間交流プログラムに含まれる「他者」概念は、子どもにとって高次な体験の提供を想起させる。

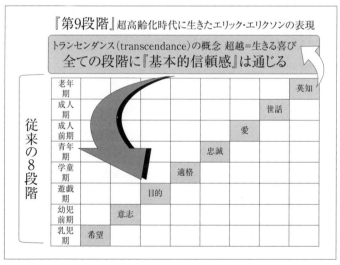

図1　エリクソンの第9段階（筆者作成）

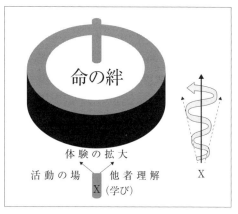

図2　ヴィゴツキーの三角形　　図3　命の絆；体験の拡大（筆者作成）

4．課題と展望

　笹島ら（1999）[21]は小・中・高校生及び大学生の世代間交流プログラム体験による他者理解の効果を調査研究し、「体験学習が他者を理解し、思いやる心を伸ばし育てる有効な手立て」であったことを示した。また、白井ら（2007）[22]は、平成10年度以降の学習指導要領が「祖父母や高齢者、地域の人々との直接的な『連携・協力・交流』を重視している」ことを指摘した。すなわち、学習指導要領の改訂で示された学校教育と福祉教育の結びつきに、世代間交流プログラムへの展開の可能性が示され始めたと言える。しかし、エリクソンは発達理論を修正したものの、「老人に向けられる通常の姿勢は、（中略）まったく遊びのない第二の幼児期が提供されている」と述べ、世代の間の基本的信頼感の確立の難しさを指摘している。

　この課題への対応は世代間交流の目指すものであると同時に、それは教育に委ねられた本質に通じる可能性を示す。これが、福祉教育と世代間交流プログラムの接点である。

　本章は、エリクソンの GENERATIVITY 理論にある「第9段階」の概念と

ヴィゴツキーの社会文化発達論から導かれる「他者」について探ってきた。すなわち、教育と融合した理論に「インクルージョン」の概念やエンパワーメントにつながる概念を考察した。これは、高齢化社会を迎えた我が国における、世代間交流概念の具体的展開を探る試みと言える。

この検証は、高齢者と子どものインフォーマルな活動のプログラムの中に子どもにとっての「他者」を明確にすることである。そして、エリクソンが述べた「基本的な信頼感（第9段階）」から世代間交流プログラムを理論化することだとも言える。

付記　本章は、2014年日本世代間交流学会誌 Vol.4 No.1 に掲載された同名の論文に加筆修正を加えたものである。

引用・参考文献

1）草野篤子・金田利子・間野百子・柿沼幸雄編著『世代間交流効果』、三学出版、2009年、1-17頁

2）エリクソン. H. *The Life Cycle Completed*, W. W. Norton.（村瀬孝雄・近藤邦夫（訳）ライフサイクルその完結、みすず書房、1989年

3）ヴィゴツキー「発達の最近接領域」の理論－教授・学習過程における子どもの発達、土井捷三・神谷英司（訳）、三学出版、2003年

4）アビルゲイル・ローレンス・ジャコブソン、マシュー・カプラン『多様化社会をつむぐ世代間交流』、三学出版、2012年、21-36頁

5）Newman,S, An Intoductory Message from the Editor. *Journal of Intergenerational Relationships* 1（1）、2003年、1-4頁.

6）田渕恵、権藤恭之（2011）、「高齢者が若者世代からポジティブなフィードバックを受け取る場面に関する研究」、日本世代間交流学会誌 VOl.1 No.1、2011年、81-87頁

7）大場宏美・藤原佳典・村山陽・野中久美子・安永正史・倉岡正高・竹内瑠美「世代間交流プログラムの評価に向けた日本語版 GENERATIVITY 尺度作成の試み」、日本世代間交流学会誌 VOl.3 No.1、2013年、59-65頁

8）日下菜穂子「超高齢化時代における世代間交流の意義－関西学研都市高齢者の世代間交流に関する調査から－」、同志社女子大学学術研究年報第59巻、2008年、69-78頁

9）今井康晴「ブルーナーにおける『足場かけ』概念の形成過程に関する一考察」、広島大学大学院教育学研究科紀第一部第57号、2008年、35-42頁

10）佐藤学『学びの快楽－ダイアローグへ－』、世羅書房、1999年

第2章　世代間交流学とエリクソン及びヴィゴツキーの概念　175

11）糸井和佳、草野篤子・内田勇人・溝邊和成・吉津晶子編著『多様化社会をつむぐ世代間交流』、三学出版、2012 年、37-44 頁

12）折出健二、日本世代間交流学会第 3 回全国大会基調講演、2012 年

13）藤原佳典、「世代間交流における実践的研究の現状と課題－老年学研究の視座から－」、日本世代間交流学会誌 VOl.2 No.1、2012 年、3-8 頁

14）吉津晶子・溝邊和成・田爪宏二、「保育者養成課程におけるクロス・トレーニングの試み」、日本世代間交流学会誌 VOl.2 No.1、2012 年、69-78 頁

15）安永正史・村山陽・竹内留美・大場宏美・野中久美子・西真理子・草野篤子・藤原佳典、「中学生の高齢者イメージに与える高齢者ボランティア活動の影響－ SD 法による測定と横断分析－」、日本世代間交流学会誌 VOl.2 No.1、2012 年、79-87 頁

16）田渕恵・三浦麻子・中川威・権藤恭之、「高齢者における世代性（Generativity）と次世代との関わり行動の因果関係　性差に着目した検討」、日本世代間交流学会誌、VOl.3 No.1、2013 年、35-40 頁

17）竹内瑠美・村山陽・安永正史・野中久美子・倉岡正高・大場宏美・鈴木宏幸・西真理子・小宇佐陽子・李相侖・藤原佳典「児童のストレスに世代間交流がもたらす効果－高齢者ボランティア"りぷりんと"特別プログラムより」、日本世代間交流学会誌 VOl.2 No.1、2012 年、49-56 頁

18）エリクソン . H. and Erikson, J. M., *The Life Cycle Completed: Extended Version*, W. W. Norton.（村瀬孝雄・近藤邦夫（訳）『ライフサイクル、その完結（増補版）』、みすず書房、2001 年

19）金田利子「命の継続発展と世代間交流」、草野篤子・柿沼幸雄・金田利子・藤原佳典・間野百子編著『世代間交流学の創造』、あけび書房、2010 年、69 － 84 頁

20）茂呂雄二、『具体性のヴィゴツキー』、金子書房、1999 年、

21）笹島浩子・神川康子・永井敏美・浦上紀子「体験学習が他者理解に及ぼす効果－高齢者疑似体験及び世代間交流の効果－」、富山大学教育学部研究論集 2、1999 年 43-52 頁

22）白井克典・土井進、「学校における世代間交流に求められる教師の力量－学習指導要領の分析と高齢者へのインタビュー調査を通して－」、信州大学教育学部附属教育実践総合センター紀要　教育実践研究 8、2007 年、113-122 頁

Chapter 2
Discussion of Intergenerational Studies and the Concepts of Erikson's "Ninth Stage" and Vygotsky's "More Knowledgeable Others"

Tsuyoshi Sasaki
Atsuko Kusano

This paper aims to explore the "Mutual reciprocity," a symbiotic concept formed in the intergenerational studies, through psychological and social development theory based on the "Ninth Stage" notion advocated by Erikson, E. and Erikson, J. and the "Others" notion based on the socio-cultural developmental theory originated by Vigotsky, L. S.

The intergenerational studies show specific exchanges between the elderly and the young people based on intergenerational programs in view of the mutual reciprocity between the elderly citizens and other generations. An idea "intergenerational contacts" underlies the notion.

Therefore, the "Others" notion based on the Eric Erikson's "Generativity theory" deriving from the "Ninth Stage" idea and the Vigotsky's idea "More knowledgeable Others" deriving from his socio-cultual development theory create "Intergenerational feuds" and "Subtle necessities of intergenerational exchanges," providing new perspectives of study.

第3章 伝統文化の世代継承に対する世代間交流学からのアプローチ

内田 勇人

1. はじめに

　私たちが暮らす社会は、緩やかに、しかし確実に日々変化している。流行（りゅうこう）という言葉があるが、まさに流れ行くように新しいライフスタイルや技術・技能、芸術、ファッション、歌などが生まれ、消費され、通り過ぎていく。これらはその時代、社会を彩り、私たちの生活に活力と息吹を与えてくれる。その一方で、「流行（はや）り廃（すた）り」という言葉があるように、時々の流行だけで終わってしまうことも珍しくない。その意味では私たちは流行を無意識のうちに評価し取捨選択しているように思われるが、反面、その国や地域の暮らしに深く根ざした時に流行は伝統文化・芸能・技能として、長くそこで暮らす人々の精神や行動、暮らし、生活に影響を与え続けるように思われる。そうした深く根ざした伝統文化・芸能・技能は、家庭や家族、親族、地域、組織、社会の共有物として、次世代へ継承されていく。

　ドイツの民俗学者ハンス・ナウマン[1]は、このような時代を超えて伝承される事柄を基層文化とよび、その時代における特殊個別的な表層文化と区別したが、こうした私たちの基層をなす文化の存在は、一種の集団としてのまとまり、共通の価値観の創出、社会の横のつながり、地域住民同士の信頼関係、安心感の構築を考える上で重要な役割を果たしていると考えられる。

　ところで、近年、わが国は世界的にも例をみない速さで社会の少子化、高齢化が進行しており、50歳以上者が人口のおよそ半数を占めるに至り、世代間の関係の希薄化とともに、これまで伝承されてきた文化・芸能・技能を次世代につなげないのではないかといった焦燥感を有している人は少なくない。

　世代間交流学が果たす役割の一つとして、こうした課題を学問として明らか

にし解決していくこと[2]も重要になるといえよう。本稿では、はじめに伝統文化・芸能・技能を次の世代へつなぐ事業・プログラムの実態について整理し、世代間交流学としてのアプローチの可能性について考察したい。

2．文部科学省、文化庁、農林水産省、厚生労働省における取り組みの一例

伝統文化・芸能・技能などを次世代へ伝承・継承していく事業・プログラムとして、近年、国（省庁）が取り組んでいる事業に焦点をあて整理した（表1）。

はじめに文部科学省であるが、2011（平成23）年度より「学校・家庭・地域の連携による教育支援活動促進事業」を創設し、地域の人々、団体のつながり、地域コミュニティの新たな構築、機能強化を目的としたプロジェクトを始めている。いわゆる学校の安全安心に配慮しながら開かれた学校を目指し、地域と連携しながら学校運営をすすめていくものである。地域に存在する様々な力を結集し、学校の内外を問わず、子どもたちの学びを支える仕組みとして地域に定着させる取り組みであり、具体的には放課後や週末等の子どもたちの学習や伝承遊び、様々な体験・交流活動の機会を地域の住民が支援する内容となっている。

文化庁は、この文部科学省の事業と連携する形で、2014（平成26）年度より、「伝統文化親子教室事業」を開始している。これは、次代を担う子どもたちが親とともに、民俗芸能、工芸技術、邦楽、日本舞踊、華道、茶道などの伝統文化・生活文化に関する活動を計画的・継続的に体験・修得できる機会を提供する取り組みである。伝統文化・生活文化の継承・発展と、子どもたちの豊かな人間性の涵養に資することを目的としている。

農林水産省は、農業・農村の持つ多面的機能として、「国土の保全、水源の涵養、自然環境の保全、良好な景観の形成、文化の伝承等、農村で農業生産活動がおこなわれることにより生ずる、食料その他の農産物の供給の機能以外の

第3章　伝統文化の世代継承に対する世代間交流学からのアプローチ　179

表1　文部科学省、文化庁、農林水産省、厚生労働省における伝統文化・芸能・技能など
　　　を次世代へ伝承・継承する事業・プログラムの一例

省庁	事業・プログラム名
文部科学省	学校・家庭・地域の連携による教育支援活動促進事業
文化庁	伝統文化親子教室事業
農林水産省	多面的機能支払交付金事業
厚生労働省	ものづくりマイスター制度
	全国健康福祉祭（ねんりんピック）

多面にわたる機能」と定義し、2015（平成27）年度より、法律によりこれら
多面的機能の補助事業を制度化した。農業・農村の持つ多面的機能の一つとし
て、文化の伝承機能があげられているが、これは全国各地に残る伝統行事や祭
りは、五穀豊穣祈願や収穫を祝うもの等、稲作をはじめとする農業に由来する
ものが多く、地域において長きにわたり受け継がれていることから、これら事
業の伝承を目指すものである。

　厚生労働省は、2013（平成25）年度より、「ものづくりマイスター制度」を
開始している。この制度は、製造・建設分野において優れた技能と豊富な経験
などを兼ね備えた技能者が、若者に実技指導等を通じて、ものづくり産業や技
能の魅力を発信し、ものづくり分野の人材確保・育成を推進する取り組みであ
る。建設業及び製造業における112職種を対象に、高度な技能を持った「もの
づくりマイスター」が技能検定や技能競技大会の課題等を活用し、中小企業や
学校において広く実技指導をおこない、効果的な技能の継承や後継者の育成を
おこなっている。小中学校等での講義や「ものづくり体験教室」等により、も
のづくりの魅力も発信している。

　また、国民の健康と福祉の向上を目的とした視点から、全国健康福祉祭（ね
んりんピック）を開催している。このイベントは、厚生省（現：厚生労働省）
の創立50周年を記念して1988（昭和63）年にはじめて開催されたが、以来、
一般財団法人長寿社会開発センター、厚生労働省、開催地の地方自治体の主催
のもと、毎年開催されている。内容は、高齢者を中心とするスポーツ、文化、

健康と福祉の総合的な祭典であるが、勝敗や優劣よりも高齢者が幅広く参加できることや楽しさに重点をおいた「スポーツ交流大会」、毎年の開催県の特色を取り入れた「ふれあいスポーツ交流大会」、ニュースポーツの楽しさを体験する「ふれあいニュースポーツ」、医療・健康・食生活などに関する展示や体験のコーナーなどの「健康フェア」が開催される。そうした中で、特筆されるべきことは、高齢者の長年にわたる知恵や経験を積極的に引き出し、広めていけるよう配慮した「文化交流大会」、各都道府県・政令指定都市より選出された美術作品を展示する「美術展」、開催県の老人クラブ連合会による地域文化・生活文化の伝承活動の実演や各世代間の交流を図る「地域文化伝承館」が開催される。

　以上のように、文部科学省、文化庁、農林水産省、厚生労働省において取り組まれている伝統文化・芸能・技能などを次世代へ伝承、継承していく事業・プログラムの一例について確認した。各省庁による種々の事業は、公募制により、主に地方自治体、各種団体、個人（一部）を対象として様々なアイデアを募り、資金助成がなされている。伝統文化・芸能・技能などを次世代へ伝承、継承していくイベント、プログラムが各地で企画・展開されている。

3．世代間交流学からのアプローチの可能性

　こうした伝統文化・芸能・技能の伝承、継承に関する世代間交流学からのアプローチであるが、日本世代間交流学会が発行している学会誌に掲載された研究論文を確認してみると、岡村と溝邊[3]による「伝承遊びを扱う小学校の世代間交流活動に見られる参加者の意識」がみられる。岡村と溝邊は、伝承遊びによる交流は児童、保護者ならびに高齢者にとって有意義であり、高齢者は伝承遊びの伝承意欲が高く、保護者は活動に対して児童への教育的意義を認め、さらに企画・運営等への積極的な参加を希望していたことを明らかにした。飯塚ほか[4]は、「囲碁を活用した世代間交流プログラムの可能性」に関する論文を発表しており、健康長寿を達成するための囲碁活動の実施効果について論究

第3章　伝統文化の世代継承に対する世代間交流学からのアプローチ　181

している。

　先述したが、私たちの基層をなす文化の存在は、集団としてのまとまりや共通の価値観の創出、社会の横のつながり、地域住民同士の信頼関係、安心感の構築を考える上で重要な役割を果たしていると考えられる。これらを伝承、継承していくことは、より良い集団や地域、社会の醸成を考える上で重要になるといえよう。と同時に、伝統文化・芸能・技能の伝承、継承は、それらを伝える側と伝えられる側の双方に及ぼす影響も大きなものがあると推察される。

　著者ほかは、身近な多世代の関係として祖父母と孫の関係に着目し、両者間の交流効果について調査研究をおこなった[5]。孫との交流が祖父母の精神的健康度に及ぼす影響について検討したところ、孫から受ける次世代への継承の期待感、命の継承の期待感や安心感、代々のつながりを感じることが、祖父母が人生を明るく前向きに生きていくことに影響を及ぼしていることが明らかになった。

　こうした祖父母と孫の間の関係性は血縁というつながりを背景とするものであるが、血縁関係はなくても、伝統文化・芸能・技能の伝承や継承といった場面においては、師匠と弟子にみられる師弟関係、地域や生活場面における教授者と被教授者の関係が存在し、この両者の間にも祖父母と孫の関係と近似した関係性が存在するのではないかと思われる。師弟関係のみならず、日常生活の中においても、自らが身につけた伝統文化・芸能・技能を次世代へつなぐ世代間交流プログラム、高齢者ボランティアプログラムを開発することで、地域在住高齢者の精神的健康度の充実を促進させることが可能であると思われるし、次世代の側への良い影響も期待される。

　こうした側面に着目し、プログラムの内容や実施効果について検討を加えていくことは、世代間交流学が有する新たな可能性の一つになると思われる。

4．課題と展望

　近年、国のいくつかの省庁（文部科学省、農林水産省、厚生労働省、文化庁）

を中心として、伝統文化・芸能・技能を次の世代へつなぐ事業・プログラムが展開されている。わが国における伝統文化・芸能・技能は多岐にわたる。建築、造園、文芸、武道、華道、茶道、熟練工技能、そして地域に根づくしきたり、風習、言い伝え、祭り、季節行事、踊り、伝統食などが例として考えられる。

　これらが次世代に伝承、継承されていくこと自体が大変重要であるが、様々な事業・プログラムの動向に着目し、そこに存在する師弟関係、地域や生活場面における教授者と被教授者の関係、世代間の交流効果等について科学的に明らかにしていくことも、世代間交流学の一つの方向性として重要になると思われる（図1）。

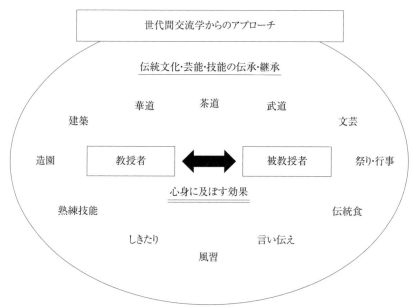

図1　伝統文化・芸能・技能の世代継承に対する世代間交流学からのアプローチ

引用・参考文献
1）和歌森太郎著『新版日本民俗学』清水弘文堂、1970年
2）草野篤子、金田利子、間野百子、柿沼幸雄編著『世代間交流効果－人間発達と共生社会

第 3 章　伝統文化の世代継承に対する世代間交流学からのアプローチ　183

　づくりの視点から-』三学出版、2007 年

3）岡村明穂、溝邊和成「伝承遊びを扱う小学校の世代間交流活動に見られる参加者の意識」
　　日本世代間交流学会誌第 1 巻第 1 号、2011 年、59-65 頁

4）飯塚あい、鈴木宏幸、高橋知也、倉岡正高、南　潮、村山陽、安永正史、藤原佳典「囲
　　碁を活用した世代間交流プログラムの可能性-「健康長寿囲碁まつり」を例に-」日本世
　　代間交流学会誌第 5 巻第 1 号、2015 年、97-103 頁

5）内田勇人、藤賀彩花、江口善章、西垣利男、山本　存、矢野真理「孫との関係が祖父母
　　の精神的健康度に及ぼす影響」日本世代間交流学会誌第 5 巻第 1 号、2015 年、29-36 頁

Chapter 3
Approach from Intergenerational Studies for the Succession of Traditional Culture

Hayato Uchida

Our fundamental culture plays a significant role to establish unity of group, creation of common values, horizontal ties within the society, trust in community residents and sense of security. It is expected that inheriting such culture is important to create a better group of residents, community and society. In addition, the succession of the traditional culture, folk entertainment and skills seems to have a considerable impact on both master and his/her successor. We think the most familiar intergenerational relationship which contributes to such succession is found in the families and relatives.

We therefore focused on a relationship between a grandparent and his/her grandchild(ren) (Uchida H et al. Effects of relationship with grandchildren on mental health of elderly persons, *Journal of Japan Society for Intergenerational Studies*, 5(1), 29-36, 2015). We researched the effects of their mutual communication and also analyzed the impact on the mental health of these grandparents. It was found that the relationship/communication contributed to their positive attitude toward life, as they have a feeling of hope brought by the next generation, a sense of anticipation or reassurance for life and generational succession.

While such relationship between grandparent and grandchild(ren) is based on blood ties, there are other types of relationship to be considered which are not blood-related ones. For example, in the succession of traditional culture, folk entertainment or skills, there is a relationship between a master and an apprentice and also one between a teacher and a student in a community or local society. We assume that those relationships are similar to the ones between grandparent and grandchild(ren).

Not only in the relationships mentioned above but also in daily lives, it is possible to promote the mental health of elderly residents. We can expect positive impacts on both the elderly and younger generation by developing an intergenerational program to carry on the traditional cultures/skills that the elderly acquired and also a senior volunteer program. It will open up a new possibility in the intergenerational study if we further investigate the contents and effects of such programs.

In fact, in recent years some programs have been developed mainly by Japanese government ministries such as Ministry of Education, Culture, Sports, Science and Technol-

Chapter 3　Approach from Intergenerational Studies for the Succession of Traditional Culture　185

ogy, Agency for Cultural Affairs, Ministry of Agriculture, Forestry and Fisheries and Ministry of Health, Labour and Welfare. Our traditional cultures, folk entertainment and skills are very diverse. For example, they include architecture, Japanese gardening, literary art, martial arts, flower arrangement, tea ceremony, trained technique, local custom, festival, event and dance, traditional foods etc. It is important that we ensure these cultures will be passed on to the next generation.

We also think it important to scientifically clarify the relationship of a master and an apprentice and also the one of a teacher and a student in a community or daily life because it shows a future direction of the intergenerational study.

第4章 都市部の新規分譲集合住宅における
多世代交流プログラム導入の試み

高橋　知也

1. はじめに

　「都道府県・主要都市の"マンション化率"2015」全国版[1] によれば、2015年における国内の全世帯数に占める分譲マンション戸数の割合（以下、マンション化率）は12.2%となっている。中でも東京都・神奈川県などの首都圏では21.6%、大阪府・兵庫県などの近畿圏では15.8%となるなど都市部におけるマンション化率が高くなっており、都市部における分譲マンションは、現代における住居形態の一つとして既に確立されているといえよう。

　本章では、都市部に新規に分譲された集合住宅における多世代交流プログラム導入のプロセスと成果および課題について、都市部の集合住宅の変遷やそれらが現在抱えている課題などにも触れながら述べることとする。

(1) 戦後から現在に至る都市部集合住宅の変遷

　都市部における集合住宅の起源は、戦後の高度経済成長期にまでさかのぼる。1960年代から70年代にかけて、都市部では労働力として地方からの急激な人口流入が生じた。その人々の受け皿として整備されたのが、集合住宅を並列に配置した「団地」である。団地は労働力を都市部に留める役割を果たすことで、戦後の経済成長を支える礎となった。

　一方で、都市部への急激な人口流入は地価の高騰や住環境の悪化を招き、80年代には都市近郊に「ベッドタウン」が整備され、都市部から郊外への人口移動が生じた。いわゆる「ドーナツ化」と呼ばれる現象の発生である。その後90年代に入り現在まで、バブル崩壊による地価の下落や都市部における高層住居誘導地区の導入、「マンション」などの集合住宅の高層化などによる「都

心回帰」、すなわち郊外から都市部への人口の再流入が進んでいる状況にある。

　以上の黎明期から現代にいたるまでの変遷に鑑みれば、都市部の集合住宅はそれぞれの年代の世相を反映しながら整備されてきたといってもよいだろう。

(2) 集合住宅コミュニティに対する住民やデベロッパーの価値観の変容

　では、集合住宅の住民によって形成されるコミュニティはどうだろうか。

　従来の団地においては、複数の棟の住民がひとつのコミュニティを作るというものが一般的[2]であった。しかし、近年の集合住宅においては、個別性や匿名性といった住民のプライバシーを重視する傾向の強まりを反映して、こうしたコミュニティを通じた繋がりは必ずしも強固なものではなくなりつつある。分譲マンションには「建物の区分所有等に関する法律」により管理組合の設置が義務付けられているものの、施設・設備の維持保全目的の側面が強く、防犯や防災、非常時相互支援等の機能が働くことは少ないとの指摘[3]もある。

　こうしたマンションコミュニティの希薄化には、居室を分譲・販売するマンションデベロッパー側の事情もある。一例として、投資から回収までのスパンが短くなるに伴い、効率性やコストを重視せざるを得ないために、旧来のように集合住宅を中心にじっくりと一つの地域を作っていくような余裕がなくなっている[4]との見方や、高い個別性や匿名性を備えたいわゆる「売りやすい住宅」が定式化され、そのスタイルからの離脱が困難になっている[4]との意見もみられる。

　このような「集合住宅におけるコミュニティの希薄化」を危惧する声が聞かれる一方で、SNSをはじめとするテクノロジーの進歩によって居住者同士の繋がり方は多様になったため、居住者全員が無理にひとつのコミュニティの中で繋がるのではなく、各自が目的に応じて参加するコミュニティを選択するというスタイルが現代における自然なコミュニティの在り方である[5]との指摘もみられる。マンションを含めた街の様相もめまぐるしく変化している現代においては、集合住宅におけるコミュニティの在り方についても、日々新しいものを模索していく必要があるといえよう。

(3) 本章における報告事例

　本章では、都市部の新規分譲マンションにおけるコミュニティ支援プログラムの1つとして多世代交流プログラムを導入する機会が得られたため、その取り組みと成果、および課題について報告する。なおこの取り組みは平成27・28年度の2期にわたって行われるものであり、報告するプログラムはその第1期に該当するものである。分譲マンションにおける交流の実態やコミュニティの形成過程は沢田ら[6]や村田ら[7]により報告されているが、多世代交流を伴った分譲マンション住民によるコミュニティ形成に関する報告や新規分譲マンションにおけるコミュニティ形成の取り組みについての報告は現在までに乏しく、本プログラムは新奇性の高いものであるといえよう。

2．プログラムの概要

　今回導入したプログラム『大人の絵本読み聞かせ教室』は、2014年から2015年にかけて新規に分譲販売が行われたマンションにて展開されている「マチTOMOプロジェクト」[8]の一事業として位置付けられているものである。マチTOMOプロジェクトとは、当該マンションのデベロッパーである大成有楽不動産株式会社が産学官の多様な団体と連携して導入しているコミュニティ支援プログラムである。集合住宅に居住する住民と産学官といった外部組織との連携は、当該事業以外に千里ニュータウン（大阪大学）や後楽町団地（北九州市立大学）などでも展開されているが、様々な団体や企業、大学が連携して一つのプロジェクトを支えているという点に、マチTOMOプロジェクトの特色があるといえよう。

　本プログラムの主たる対象は高齢者を含む大人を想定しており、絵本という一般に「子どものためのもの」という印象の強い題材を用いて、大人にもその面白さを再発見する機会を提供するとともに、ひいてはマンション内でのグループ作りも視野に入れたプログラムを用意した。ただし、事前に居住者の年齢層について検討を行ったところ、都心部へのアクセスの良さや周囲に幼稚園

や小学校などの教育施設が充実していることを反映して、比較的若い世代や核家族世帯が多く居住していることが確認された。そのため、プログラムへの子ども単独での参加や親子での参加も可とした。

　プログラムの運営にあたっては、講師として絵本読み聞かせ専門のインストラクターを招へいした。また活動の会場確保や全戸へのチラシ配布は、同じくマチ TOMO プロジェクトに参画する株式会社フォーシーカンパニーの協力により行われた。さらに、近隣地域に活動拠点を持つシニアの絵本読み聞かせボランティアグループ『りぷりんと・かわさき』より、毎回 3 ～ 4 名の高齢者に運営サポーターとして活動への参加を依頼した。プログラムは 2015 年 4 月から 12 月にかけて、およそ 3 週間に 1 度の頻度で開催した（表 1）。

表 1　プログラムの開催日時、活動内容および参加人数

開催日	曜日	時間	内容	大人	子ども
2015/04/25	土	10：00 ～ 11：50	お子様と楽しむ絵本	8	5
2015/05/16	土	11：00 ～ 11：50	大人が楽しむ絵本	4	4
2015/06/20	土	15：00 ～ 16：30	仕掛け絵本に触れる	1	1
2015/07/04	土	15：00 ～ 16：30	季節の絵本 1（七夕）	4	6
2015/08/01	土	14：00 ～ 15：30	季節の絵本 2（夏）	2	2
2015/08/22	土	14：00 ～ 15：30	季節の絵本 3（おばけ）	4	3
2015/09/19	土	14：00 ～ 15：30	季節の絵本 4（月）	2	1
2015/10/04	土	14：00 ～ 15：30	大人の絵本 1（柳田邦男）	2	2
2015/10/24	土	14：00 ～ 15：30	大人の絵本 2（村上春樹）	2	2
2015/11/21	土	14：00 ～ 15：30	大人も子供も楽しめる絵本	6	5
2015/12/05	土	14：00 ～ 15：30	クリスマスの絵本	3	2
2015/12/26	土	15：30 ～ 16：30	お正月の絵本	0	1

3. プログラム実施の結果と考察

(1) マンション居住者の参加状況

　全12回の活動を通じ、延べ72名（大人：38名、子ども：34名）の居住者が参加した。参加者層としては、子どもや、子どもに連れ添って参加する子育て世代の居住者が多く、親子揃って絵本に触れる様子もよくみられた。男性の参加者も比較的多く、昨今の絵本ブームの影響が感じられた。一方で、高齢者の参加はプログラム全体を通じて2名に留まった。

　活動においては、全12回とも開催月や季節によって異なるテーマを設定し、初めての参加者はもちろん、リピーターの参加者も楽しめるよう配慮した。例えば8月下旬のおはなし会では「おばけ」が登場する絵本で構成したが、参加した子どもが家族に寄り添ってお話を聞く様子がみられた。また11月のおはなし会では、大人も子どもも楽しめる絵本として『スイミー』（好学社）などのロングセラーや『あかにんじゃ』（岩崎書店）などのシュールさに富んだ絵本を紹介し、親子が一緒になって絵本の楽しさに触れられるようなきっかけを提供した。

(2) 本プログラムに対する信頼感や理解の深まり

　本プログラム開始当初は終始インストラクターが活動を主導し、参加者はインストラクターの言葉に耳を傾けるのみであったが、中盤以降は参加者自らがインストラクターに対してリクエストを出したり、参加者自らが絵本を読み聞かせたりといった場面もみられるようになった。また活動を継続する中で、リピーターが少しずつ増え始めたほか、子どものみで教室に参加するといった様子もみられるようになった。回を重ねるにつれ、プログラムに対する信頼や理解を得られるようになってきた証左であると考えられる。

第 4 章　都市部の新規分譲集合住宅における多世代交流プログラム導入の試み　191

(3) 多世代交流の実現と限界

　参加者からは「子どもや孫に読ませてあげるべき本」や「子育てのコツ」などについての質問が挙がることもあり、その際はインストラクターのほか、運営サポーターとして参加した高齢者が自らの経験を踏まえたアドバイスを提供するといった様子もみられた。多世代交流という観点からも望ましい形で本プログラムが展開されたものと思われる。

　ただし、当初プログラムの対象として想定したマンションに居住する高齢者の参加は、居住する高齢者が少ないこともありほとんどみられなかった。結果として多世代交流はサポーターとして参加した高齢者と若年層の居住者の間でなされることとなったが、今後はより幅広い世代に興味を抱かせるプログラムの開発が必要であると考えられる。

4．プログラム運営上の課題

　実質的にマンション居住者のみが対象となっているため、他のイベントとの同時開催となった場合などに、参加者が少ないことがあった。リピーターを増やせるよう、より一層魅力的なコンテンツを目指す必要がある。改善案として、趣旨の異なる複数のプログラムを用意できるよう計画を進めている。

　また当初の計画では、居住者同士での世代間交流の実現と絵本の読み聞かせに特化した自主グループの設立までを見据えていたが、居住者層のニーズとの間に相違があり、結果としてプログラムの一部見直しを行うこととなった。居住者のニーズに沿ったプログラムを提供できるよう、今回の実施結果を再度見直し、第 2 期プログラムの改善に取り組みたい。

引用・参考文献

1）東京カンテイ　2016　都道府県・主要都市の "マンション化率" 2015　全国版、(2016 年 2 月 1 日閲覧)　http://www.kantei.ne.jp/release/PDFs/86karitsu-zenkoku.pdf

2）片桐新自　2007　「昭和ブーム」を解剖する、関西大学社会学部紀要 38(3), 2007, 43－60

3）村田明子・田中康裕・山田哲弥　2012　集合住宅の安全安心なコミュニティ構築の促進

に向けた居住者相互交流支援システムの開発、清水建設研究報告 89, 135-142

4）つなぐネットコミュニケーションズ　2012　つながり　～マンションコミュニティの話をしよう～　Vol.5 コミュニティ×建築（2016 年 2 月 1 日閲覧）、http://www.mlab.ne.jp/columns/community02_20120830/

5）ログミー　2014　マンションコミュニティを考える（2016 年 2 月 1 日閲覧）、http://logmi.jp/30337

6）沢田知子・曽根里子・染谷正弘　2008　大規模分譲集合住宅におけるコミュニティ形成過程に関する研究 その2：経年時 (入居後 3 年) における共用施設利用頻度の推移の要因考察、日本建築学会大会学術講演梗概集 E-2,257-258

7）村田明子・田中康裕・山田哲弥・鈴木毅・北後明　2010　分譲マンションにおける交流活動の実態，都市集合住宅のコミュニティと相互支援に関する調査研究 その3、 日本建築学会大会学術講演梗概集 E-2, 305-306

8）大成有楽不動産株式会社・京浜急行電鉄株式会社・菱重エステート株式会社・株式会社長谷工コーポレーション・ナイス株式会社 2013 ニュースリリース 「オーベルグランディオ横浜鶴見アリーナテラス」12 月 7 日（土）より第 1 期販売開始（2016 年 2 月 1 日閲覧）、https://www.taisei-yuraku.co.jp/wp-content/uploads/b379c52724966eca2140bde-9f8eb6e89.pdf

Chapter 4

A Trial of Intergenerational Exchange Programs Introduced in the newly Developed Collective Housing in an Urban City

Tomoya Takahashi

This chapter describes the process, achievements and challenges of intergenerational exchange programs introduced in the newly developed collective housing in an urban city by referring to the changes and problems to collective housing in urban areas.

The mainstream of collective housing in urban areas changed from a housing complex in the 60's and the 70's to a bedroom town in the 80's to a condominium after the 90's. Up to now, the residents of some housing complexes made a community in general, but recently the connection through the community is becoming loose. As a condominium is rapidly changing, it is necessary to explore the new way of making a community.

The program introduced in this chapter is named "reading aloud picture books for adults". This program aims to give an occasion for adults to rediscover a feeling of interest and to make a group of reading picture books for children and adults. But, the preliminary survey showed that many of the residents were composed of younger generations and nuclear families due to good traffic accessibility and proximity of good education facilities such as kindergartens and elementary schools before the program was enforced. Thus this program included children or families living in this condominium. An instructor of reading aloud picture books was invited to give lectures to participants. Some volunteers who engaged in reading aloud picture books near the collective housing were also invited as supporters of conducting this program.

The program was conducted from April to December 2015, and had twelve sessions. 72 residents (38 adults, 34 children) participated in the program in total. Many of the participants were parents who joined with their children. Otherwise, only two elderly people participated in the program. All sessions set different themes according to the seasons to amuse not only the first time participants but also repeaters.

At first, the session was mainly conducted by an instructor and the participants only listened to her. However, from the middle of the program, participants requested the instructor to teach them how to read picture books and then some participants started to read picture books to others by themselves. Moreover, the number of repeaters gradually increased, and some children participated in the program by themselves. The reason may be that participants regarded this program as reliable or satisfactory as the program went on.

During the sessions, the participants were free to ask questions, and the instructor and the supporters answered the questions or provided their experimental knowledge. However, only a few elderly residents participated in the program. This may be due to the small number of elderly people living in the condominium. As a result, intergenerational exchanges were conducted among the participants and elderly supporters, Therefore the development of a new program is needed to involve wider generations in the future.

第5章　高齢者ボランティア活動によるソーシャル・キャピタル醸成に関する日米比較
—— REPRINTS と Experience Corps の比較より

安永　正史

1. はじめに

　世界に先駆けて急速に進む我が国の少子高齢化によって、社会保障のための財源の確保が困難になりつつあり、社会システム全体の崩壊が危ぶまれている。また、それに伴う核家族の拡大は、幼児・児童の人格形成に良好な影響を与える世代間交流の希薄化を生んでいる。そのため、高齢者には自身の健康寿命の延伸と次世代支援の両者の観点から社会参加・社会貢献活動、特にボランティア活動への参加が期待されている。近年、こうした社会的要請に応えるために、高齢者による学校支援活動や子育て支援といったボランティア活動によって、住民相互の信頼、規範、ネットワーク、すなわちソーシャル・キャピタル（以下、SC）[1] の醸成を促しつつ、高齢者自身の健康増進を目指す取り組みが、高齢福祉・地域連携に関わる公的機関を中心に各地で行われている。

　SC は人間関係資本と訳され、「ご近所のつながり・信頼感から生まれる力」などと解釈されてきた概念であるが、公的機関が行う各種事業が健康や生活など社会福祉にもたらす効果を強化したり、事業自体を評価する際に活用可能な理論基盤となっている[2]。近年、SC はマクロレベル（国や自治体）、メゾレベル（近隣地域）、ミクロレベル（グループ・団体）、個人レベル（信頼、規範）の４つのレベル[3] の観点から分析され、事業の質だけでなく、各レベルでの普及・浸透の程度を規定する特性・要因について、より精緻に検討されはじめている。

　米国の Experience Corps Study（以降 EC）[4] は高齢者という個人レベルを起点に健康増進と SC の醸成を目指した数少ない介入研究の一つである。こ

の研究で高齢者は貧困層が多く通う小学校で学力の遅れや問題行動のある子どもの学習支援者としてボランティア活動に従事している。活動の結果、高齢者には認知機能および心身機能の向上、子どもには学力の向上が見られた他、学校全体の雰囲気の改善に効果が示されている。また、ECは全米退職者協会の支援のもと事業運営されており、ボルティモア市を始め全米20都市に2000名あまりのボランティア会員が所属する組織にまで発展している。

　一方、我が国において、このECを先行モデルとして2004年より東京都健康長寿医療センター研究所の社会参加と地域保健研究チームが開始したのが、高齢者と子どもの世代間交流による相互効果の検討を目的とした介入研究REPRINTS（Research of Productivity by Intergenerational Sympathy）である。当該研究で高齢者は小学校等の教育施設において、子どもに絵本の読み聞かせを行う等のEC同様に学校支援ボランティアとして従事している。活動の結果、これまでに高齢者[5]、保護者[6]、子ども[7]の3者に多面的な活動の効果が報告されている。現在、REPRINTSは研究開始から13年あまりが経過し、研究スタートの時点で70名あまりであったボランティアが現在では260名あまり、参加団体は7団体となり、組織としての活動の輪を地域レベルにまで広げ、EC同様に高齢者個人の健康増進との関連のみならず、メゾレベル、ミクロレベルにおいて、SCへの効果の調査・研究が進められている。

　ECとREPRINTSはどちらも地域在住の高齢者による学校支援活動を通した健康づくり、SC醸成を目的としたプログラムであるが、組織運営上、少なくとも次の点で異なる。（1）ECは基本的にボランティアの配置を有給の専門コーディネーターが行っている。一方、REPRINTSのボランティアのコーディネートは、ボランティア内で役割分担をして行っている。（2）ECではコーディネーターが各学校、各クラスの活動に各ボランティアを配置している。一方、REPRINTSでは、学校、幼稚園、保育園などの活動先との連絡調整、スケジュール決め、人員配置などボランティア自身が役割を交代しながら行っている。（3）ECは組織の維持、新人ボランティアの養成などもコーディネーターが行っている。一方、REPRINTSは、ボランティア自身がこの組織の維持や

新人養成を行っている。そのため、40 〜 50 名程度からなる各団体は、組織運営のために、どの団体も一月に一回の割合で定期ミーティングを開き、情報や意見の交換を行い、読み聞かせの勉強会を行っている。

こうした組織運営上の相違は、活動内容、性質に依拠するところが大きいが、ボランティアや教育に対する考え方など日米の文化的な要因も SC の醸成に異なる影響を及ぼしていると推測される。

そこで、本稿では、REPRINTS と Experience Corps® のボランティアに対して行った SC に関するパイロット研究について紹介する。

2．方法

(1) 調査期間

2014 年 5 月〜 2015 年 12 月。

(2) 調査対象者

REPRINTS 参加ボランティア 22 名、Experience Corps®（フィラデルフィア）参加ボランティア 45 名。

(3) ボランティアの活動状況

REPRINTS に参加する高齢者ボランティアの主たる活動は絵本の読み聞かせによる学校支援活動である。参加者は 60 歳以上の高齢者であり、一般的な退職年齢を基準に設けられている。その理由は退職後に期間を置かずに社会的な活動に参加することで社会的役割と知的能動性を賦活し、心身の機能を維持することが当該プログラムの第一のねらいであるからである。当プログラムにはもう一つのねらいがあり、それは絵本の読み聞かせを通して若年世代の図書・文学への関心を高めるとともに、高齢者への敬愛の念を深めることで若年世代の情操教育の一助になること、更には地域における世代間の信頼を維持・促進し、SC の醸成に寄与することである。

プログラムに参加するにあたり、高齢者は絵本の読み聞かせによる学校ボランティア活動を始めるための準備として、週1回2時間のボランティア養成のためのセミナーを3カ月間受講している。セミナーの内容は、絵本に関する知識と読み聞かせの実技、ボランティアについての基礎知識、地域における子育て事情、学校教育の現状、健康づくりなどである。実際にボランティアとして活動する際には、幼稚園、保育園、小学校、図書館など1つの校あたり6～10人程度の小グループに分かれて担当している。

一方、Experience Corps® (FRIED et. al. 2004) における高齢者の主たる活動は、小学校低学年までの子どもを対象に読み書きを中心とした基礎学力の向上を目的とする授業サポートである。活動時間は朝から放課後まで、週3日以上が基本であり、週に最低15時間程度、1クラスに1ずつ入るのが基本である。

(4) 調査項目

性別、年齢などの他に、【信頼】に関して2項目（①「一般的に人は信頼できる」、②「近隣の人は信頼できる」）、【互恵性】に関して2項目（③「多くの場合、人は他人の役に立とうとする」、④「近隣の人は、多くの場合、他人の役に立とうとする」）、【ネットワーク】に関して2項目（⑤「自分と同じ世代の人との付き合いは多いですか」⑥「自分と違う世代の人との付き合いは多いですか」尋ね、「1．そう思う」「2．どちらかというとそう思う」「3．どちらかというとそう思わない」「4．そう思わない」の4段階で回答を求めた。

(5) 分析方法

(1) 得点化：信頼感が高いほど得点が高くなるよう4段階の評定値を1～4点に再配点した（互恵性、ネットワークも同様）。

(2) 分析方法：①～⑥の項目に対して2要因混合計画（参加者間：日米、参加者内：ボランティア活動開始前と1年後）の分散分析を行った。

3．結果

　表1に調査協力者の基本属性を示した。また、SC に関する項目①～⑥について、ボランティア活動開始前と1年後の結果を図1～6に示した。分散分析の結果、【信頼】【互恵性】【ネットワーク】①～⑥のすべての項目で有意な交互作用が認められ、下位検定の結果、REPRINTS 参加ボランティアにのみ得点の上昇が示された。

表1　REPRINTS と Experience Corps における調査協力者の基本属性

	日本：REPRINTS	米国：Experience Corps	p
対象者（人）	22	45	
女性／男性（人）	21/1	41/4	
平均年齢（歳）	68.41	61.33	.31
（SD）	5.71	7.13	
教育年数	13.91	15.50	.01**
（SD）	2.00	2.59	

4．考察

　SC 醸成の効果が REPRINTS 参加ボランティアに示された。これは、Experience Corps® がコーディネーターを中心に活動が進められているのに比べて、REPRINTS 参加の高齢者は事前打ち合わせ、勉強会、反省会などグループ単位での活動や組織運営に多くの時間を割いており、学校などの読み聞かせ先の開拓、連絡調整など地域へのつながりも高齢者自身が行っていることが影響していると推測される。

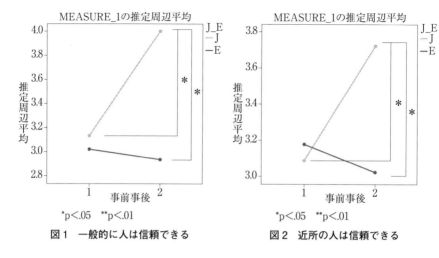

図1 一般的に人は信頼できる　　　　　図2 近所の人は信頼できる

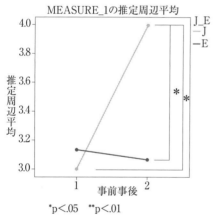

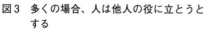

図3 多くの場合、人は他人の役に立とうとする

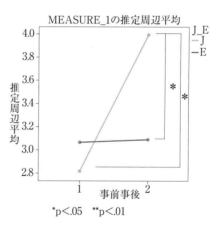

図4 近所の人は多くの場合他人の役に立とうとする

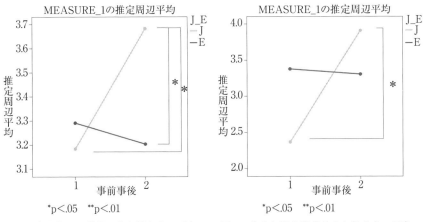

図5　自分と同じ世代の人と付き合いが多い　　図6　自分と違う世代の人と付き合いが多い

引用・参考文献

1) Putnam R. Making democracy work: civic traditions in modern Itary. New Jersey: Princeton University Press; 1993.
2) Murayama H, Fujiwara Y, Kawachi I. Social capital and health: a review of prospective multi-level studies. J Epidemiol. 2012;22:179-87.
3) Machinko J, Starfield B. The utility of social capital in research on health determinants. Milbank Quarterly. 2001;79:387-427.
4) Fried LP, Carlson MC, Freedman M, Frick KD, Glass TA, Hill J, et al. A social model for health promotion for an aging population: initial evidence on the Experience Corps model. J Urban Health. 2004 Mar;81(1):64-78. PubMed PMID: 15047786. Pubmed Central PMCID: 3456134.
5) Fujiwara Y, Sakuma N, Ohba H, Nishi M, Lee S, Watanabe N, et al. REPRINTS: Effects of an Intergenerational Health Promotion Program for Older Adults in Japan. Journal of Intergenerational Relationships. 2009;7(1):17-39.
6) Fujiwara Y, Watanabe N, Nishi M, Ohba H, Lee S, Kousa Y, et al. Indirect effects of school volunteering by senior citizens on parents through the "REPRINTS" intergenerational health promotion program. Japanese journal of Public Health. 2010;57(6):458-66.
7) Fujiwara Y, Watanabe N, Nishi M, Lee S, Ohba H, Yoshida H, et al. Regulatory factors for images of the elderly among elementary school students assessed through secular trend analyses by frequency of inter-exchange with "REPRINTS" senior volunteers. Japanese journal of Public Health. 2007;54(9):615-25.

Chapter 5

Comparison between Japan and the US on Social Capital Fostering through Elderly Volunteer Activities: Comparison between REPRINTS and Experience Corps

Masashi Yasunaga

We have many problems related to a declining birth rate and increasing aging population and need to suppress the increase in social security expenses in order to avoid the collapse of social system in Japan. Moreover, the increase of the nuclear family bring to a decrease of the intergenerational exchange which has a good influence on the personality development.

Therefore much is expected of older adults, such as maintaining their health, engaging in social participation or social contribution, especialy volutieer activity.

Recently, promoting social capital (SC) and health of older adults is receiving a lot of attention, because of the social request. However, as it is difficult to instantly boost SC spontaneously due to drastic changes in family and community structures in today's Japan, well-considered intervention programs are needed.

We examined to compare the impact of the intergenerational program "REPRINTS" (Research of Productivity by Intergenerational Sympathy) and Experience Corps program on SC. 22 Japanese and 45 American community-dwelling older adults participanted in both baseline and follow-up survey. Participants was asked about SC, for example, "Can you basically anyone (neighberhood)?", "Do you think anyone want to have a role for others?"and "Do you have many exchange for same(different) generation?"

The comparison of SC scores between participant in REPRINTS and Experece Corps revealed that SC scores from REPRINTS senior volunteers was significantly improved.

The intergenerational program REPRINTS might be effective for boosting SC by providing them with conection and alternative support between members.

第6章　高齢者のシームレスな社会参加と世代間交流
―― ライフコースに応じた重層的な支援とは

藤原　佳典

1．はじめに

　少子高齢社会が進行する我が国では、高齢者は健康や社会経済的側面から最大多数の弱者となり得る。一方で、円滑な共生社会の実現をめざす上では、就労やボランティアといった有償・無償の社会貢献の担い手としても期待される。シュロック、M.M. は、高齢者の健康度を生活機能の側面から見た分布を示した。高齢期における健康度の推移は加齢に伴うライフコースと言える[1]。そこで、筆者はその分布図をもとに、ライフコースに応じた社会参加活動の枠組みを体系的に示した（図1）。これまで世代間交流に関する研究の大半は、

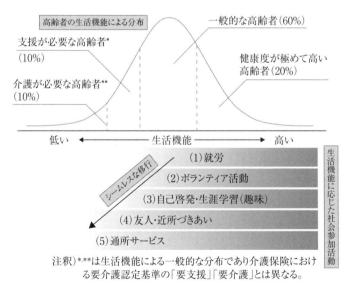

図1　高齢者の生活機能（＝健康度）による分布と社会参加活動の枠組み

多様な世代間交流プログラムの効果を介入前後の数日ないし、数か月間評価するにとどまることが多い。本来、世代間交流とは長い人生の中で徐々に対象や形態を変えながらシームレスに継続されていくべきものである。本稿の目的は、世代間交流について単一のプログラム評価に終始することなく、ライフコースに応じた研究のあり方について整理してみたい。

2. 高齢者の多重役割と社会参加のステージ

　社会参加活動とは、本来多種多様であり、一元的に価値づけされるべきものではない。また、我々は単一の社会参加活動のみに従事しているわけではなく、重層的に参画している。例えば、定年退職後に、非常勤職員として、元の職場に週3日勤務し、後輩の育成に励むとともに、週2日は、地元小学校の周辺で通学児童の見守りボランティア、日曜日の朝は、地域の剣道教室に参加して、子どもから長老まで幅広い年代の剣士と汗を流すといったアクティブシニアもいる。

　このように、一人の人間が多くの社会的な役割を担うことについての概念は社会学領域においては、多重役割理論として知られる。多重役割理論においては、従来は現役世代である青壮年層が仕事や家事・育児といった家庭の内外で複数の役割を担うことの心身の負荷・ストレスの多寡が議論された。この中で、60歳以上の世代に着目した研究は米国における全国調査が有名である。この研究においては就労、ボランティア、家事、家族としての役割が多いほど生活満足度、自己効力感や抑うつに対して好影響が見られることが示された[2]。

　更に近年では、老年学領域において、退職後世代の社会参加のあり方や、町会や自治会などの地域組織が空洞化する中で、地域活動の担い手として、また、人口減少社会における労働力として、高齢者こそが多重役割研究の対象となるにふさわしいと考えられるようになってきている。

　高齢期の望ましい生き方を「サクセスフル・エイジング」と呼び、柴田はそ

の条件を 1）長寿、2）高い生活の質、3）社会貢献としている[3]。特に、第三の条件である社会貢献は、生産性の側面から捉えてプロダクティビティ（productivity）と称される[4]。

　我が国では、安息よりも仕事をもつことが、美徳であり、健康の源とする文化的背景が根強い。そして、仕事など何らかの社会的役割をもって、それを果たす達成感こそが、いわゆる「生きがい」であると考える傾向がある。従って、社会的役割を喪失し、社会的に孤立することは、高齢者の心身の健康までも蝕むのではないかと危惧される。

　本章では、まず高齢者の社会参加・社会貢献を productivity の理論に基づき操作的に (1) 就労、(2) ボランティア活動、(3) 自己啓発（趣味・学習・保健）活動、(4) 友人・隣人等とのインフォーマルな交流、(5) 要介護期のデイ（通所）サービス利用の5つのステージを定義する。

　高齢者の社会参加のステージは重層的であり、求められる生活機能により高次から低次へと階層構造をなす。例えば、金銭的報酬による責任が伴う就労を第一ステージとすると、就労が困難になった者の主な社会参加のステージは、次に原則として無償の社会貢献である第二ステージのボランティアへ移行する。他者への直接的な貢献に負担を感じるようになると第三のステージである自己啓発（趣味・生涯学習）活動へと移行する。趣味・稽古ごとといった自己啓発活動は原則として団体・グループ活動である。更に、生活機能が低下すると、これらの制約に縛られない第四ステージの友人・知人などとの私的な交流や近所づきあいへと移行することが望ましい。更に、要支援・要介護状態に進むと送迎を伴う受動的な社会参加も可能である第五ステージの通所サービス（デイサービス）や地域のサロン、カフェの利用へと移行する。

　こうした移行のプロセスは、社会的責任とそれに伴う活動継続における難易度という視点からも妥当であると考えられる。ここで、(3) 自己啓発における保健行動についてであるが、本来、自分自身のための健康づくりや疾病予防の活動が、なぜ社会参加・社会貢献活動と位置付けられるのか若干の違和感を持つ読者も少なくないと推察される。しかし、高齢者が可能な限り元気で自立生

活を延長すること、つまり健康寿命を延伸することは、一つにはその家族にとって、看病や介護の負担を強いられることがなく家族の productivity を後押しできるという直接のメリットがある[5]。公的介護保険が適用される我が国においても、子ども世代が介護のために早期退職をせざるを得ないニュースが散見される世情を鑑みると、高齢者が元気でいてくれることの意義は実感されよう。

一方、社会保障費の世代間格差についての論争は小泉内閣下の 2001 年に「改革なくして成長なし」と題した年次経済財政報告において、個人の生涯を通じた受益と負担（世代会計）の観点から、60 歳以上世代が 5 千 7 百万円の受益超過であるのに対して、40 歳代以下世代は負担超過であると発表されたことに端を発する。

その後の推計からも、生年が下るにつれて支払い超過の傾向にあることが指摘された[6]。このように、社会保障を通じた世代間不均衡は国民の間で無視できないことが明らかとなっている。ともすれば世代間対立を招きかねない状況を少しでも打破するためにも、高齢者が健康寿命を伸ばすことにより productivity を維持することが期待されている。

3. ボランティアや生涯学習に見る世代間交流

先述の高齢者の productivity の操作的な 5 つのステージに基づき、筆者らは就労から通所サービスの利用（図 1）に至るまで高齢者が社会参加・社会貢献することによる健康維持・増進への好影響について報告してきた。

とりわけ世代間交流を基盤とした社会貢献の代表例としては、高齢者による学校支援ボランティアプロジェクト "REPRINTS" がある[7][8]。高齢者ボランティアグループによる定期的な絵本の読み聞かせ活動を通した世代間交流により、聞き手である子ども、読み手である高齢者ボランティア自身、子どもの保護者への多面的な効果を検証してきた。

"REPRINTS" の 9 ヶ月間の短期的な効果として、ボランティア群は対照群に比べて、健康度自己評価や社会的ネットワーク、体力の一部において有意な

改善または低下の抑制がみられた。子どもへの影響については、高齢者イメージは児童の成長とともに低下する可能性があるが、"REPRINTS"ボランティアとの交流頻度が高い児童では、1年後も肯定的なイメージを維持しうることが示された[9]。また、2年間における追跡からは"REPRINTS"ボランティアにより保護者の学校への奉仕活動に関する心理的・物理的負担の軽減がみられた[10]。

以上より、"REPRINTS"プロジェクトによる高齢者ボランティアと児童、保護者にわたる互恵的効果が検証された。

2004年に開始したREPRINTSプロジェクトは今年で13年目を迎える。現在、活動地域は全国2市1特別区から3市5特別区に広がりボランティアは総勢300名を超す。第一期から13年間活動を続けるボランティアも散見される。筆者は13年間の本プロジェクトに関わる中で、個々人のライフコースに合わせて世代間交流のありようが変遷する事例を数々経験してきた。

Productivityのステージが重層的であることを考えると、REPRINTSボランティアは原則60歳以上であり、就労や家事・子育て中心の現役世代を経験している。職場内の先輩後輩や家事・子育てにおいても親や子どもとの世代間交流が必要不可欠なものとして行われたことが容易に想像できる。彼らは現役生活を引退した後にREPRINTSプロジェクトへの参画といった第二のステージであるボランティア活動への移行に成功した人々である。また、絵本の読み聞かせに伴う選書や読解、音読といった活動は知的探究心を伴う高度な生涯学習である。これはProductivityの第三ステージである自己啓発・趣味活動に相当する。そして10年以上の年月で高齢者ボランティアの心身の健康状態は着実に変化していく。

4. 高齢者と子どもの生活機能の変化

高齢期における心身の機能の変化について、筆者らのこれまでの研究をまとめると、体力や認知機能の低下にみられる老化現象や、脳卒中、心臓病といっ

た生活習慣病の影響により60歳台になると徐々に衰えが目立ってくる。心身の機能が低下することによって、日常生活に支障が出てくるようになることを、「生活機能の低下」と呼ぶ。

人間の活動能力を7つの段階に体系化した米国の老年学者ロートン、M.P.のモデル（図2）で言えば、日常の活動能力の中で「身体的自立」のさらに上位に位置する「手段的自立」「状況対応」「社会的役割」が社会生活における高次の生活機能に対応している[11]。「手段的自立」とは在宅で独力でも生活できるだけの能力であり、具体的には交通機関を利用した外出、日用品の買い物、金銭管理等の能力を問うものである。「状況対応」とは余暇活動や創造性などの「知的能動性」が維持されているかを問う。また、「社会的役割」では周囲の人々との親密な付き合いや、社会との交流に関する能力の維持が期待される。

そこで、東京都老人総合研究所（現、東京都健康長寿医療センター研究所）では、独力で社会生活を維持する能力「高次生活機能」を測る尺度として、「老研式活動能力指標」（1991年）を開発し、健康調査や健診などの場で用いられている（表1）。この尺度のうち、表1の（1）から（5）が「手段的自立」、（6）から（9）が「知的能動性」（図2の状況対応に相当する）、（10）から（13）

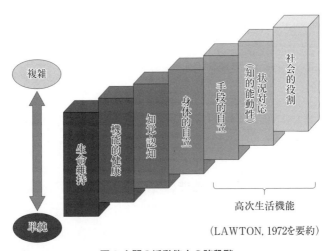

図2 人間の活動能力の諸段階

が「社会的役割」の三つの下位尺度に分類される。この13項目がすべて「はい」と回答できる人は社会生活において完全に自立しており、REPRINTSボランティアも活動開始当初は殆どの人が13点満点であった。しかし高齢者の高次生活機能は男性では75歳、女性では70歳を境に低下しやすい。「社会的役割」、「知的能動性」から順に低下しやすく[12]、更に「手段的自立」が維持できなくなると、いわゆる「要支援」状態となり、更に「身体的自立」が維持できなくなると「要介護」状態となる。

　このモデルを子どもの発達のプロセスに置き換えるとどうなるであろうか。子どもと高齢者の生活機能を同じ尺度を用いて学術的に比較した研究はないので、正確なことは言えないが、図1における「身体的自立」が幼稚園児、「手段的自立」が小学校低学年、「知的能動性」が小学校高学年から中学生、「社会的役割」が高校生以上に求められる能力と言えよう。

　人間の生活機能において最も高尚であり、かつ維持することが困難な「社会的役割」をなんとか維持し、自立した生活を延伸しようとする高齢者と、成長

表1　高次生活機能を測る尺度 - 老研式活動能力指標

1. バスや電車を使って一人で外出できますか。
2. 日用品の買い物ができますか。
3. 自分で食事の用意ができますか。　　　　　　　　　　　手段釣自立
4. 請求書の支払いができますか。
5. 銀行預金・郵便貯金の出し入れができますか。

6. 年金などの書類が書けますか。
7. 新聞を読んでいますか。　　　　　　　　　　　　　　知的能動性
8. 本や雑誌を読んでいますか。　　　　　　　　　　　（状況対応能力）
9. 健康についての記事や番組に関心がありますか。

10. 友だちの家を訪ねることがありますか。
11. 家族や友だちの相談にのることがありますか.
12. 病人を見舞うことができますか。　　　　　　　　　　社会的役割
13. 若い人に自分から乱しかけることがありますか。

　　注)「はい」に1点、「いいえ」に0点を与える。満点は、13点となる.

とともに少しずつ生活機能を獲得していきながら「社会的役割」を担っていく小学校高学年から高校生の若者との関係を、筆者は山の頂上の少し手前ですれ違う登山家に例える。長い下り坂を転ばぬようにゆっくりと慎重に下りていく高齢者と、山頂目指して歯をくいしばりながら駆け上がろうとする若者が、すれ違い際に、お互い、「あと少し、頑張って」と励まし、「有難うございます。お気をつけて」と労う、そのような関係に例えられる[13]。

5．友人・隣人等とのインフォーマルな交流に見られる世代間交流の分岐点

　このような生活機能における世代間の分岐点については、現実には支える側が支えられる側へ移行する際には自尊感情やプライドを封印すべき状況もあろう。しかし、この分岐点を乗り越えることこそが、数々の喪失体験が待ち受ける高齢者にとって世代間の互助のスタート地点であり、シームレスな社会参加ではなかろうか。

　更には、心身機能が減弱していく過程において、直接的に子どもを支援する活動が困難になってきたとしても、次世代を支援する術として、例えば、子育て世代への支援がある。

　核家族化の進行に伴い、母親の育児不安や孤立が問題となる中で、親だけでなく多様な人々が子育てに関わることの重要性が指摘されている[14) 15)]。2015年4月から本格スタートした、国の「子ども・子育て支援新制度」は、すべての子どもの良質な成育環境を保障し、子ども・子育て家庭を社会全体で支援することを目的としている[16]。

　一方で、バス・電車内でのベビーカー使用や、保育園や小学校等からの子どもの声が騒音だとの近隣からのクレームがしばしば見られ、子ども・子育てに対して寛容な意見ばかりではないことが伺われる。「子育てのしやすさ」には、保育施設・公的サービスの充実といった「手段的サポート」はもちろんのこと、親世代が、子どもが地域社会の中で受け入れられ、大切にされていると

感じられることや、子育ての大変さが理解されているといった「情緒的サポート」も重要である。こうした「情緒的サポート」は日常での路上や商店などでの挨拶や声かけをきっかけに始まることがあり、生活機能が低下した高齢者でも心がけや思いやり次第で実践できる可能性がある。地域の中高年者は子どもや子育て中の親にとって、親族や同世代の子育て仲間とは異なる種類のサポートを提供してくれる存在となり得る。松田の研究では、母親の育児不安度が低く生活満足度が高いのは、世帯外の育児ネットワークの規模が大きく、親族以外の多様なサポート提供者から多様な種類のサポートを得られることの利点が示唆された[17]。

　そこで、小林らは中高年者を対象として、地域の子育て支援行動尺度を開発し地域の子育て支援をよく行っている住民の特徴を明らかにした[18]。その結果、子ども・子育て世代との接触機会が多いこと、女性であること、孫の世話をしていること、generativity の得点が高いことが挙げられた。しかしながら、健康的・経済的資源を有する人ほど地域の子育て支援をしているわけではなかった。よって、生活機能が低下しがちな高齢者であっても、情緒的サポートは十分可能であることが再確認できた。

　Productivity モデルの第四ステージである近所づきあいにおける社会参加と世代間交流については、認知症の問題が不可避である。REPRINTS ボランティアの中でも認知症を発症し活動からの引退を余儀なくされる人もいる。認知症高齢者には、障害に対する偏見とともに加齢による偏見（エイジズム）を受ける危険も指摘されている[19]。認知症になっても閉じこもらずに地域で安心して暮らせる社会を創生することを目指し、地域の認知症サポーターを養成する「認知症サポーター 100 万人キャラバン」が展開されている[20]。このキャンペーンでは、認知症の知識と具体的な対応を地域住民に伝える講師役である「認知症キャラバン・メイト」（以下、キャラバン・メイト）を養成している。養成されたキャラバン・メイトは、講師役として、地域、職場、学校などで認知症サポーターを養成する「認知症サポーター養成講座」を開催している。認知症サポーターとは、認知症者とその家族に対するよき理解者・支援者となる

市民のことである。

2016 年 12 月末現在、認知症サポーターは合計 8,497,194 人、その内、キャラバン・メイトは 12 万 6401 人を数える。

筆者らは、滋賀県近江八幡市内の小中学校で実施されているシニア世代のキャラバン・メイトによる認知症啓発授業の効果として認知症高齢者イメージの変化を検証した。市内の 4 校の中学 3 年生 424 名、2 校の小学 5、6 年生 143 名を対象に、授業前と授業後に認知症高齢者イメージについて自由記述形式により回答を求めた。その結果についてテキストマイニング手法によるコレスポンデンス分析およびクラスター分析を実施した。その結果、啓発授業前には認知症高齢者に対する忌避的イメージ（例えば、「近寄りがたさ」「危険」）が多く想起された。啓発授業後には、認知症高齢者の心理状態（例えば「不安・焦燥」「寂しい」）やケア意識（「助けてあげたい」「憐み・共感」）が特徴的に想起された。以上より、近江八幡市の認知症啓発授業の実施と小中学生の認知症高齢者イメージの肯定的な変容に関連があることが示された[21]。

小中学生が成長する一方、認知機能障害から生活機能が低下する高齢者への理解が促される。世代間交流の分岐点についての啓発の機会を高齢者が主体のキャラバン・メイトが提供する、まさに熟慮された世代間交流プログラムと言えよう。

6．通所サービスにおける世代間交流

最後に、Productivity の第五ステージである介護・福祉サービスにおける社会参加と世代間交流について筆者らはデイサービス（以降、DS）の利用の有効性について検討した。

対象は当センターもの忘れ外来に通院し、筆者が主治医として 2 年間の継続診療が可能であった認知症患者 35 名（DS 利用群 21 名、非利用群 14 名）とした。DS 利用群においては、軽度認知機能低下者向けの認知機能検査 Montreal Cognitive Assessment（MoCA-J）の得点が 2 年間維持されたが、非利用群は

後半の1年間で有意に低下した[22]。MoCA-J の下位項目で同様に検討すると、日時や場所など自分が現在置かれている状況を理解する能力である見当識領域において非利用群は、後半の1年間で有意な得点低下を認めた[23]。DS の利用に際しては体操や音楽といった基本的なプログラムに加えて、様々な見当識の維持に寄与するプログラムが定期的・継続的に行われる。これらのプログラムの影響もさることながら、定期的な外出やコミュニケーションの促進こそが好影響の要因であると考える。

　要支援・要介護状態となり介護サービスを受ける立場になったとしても、世代間交流の場は存在する。例えば、DS における利用高齢者と職員との交流である。確かに、DS は高齢者の利用者が多数参集するが、認知機能や身体機能が低下した人が多いため、高齢者同士の交流・コミュニケーションは案外期待できない。むしろ、DS への送迎から DS におけるサービスの提供まで、コミュニケーションの中心は高齢者と若い職員である。

　全国で4万事業所以上あるデイサービスでは、連日、若い職員が「サービス」という名のもとで利用高齢者と世代間交流を続けている。利用者の定員が20〜30人だとすると介護職員や看護職員など5、6人の職員が勤務していることになり、20万人以上の若者の雇用を生み出していることになる。筆者が主治医として担当する独居の高齢患者が会話する若者とは殆どが介護サービス関係者である。そして、週1日でもその若者との交流を待ち望んでいる。「仕事」とはいえ、デイサービスでの世代間交流に私たち周囲の者まで、ぬくもりを感じるのは、彼ら若者のひたむきさ、明るさによるからではなかろうか。

　我が国、最大かつ全国一律の世代間交流の現場を活性化することは、超高齢社会における世代間交流を支援する上で、更には、若者の雇用という意味では、持続可能な社会の創生という点からも極めて重要である。

　こうした第五ステージにおける世代間交流の普及啓発に向けて、今後は、世代間交流がもたらす互恵的効果の検証、つまりサービス利用高齢者へのメリットのみならず、職員側へのメリットについてもエビデンスを蓄積する必要がある。

7．シームレスな社会参加・世代間交流と地域包括ケアシステム

　本章では、ライフコースに応じた5つのステージにおける社会参加・世代間交流の枠組みと効果について紹介してきた。

　第一のステージである就労と世代間交流については、熟練者から若輩者への技術・経験の継承という視点での世代間交流は、様々な職場において日常行われている。更に、子育て世代が働く際に、早朝や土日、休日の勤務は家事育児との両立の点から避けたいとの声が多い。一方、長時間の就業は負担が大きくても、勤務時間には融通が利きやすい高齢者は、子育て世代とのワークシェアリングのパートナーとして期待が大きい。しかしながら、職域における世代間交流の研究は見当たらない。この種の世代間交流は高齢者と若者における相互の効果を期待するだけでなく、雇用者や事業組織ひいてはその産業界全体の持続・発展に寄与しうる点からも、職域における世代間交流についての研究は今後、求められる。

　ライフステージに応じた社会参加・世代間交流の重要性は学術的にも、実務的にも重要であることは認識されるものの、現実には図1の社会参加活動において、円滑に次のステージへ移行することは容易ではなく、移行に失敗し、孤立・閉じこもりに陥る高齢者も少なくない。その背景には高次から低次の社会参加へと高齢者をライフコースに沿った形で縦断的、継続的にシームレスな支援を行う体制が十分整備されていないことが考えられる。

　筆者は世代間交流の普及を阻害する要因として、高齢者、子ども、地域づくり施策といった行政の縦割りシステムの弊害を指摘してきた[24]。

　本稿では、例えば、高齢者施策という縦割りシステムに加えて、更に横割りシステムの弊害を指摘したい。高齢者のライフコースの5つのステージに応じて、就労支援、ボランティア支援、生涯学習支援、みまもり・生活支援、介護サービスというように、施策を担当する部署は多くの自治体において異なる。生活機能が低下し現状のステージでの社会参加が困難になった高齢者に対

第6章　高齢者のシームレスな社会参加と世代間交流　215

して、円滑に次のステージの社会参加・世代間交流の機会を紹介・勧奨できる
コーディネートシステムが必要となる。

　我が国の地域保健福祉介護施策の実情を緊急度や均質性、普及性の面から鑑
みると、このコーディネートシステムは地域包括ケアシステム（以下、包括ケ
ア）へ包含されることが最も妥当と考えられる。国策としての包括ケアは、高
齢者が住み慣れた地域の一員として社会参加し尊厳を持ち暮らし続けることが
できるよう支援する包括的な社会システムである。そこでは、住まい・医療・
介護のみならず、就業、趣味・生きがい活動や生活支援サービスをも提供する
多様な社会資源が地域のネットワークとなることが期待されている。そして、
包括ケアの核である地域包括支援センター（以降、包括C）は、このネット
ワークを活用し、高齢者の心身の状況に応じた適切な活動に適切な時期に移行
できるよう支援・コーディネートすることが求められる。今後、国は、共生社
会の実現に向けてこうした包括ケアのシステムを子ども子育ての分野にも応用
していく施策を打ち出している。

　一方で、多忙極まる包括Cにおいてネットワーク化が進まない理由には、
包括Cの連携スキル不足や他の実務者が連携の必要性を理解していないこと
が指摘されている[25]。

　欧米諸国に比べて、急激な少子超高齢化や人口減少が進行する我が国におい
ては，多世代の相互扶助を循環させる"Circle of care"の概念を更に，普遍
化し加速させなければならない。そのためには現場レベルの単一の世代間交流
プログラムに留まるのではなく社会システムや政策にまで反映させることに
より、持続可能な社会を実現しようとする概念"Positive spiral of care"に基
づく、「多世代循環型相互扶助システム（以降、多循システム）」の構築が求め
られる[26]。多循システム における緊喫の対象領域は第一に子ども・子育て支
援、第二に障害者支援、第三に生活困窮者自立支援、第四に高齢者への支援と
した。これらの四領域で多世代の相互扶助を継続して循環させるプラットホー
ムとして「（仮称）多世代総合支援センター」の導入を試案する。その基盤と
して全国の先進事例を調査した結果4つのタイプに分類された。事例はいずれ

も多世代の個別ハイリスク支援に留まっていた[27]。リスク予防的視点から多世代アプローチを地域づくりに活用する策を導入する必要がある。

　従って、世代間交流に関わる研究者においては、高齢者と子どもの現場レベルでの単一の交流プログラムのみに注目するのではなく、今後は、その支援者である社会資源の交流・連携を促進するような方策を提言することが求められるであろう。

引用・参考文献

1) SCHROCK, M.M.(1980), Holistic assessment of the healthy aged, Wiley, New York. 7-9.

2) ADELMANN, PK. (1994), Multiple Roles and Psychological Well-being in a National Sample of Older Adults, Journal of Gerontology: SOCIAL SCIENCES, 49(6):S277-S285.

3) 柴田博（2002）サクセスフル・エイジングの条件. 日本老年医学会誌,39:152-154

4) ROWE, J. W., KAHN, R. L. (1997), "Successful Aging". The Gerontologist, 37 (4): 433-440

5) KAHN RL.(1983), Productive behavior: assessment, determinants, and effects. Journal of American Geriatric Society, 31(12):750-757.1

6) 鈴木亘,増島稔,白石浩介,森重彰浩（2012），社会保障を通じた世代別の受益と負担. ESRI Discussion Paper Series No.281. 内閣府経済社会総合研究所．(2012)．
http://www.esri.go.jp/jp/archive/e_dis/e_dis281/e_dis281.pdf

7) FUJIWARA, Y., SAKUMA, N., OHBA, H., NISHI, M., LEE, S., WATANABE, N., KOSA, Y., YOSHIDA, H., FUKAYA, T., YAJIMA, S. and AMANO, H. (2009), Intergenerational health promotion program for older adults: "REPRINTS" the experience and its 21 months effects. Journal of Intergenerational Relationship, 7:7-39

8) 藤原佳典,西真理子,渡辺直紀,李相侖,吉田裕人,佐久間尚子,呉田陽一,石井賢二,内田勇人,角野文彦,新開省二（2006）都市部高齢者による世代間交流型ヘルスプロモーションプログラム "REPRINTS" の1年間の歩みと短期的効果. 日本公衆衛生雑誌,53:702-714

9) 藤原佳典,渡辺直紀,西真理子,李相侖,大場宏美,吉田裕人,佐久間尚子,深谷太郎,小宇佐陽子,井上かず子,天野秀紀,内田勇人,角野文彦,新開省二（2007），児童の高齢者イメージに影響をおよぼす要因 "REPRINTS" 高齢者ボランティアとの交流頻度の多寡による推移分析. 日本公衆衛生雑誌,54:615-625

10) 藤原佳典,渡辺直紀,西真理子,大場宏美,李相侖,小宇佐陽子,矢島さとる,吉田裕人,深谷太郎,佐久間尚子,内田勇人,新開省二（2010）高齢者による学校支援ボランティア活動の保護者への波及効果―世代間交流型ヘルスプロモーションプログラム "REPRINTS" から―. 日本公衆衛生雑誌,57:458-466

11) LAWTON M. P.(1972), Assessing the competence of older people. In: Research Planning and Action for the Elderly: the Power and Potential of Social Science, Human Sciences Press, New York. pp 122-143

12) FUJIWARA,Y., SHINKAI, S., KUMAGAI, S., AMANO, H., YOSHIDA, Y., YOSHIDA, H., KIM H., SUZUKI, T., ISHIZAKI T., HAGA, H., WATANABE, S. and SHIBATA H.(2003), Longitudinal changes in higher-level functional capacity of an older population living in a Japanese urban community. Archives Gerontology and Geriatr.ics,36(2):141-153.

13) 藤原佳典, 渡辺直紀, 西真理子, 大場宏美, 李相侖, 小宇佐陽子, 矢島さとる, 吉田裕人, 深谷太郎, 佐久間尚子, 内田勇人, 新開省二 (2010) 高齢者による学校支援ボランティア活動の保護者への波及効果—世代間交流型ヘルスプロモーションプログラム "REPRINTS" から—. 日本公衆衛生雑誌, 57:458-466

14) 大日向雅美著『子育てと出会うとき』日本放送出版協会、1999 年

15) 柏木恵子著『子どもが育つ条件：家族心理学から考える』岩波書店、2008 年

16) 内閣府ホームページ
   http://www8.cao.go.jp/shoushi/shinseido/index.html

17) 松田茂樹. 育児ネットワークの構造と母親の Well-Being. 社会学評論 2001; 52(1): 33-49.

18) 小林江里香, 深谷太郎, 原田謙, 村山陽, 高橋知也, 藤原佳典. 中高年者を対象とした地域の子育て支援行動尺度の開発. 『日本公衛誌』,Vol.63,No.3,2016 年 ,101-112

19) WHO-WPA Geneva (2002), Reducing stigma and discrimination against older people with mental disorders ; a Technical Consensus Statement, 1-26.

20) 厚生労働省「認知症サポーター 100 万人キャラバン」
   http://www.caravanmate.com/index.html,

21) 村山陽, 小池高史, 倉岡正高, 藤原佳典 (2013), 認知症啓発授業が小中学生の認知症高齢者イメージに及ぼす影響 - テキストマイニング手法による分析 -, 日本認知症ケア学会誌 ,12（3）：593-601

22) FUJIWARA Y., SUZUKI, H., YASUNAGA, M., SUGIYAMA, M., IJUIIN, M., SAKUMA, N., INAGAKI, H., IWASA, H., URA, C., YATOMI, N., ISHII, K., TOKUMARU, A.M., HOMMA, A., NASREDDINE, Z. and SHINKAI, SHOJI. (2010), Brief screening tool for mild cognitive impairment in older Japanese: validation of the Japanese version of the Montreal Cognitive Assessment. Geriatric & Gerontology International,. 10（3）:225-232.

23) 長沼亨, 鈴木宏幸, 安永正史, 竹内瑠美, 扇澤史子, 吉田光, 藤原佳典 (2013), 認知症高齢者における通所介護（デイサービス）利用の有無が認知機能へ及ぼす影響 - 物忘れ外来通院患者を対象とした縦断的検討 -, 老年精神医学雑誌 ,24（5）:493-501.

24) 藤原佳典 (2012), 世代間交流における実践的研究の現状と課題 - 老年学研究の視座から -. 日本世代間交流学会誌, 2:3-8

25) 厚生労働省「我が事・丸ごと」地域共生社会実現本部
   http://www.mhlw.go.jp/stf/shingi/other-syakaihosyou,html?tid=368203

26）藤原佳典，倉岡正高，長谷部雅美，南潮，村山陽，安永正史，野中久美子（2017），多世代の互助・共助による社会システムは構築できるか－持続可能な社会の処方箋"Positive spiral of care"を目指して－．日本世代間交流学会誌，(3-8)．

27）国立研究開発法人科学技術振興機構（JST）社会技術研究開発センター（RISTEX）平成26年度戦略的想像研究推進事業（社会技術開発）『「持続可能な多世代共創社会のデザイン－プロジェクト企画調査』「多世代循環型相互扶助システムの開発に向けた検討」報告書（代表者：藤原佳典）

Chapter 6

Seamless Social Participation and Intergenerational Relationships for the Elderly: A Viewpoint from Multiple Support System in Accordance with One's Life Course

Yoshinori Fujiwara

Essentially, intergenerational relationships should seamlessly continue while gradually changing its targets and forms.The purpose of this manuscript is to review the outcomes and future prospects of intergenerational studies in accordance with one's life course. Based on productivity theory, we have operationally defined social participation and social contribution as five stages: (1) employment; (2) volunteer activity; (3) self-development: hobby, lifelong Learning, and health promotion; (4) informal communication with friends or neighbors; (5) care service usage.In fact, as it is difficult for the elderly to shift to the next stage smoothly, some elderlies become socially isolated or homebound. One major reason may be because we have not established an adequate system to support seamless shift from a higher stage to a lower stage for the elderly with declining functional capacity. Therefore, the support system is required in the Integrated Care System in Japan. Furthermore, we should propose "multigenerational mutual support system" based on the concept of "Positive spiral of care". The concept aims at developing social policies that include the concept "circle of care", which may contribute to achieve sustainable society.

第7章　子どもとふれ合うことによる高齢者の感情体験

村山　陽

1．はじめに

　世代間交流プログラムに参加した高齢者から「子どもから元気をもらった」「子どもとのふれ合いが刺激になった」のような感情の体験が語られることがよくある[1]。こうした高齢者から聞かれる感情体験は、どのような心の動きを表しているのだろうか。心理学の領域では、快体験（喜び、安堵など）を伴う感情は「ポジティブ感情」と称されており、多くの研究においてポジティブ感情を経験することが心身の健康をもたらす効果があることが報告されている[2]-[6]。高齢者の感情については、若者に比べて新しい体験を積極的に希求する刺激欲求性（Sensation Seeking）が弱まるため、ポジティブ感情が体験しづらいことが報告されている[7]。しかしながら、子どもとのふれ合いにより高齢者がどのような感情を生起するのかほとんど検証されていない。

　ここ数年間で地域における世代間交流プログラムの効果検証を目的とした研究は蓄積されており、高齢者の身体的 well-being、主観的健康感および QOL の向上に及ぼす効果が明らかにされている[8]-[11]。例えば、藤原ら[8] は、絵本の読み聞かせを通した世代間交流ヘルスプロモーションプログラムの効果として、高齢者の主観的健康感や社会的ネットワークが増進することを見いだしている。亀井ら[9] は、都市部在住高齢者と小中学生を対象とした多世代交流型デイプログラムが、高齢者の QOL（生活の質）に影響することを明らかにしている。しかしながら、子どもとの世代間交流がどのような機序で高齢者の心身の健康につながるのか明確なモデルはほとんど提示されてこなかった。言いかえれば、世代間交流の効果は認められるが、その効果が生じるメカニズムはほとんど検討されてこなかったと言える。地域の世代間交流プログラムの現場

では、高齢者と子どもとの交流が思いのほか進まない現状も報告されており、その原因を考えるうえでも「世代間交流が高齢者の健康に及ぼす効果の機序」を解明することは必要であろう[12]。

こうした課題に対して筆者らは、子どものふれ合いにより生起する高齢者の「ポジティブ感情」に焦点をあてた研究を行ってきた。本章では、子どもとふれ合うことにともなう高齢者の感情体験（以下、子どもとのふれ合い感情体験）に関するこれまでの研究成果の一部を紹介したい[13) 14)]。

2．高齢者の子どもとのふれ合いにともなう感情体験エピソードの収集

筆者らは、高齢者の子どもとのふれ合いにともなう感情体験エピソードを収集することを目的として、2013年6月に東京都A区のシルバー人材センターに登録している65歳以上の高齢者47名に対してインタビュー調査を行った。日常的な世代間交流によるポジティブ感情体験に関する語りを収集するために、「日常的な世代間交流体験」をテーマとした。なお、その際に「子ども」を5歳～10歳までの子ども（孫、親せきの子ども、近所の子どもを含む）と定義した。また、子どもへのあいさつや会話を含めた交流を表す用語として「ふれ合い」を用いることにした。収集したデータは、子どもとのふれ合いにより生じたポジティブ感情にあたるエピソードと思われる部分を抽出して分類作業を行った。

その結果として表1に示すように高齢者の子どもとのふれ合いにともなう感情体験は、5つのカテゴリー（①認められた嬉しさ、②満たされた心、③交流自体の楽しさ、④高揚感、⑤爽快感）に分類された。具体的に、①認められた嬉しさとは、自分自身の役割や存在が子どもから承認されたことに対して喜びを感じる体験である。例えば、Aさんは、近所の子どもとの交流の中で、「知っているおばあちゃん」と子どもから認識される嬉しさを語っていた。②満たされた心とは、子どもとのおしゃべりや遊びを通して幸福感や心の豊かさを感じ

る体験である。③交流自体の楽しさは、交流自体に没頭して楽しいという感情体験である。例えば、児童館に勤めているBさんは、館内での幼児や小学生との遊びを通して「やっぱり楽しいですよね。楽しいし、長く続けていても、え、もう1時間たったの？と思っても、まだ20〜30分な感じしているし。」と語っていた。④高揚感は、交流を通して子どもから「元気をもらった」「若返った」「刺激をもらった」というように子どもとの交流を通して心が高ぶるような感情体験である。見体的に、「子どもの元気な姿や積極的な声かけ」のような場面で多く示された。例えば、少年野球の監督をしているCさんは、「自分も活き活き、子どもたちもみんなが揃うと活き活き。」と述べていた。⑤爽快感は、日常的なわずらわしさや嫌な事柄を忘れて気分が晴々するような感情体験である。例えば、Dさんは、定年まで勤めていた社内の人間関係について「大人の人間関係がすごく嫌だったんですね。」と発言し、地域の小学生との交流を通して「あのなんかギスギスしてた私の気持ちがすごくこう和らいだんですよ。」と語っている。こうした調査インタビューの結果から、高齢者は子どもとふれ合う際に、多様なポジティブな感情体験を経験していることが明らかになった。

表1. 子どもとのふれ合いにともなう高齢者のポジティブ感情体験

カテゴリ名	発話例
認められた嬉しさ	「今日、こんなことやんなっちゃったとか、そういってくれる子がいて、その子と話してるとなんか嬉しいなあって、少しでも役に立つたかなあって気持ちに。」
満たされた心	「すごく幸せな感じでしたね。いきいきしてるっていうか、張り合いがあるっていうか」
交流自体の楽しさ	「やっぱり楽しいですよね。楽しいし、長く続けていても、え、もう1時間たったのか？と思っても、まだ20〜30分な感じしているし。」
高揚感	「やっぱり1日明るく、その日が一日楽しく過ごせるね。やっぱり、顔見たり、それから子どもの声を聴いたり、姿を見たりすると、なんとなくね。その一日がね、なんか楽しい。見ているだけで楽しい。」
爽快感	「大人だけを見ているので、中にはなんて失礼なと思うような場合もあるんですよ。そういう大人だけを見ているとやっぱり子どもってかわいいなと思う。」

3. 「世代間ふれ合い感情尺度」の作成

筆者らは、インタビュー調査での結果をもとに、高齢者が子どもとのふれ合いによって生じる様々なポジティブな感情経験の程度を測定するための“ものさし”を作成することを試みた。心理学の領域では、この“ものさし”のことを「尺度」という言葉で表し、目に見えない心を測るために使用されている。先のインタビュー調査では、子どもとのふれ合いにともなう感情体験に関する様々な語りがあげられたが、それぞれの体験が似ているのか似てないのかを主観的に判断するのはとても難しい作業になる。そこで、「因子分析」という統計的手法を用いて、統計的に要約する必要がある。「因子分析」とは、同じような反応を示す項目をグループに分類しようとする統計手法でり、それにより取り出される共通して影響を与えていると仮定される要素のことを「因子」と呼んでいる。本研究では、先のインタビュー調査により収集したポジティブな感情経験のエピソードをもとに 15 項目（社会や地域のために役立てると感じる、一緒にいるのが楽しいと感じる、日常の嫌なことを忘れられると感じる等）を作成し、「あなたが子どもとふれ合うとき、どのように感じると思いますか。」との教示に対して、「とてもそう思う」「少しそう思う」「どちらともいえない」「あまりそう思わない」「まったくそう思わない」の 5 件法で回答を求める尺度「世代間のふれ合いにともなう感情尺度」の開発を試みた。

2013 年 8 月に 65 歳以上の高齢者 291 名を対象に質問紙調査を実施した。質問紙調査への協力者 291 名のうち、日常的に子どもとのふれ合いがある高齢者204 名（男性 84 名、女性 120 名）を分析対象者とした。因子分析を行うにあたりいずれかの選択肢に全回答数の 70% 以上の回答があった 3 項目を削除し、残りの 12 項目について因子分析を行ったところ、最終的に 3 つの因子（被承認感、高揚感、自己充足感）が取りだされた。第 1 因子は、「社会や地域のために役立てる」「年配者として社会に貢献できる」「自分が持つ知識や技術を伝えられる」といった項目から構成されており、これらの項目は子どもとのふれ

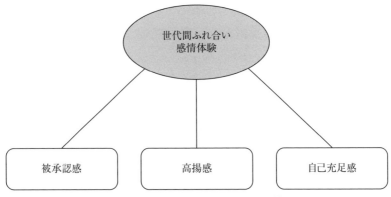
図1. 世代間ふれ合い感情尺度の因子構造

合いを通して自分自身の役割や存在が承認されたと感じていることから「被承認感」とした。第2因子は、「一緒にいるのが楽しい」「うれしい気分になる」「自分の心の成長につながる」の項目からなり、これらの項目は子どもとのふれ合いを通して心が高ぶる感情を表していることから「高揚感」とした。第3因子は、「日常の嫌なことを忘れられる」「時間つぶしになる」「自分の健康の維持に役立つ」の項目から構成され、子どもとのふれ合いを通して自分自身に満足や充足を感じていることからこれらの項目を「自己充足感」とした。

こうした結果から、図1で示すように、高齢者が子どもとのふれ合いによって生じるポジティブな感情経験「世代間ふれ合い感情体験」は、「被承認感」「高揚感」「自己充足感」という3つのものさしで測定されることが明らかになった。なお、「世代間ふれ合い感情尺度」の項目数について、尺度使用の簡便性を考慮して、因子負荷量および項目の意味内容を検討したうえで、最終的に9項目を採用した。

4．世代間ふれ合い感情体験と高齢者の個人属性との関連

「世代間ふれ合い感情尺度」の3つの因子（被承認感、高揚感、自己充足感）と個人属性との関連を検討するためにt検定という統計的手法を用いた（表

第 7 章　子どもとふれ合うことによる高齢者の感情体験　225

表 2．ふれ合い感情尺度の個人属性による得点差

		被承認感			高揚感			自己充足感		
		平均値	(SD)	P 値	平均値	(SD)	P 値	平均値	(SD)	P 値
＜個人属性＞										
性別	男性（n=84）	3.92	(0.85)	0.40	4.40	(0.61)	0.32	3.69	(0.91)	0.37
	女性（n=120）	3.81	(1.01)		4.49	(0.60)		3.81	(0.98)	
年齢	65 ～ 74 歳（n=117）	3.86	(0.86)	0.84	4.41	(0.64)	0.29	3.80	(0.93)	0.51
	75 歳以上（n=87）	3.84	(1.05)		4.45	(0.56)		3.71	(0.98)	
同居者	あり（n=51）	3.69	(1.14)	0.17	4.41	(0.71)	0.64	3.67	(1.02)	0.45
	なし（n=153）	3.90	(0.87)		4.46	(0.56)		3.80	(0.93)	
孫との同居	あり（n=21）	4.08	(0.85)	0.21	4.71	(0.40)	0.04*	3.84	(0.98)	0.71
	なし（n=183）	3.83	(0.96)		4.42	(0.62)		3.76	(0.95)	
外出頻度	高群（n=169）	3.92	(0.89)	0.02*	4.43	(0.64)	0.38	3.75	(0.96)	0.70
	低群（n=35）	3.51	(1.14)		4.53	(0.41)		3.82	(0.91)	
主観的健康感	健康群（n=166）	3.91	(0.94)	0.10	4.47	(0.59)	0.41	3.79	(0.94)	0.41
	不健康群（n=38）	3.61	(0.96)		4.38	(0.67)		3.65	(1.01)	
1 ヶ月間の医療機関受診	あり（n=157）	3.80	(0.98)	0.16	4.44	(0.62)	0.62	3.70	(0.96)	0.06
	なし（n=47）	4.02	(0.78)		4.49	(0.54)		3.99	(0.89)	
＜既往＞										
心臓病	既往あり（n=30）	3.43	(1.08)	0.00**	4.19	(0.70)	0.01*	3.47	(0.92)	0.06
	既往なし（n=174）	3.92	(0.90)		4.50	(0.58)		3.82	(0.95)	
高血圧	既往あり（n=166）	3.91	(0.94)	0.09	4.47	(0.59)	0.41	3.79	(0.94)	0.41
	既往なし（n=38）	3.61	(0.96)		4.38	(0.67)		3.65	(1.01)	
糖尿病	既往あり（n=43）	3.93	(0.82)	0.54	4.40	(0.67)	0.50	3.65	(1.04)	0.38
	既往なし（n=161）	3.83	(0.98)		4.47	(0.59)		3.80	(0.93)	
脳卒中	既往あり（n=20）	3.97	(0.69)	0.46	4.33	(0.58)	0.35	3.68	(0.95)	0.69
	既往なし（n=184）	3.84	(0.97)		4.46	(0.61)		3.77	(0.96)	
がん	既往あり（n=25）	3.65	(1.10)	0.34	4.45	(0.76)	0.98	3.45	(0.96)	0.09
	既往なし（n=179）	3.88	(0.92)		4.45	(0.58)		3.81	(0.95)	
＜子どもとのふれあい＞										
子どもとのふれあい志向	高群（n=165）	4.00	(0.86)	0.00**	4.58	(0.51)	0.00**	3.88	(0.92)	0.00**
	低群（n=39）	3.23	(1.06)		3.91	(0.69)		3.27	(0.96)	
子どもとのふれあい頻度	高群（n=90）	4.03	(0.90)	0.01*	4.56	(0.59)	0.02*	3.89	(1.02)	0.11
	低群（n=114）	3.71	(0.96)		4.37	(0.61)		3.67	(0.89)	

* *p* ＜ .01 * *p* ＜ .05

2）。t 検定とは、2 つのグループの平均値を差があるどうかを調べる手法である。その結果、「孫との同居あり / なし」、「外出頻度高い / 低い」、「子どもとふれあい志向（子どもとふれ合いたいという意識）高い / 低い」、「子どもとふ

れ合う頻度高い / 低い」、「心臓病の既往あり / なし」について、世代間ふれ合い感情尺度との関連が見られた。具体的にみると、「孫との同居」では、「高揚感」が、「孫との同居なし（孫と別居している高齢者）」よりも「孫との同居あり（孫と同居している高齢者）」の方が高いことが認められた。「外出頻度」に関しては、「被承認感」が、「外出頻度低群」よりも「外出頻度高群」の方が高いことが見いだされた。「子どもとのふれ合い志向」では、「被承認感」「高揚感」「自己充足感」ともに、「ふれ合い志向高群」の方が、「ふれ合い志向低群」よりも高いことが示された。「子どもとのふれ合い頻度」に関しては、「被承認感」「高揚感」において、「ふれ合い頻度高群」の方が「ふれ合い頻度低群」よりも高いことが認められた。また、心臓病の既往について、既往がある者よりも既往がない者の方が「被承認感」「高揚感」が高いことが示された。こうしたことから、高齢者は子どもとのふれ合いを通して、ポジティブな感情を抱きやすく、それが心身の健康の維持や向上につながる可能性が示唆された。

5．世代間ふれ合い感情体験と高齢者の精神的健康との関連

　筆者らは、「世代間ふれ合い感情尺度」が、実際に感情体験をどれくらい的確に測定できているのか（妥当性）、および、他の調査でも同じような結果が出るのか（信頼性）について検証するために数度にわたり調査を行い、その結果をもとに調査項目の文言を修正した「改訂版 世代間ふれ合い感情尺度」（全9項目）を新しく開発した（資料1）。そして、本尺度を用いて、高齢者の子どもとのふれ合いにともなうポジティブな感情体験と精神的健康にどのような関連があるのかを明らかにするために検証を行った。2015年3月に川崎市A区の20歳から84歳の市民から無作為に抽出された2,500人を対象に行った郵送調査の中から、分析には65歳以上の275人を対象にした。「改訂版 世代間ふれ合い感情尺度」について因子分析を行ったところ、改定前の尺度と同様に3因子の構造（被承認感、高揚感、自己充足感）であることが認められた（表3）。
　次いで「世代間ふれ合い感情」が「精神的健康」に及ぼす影響を検討するた

めに、「共分散構造分析」という要因間の関係を調べる統計的手法による検証を行った。本研究の場合は、「世代間ふれ合い感情」の３つの因子（被承認感、高揚感、自己充足感）が、それぞれ「精神的健康」に影響するという仮説モデルを立て、それが正しいかどうかを検証した。また、分析に際しては、「世代間ふれ合い感情」と「精神的健康」との関連を見る上で、「性別」、「就学年数」、「子どもとの接触」、「孤立状態（社会からどれくらい孤立しているかの指標）」、「主観的健康感（自らの健康について主観的に評価する指標）」の影響を考慮した。結果の見方として、図２の場合では、要因が四角、矢印の向きが要因間の影響の向きをそれぞれ示している。検証の結果、世代間ふれ合い感情体験の因子の中で、「被承認感」のみが「精神的健康」の向上に影響することが示された。こうしたことから、子どもとのふれ合いを通して高齢者が自分自身の役割や存在が承認されたと感じられる体験をもつことが、精神的健康の維持と向上につながることが考えられる。また、「被承認感」には、「性別」、「孤立状態」、「主観的健康感」が影響しており、女性、社会的に孤立していない、主観的な健康感が高い高齢者ほど、被承認感を経験することが示された。

表3.「改訂版　世代間ふれ合い感情尺度」因子分析結果

	1	2	3
社会や地域のために役立てる	.792	.098	－ .095
年配者として社会に貢献できる	.969	－ .097	－ .069
自分が持つ知識や技術を伝えられる	.613	－ .072	.195
一緒にいるのが楽しい	－ .192	.985	－ .027
うれしい気分を感じる	.147	.677	－ .023
自分の心の成長につながる	.305	.513	.052
日常の嫌なことを忘れられる	－ .066	.042	.904
退屈な気分がまぎれる	－ .045	－ .083	.733
自分の健康の維持に役立つ	.290	.094	.524
因子間相関：			
1　被承認感	－		
2　高揚感	.570	－	
3　自己充足感	0.64	0.55	－

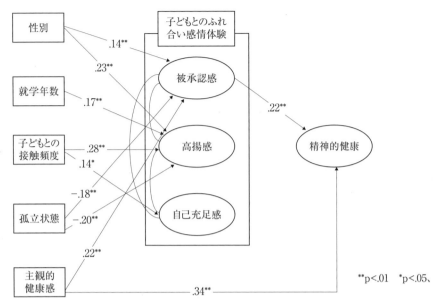

図2. 子どもとのふれ合い感情体験と精神的健康との関連

6．まとめ

　本節では、高齢者が子どもとのふれ合いによって生じる感情状態を明らかにするとともに、それを測定するための"ものさし"となる「世代間ふれ合い感情尺度」を作成した。さらに、「世代間ふれ合い感情尺度」を用いて、高齢者の子どもとふれ合うことにともなうポジティブ感情と個人属性および精神的健康との関連について検討した。

　高齢者が子どもとのふれ合いにより生起した感情として、子どもとのふれ合いを通して社会や次世代から受容されていると感じる「被承認感」、子どもとのふれ合い自体に楽しさや嬉しさを見いだす「高揚感」、子どもとのふれ合いの中に自分自身の充足感や満足感を見いだす「自己充足感」が抽出された。これら3つの感情はそれぞれがポジティブな感情である一方で、それらの感情が

子どもとふれ合う「動機」の違いに関連していることが考えられる。具体的に、「被承認感」は社会や子どもに対する利他的な動機づけによる感情、「高揚感」は子どもとのふれ合い自体への没頭から内発的に動機づけられた感情、「自己充足感」は自分自身の利己的な動機づけによる感情、とそれぞれ推測される。

　世代間ふれ合い感情体験と個人属性との関連を見ると、子どもとのふれ合う意識（ふれ合い志向）が高い高齢者ほど、3つの感情（「被承認感」「高揚感」「自己充足感」）がそれぞれ高いことが示されていることから、子どもとのふれ合いにより生じるポジティブな感情が、高齢者の子どもとふれ合いたいという欲求に結びついている可能性が示唆される。その一方で、子どもとふれ合う頻度を見ると、2つの感情（「被承認感」「高揚感」）において、ふれ合う頻度が少ない者よりも多い者の方が高いことが示された。こうしたことから、子どもとふれ合う行動には利己的なポジティブ感情ではなく、利他的または内発的なポジティブ感情が関連することが推測される。また、孫と同居している者は、同居していない者よりも「高揚感」が高く、外出をよくする者は外出をあまりしない者よりも「被承認感」が高いことが示された。孫と同居している高齢者は、日常生活の中で孫とふれ合う機会や時間が多くあるために、孫とのふれ合いに没頭して「高揚感」を高める体験をよくするのではないかと推測される。外出頻度と「被承認感」との関連について、先行研究[15) 16)]では高齢者の外出頻度と社会的役割機能や役割意識との関連が認められており、外出をよくする高齢者は子どもとのふれ合いにおいても社会、地域または家族に認められたいという欲求が強く、それが「被承認感」の高さにつながるのではないかと思われる。また、心臓病の既往がある高齢者よりも心臓病の既往がない高齢者の方が「被承認感」「高揚感」が高いことが認められた。「心臓病」の既往とポジティブ感情との関連について、Davidson らの研究[17)]によれば、ポジティブ感情が強いほど心筋梗塞などの心臓病のリスクが低いことが示されている。こうしたことから、子どもとのふれ合いにおいて生じる「被承認感」「高揚感」が心臓病のリスクを下げる要因になる可能性が考えられる。

　さらに、「改訂版世代間ふれ合い感情尺度」を用いて子どもとのふれ合いに

ともなう感情体験と高齢者の精神的健康との関連を検討したところ、子どもとのふれ合いを通して高齢者が自分自身の役割や存在が承認されたと感じられる体験をもつことが、精神的健康の維持と向上につながることが示唆された。

　以上のことから、高齢者は子どもとのふれ合いを通して、ポジティブな感情を抱きやすく、それが心身の健康に関連すると思われる。ただし、子どもとのふれ合いによる感情のタイプに応じて、高齢者の心身の健康に対する影響力が異なることが考えられる。今後、「改訂版世代間ふれ合い感情尺度」の精度を高めるとともに、高齢者の心身の健康のどの側面に、どのような影響を及ぼすのかさらに検証を進めることが必要であろう。また、本研究ではネガティブな感情が見いだされなかったが、さらに探索的に知見を蓄積していく中で、子どもとのふれ合いを通した否定的な側面を含めてさらに尺度を精査していく必要があろう。さらに、これまでの研究では横断研究にとどまっている、時系列調査や実験法を用いることで、「世代間ふれ合い感情体験」と心身の健康との因果関係を明らかにすることが求められよう。

資料1.「改訂版 世代間ふれ合い感情尺度」

教示文1. あなたは、日常生活で子ども（幼児から小学生くらい）とふれ合うことは、どのくらいありますか。（○は1つ）

　　　　　　＊ふれ合いとは、あいさつや会話、孫・ひ孫などとの付き合いを含む子どもとの関わりを指します。

1. よくふれ合う　　　2. たまにふれ合う　　　3. ふれ合うことがない

＜「よくふれ合う」または「たまにふれ合う」と回答した方にお尋ねします＞

教示文2. あなたが子どもとふれ合う時、どのように感じますか。（○は1つずつ）

あまり考え込まずに思ったことを そのままお答えください。	とてもそう思う	少しそう思う	どちらともいえない	あまりそう思わない	全くそう思わない
(1)　一緒にいるのが楽しい	1	2	3	4	5
(2)　自分の心の成長につながる	1	2	3	4	5
(3)　社会や地域のために役立てる	1	2	3	4	5
(4)　退屈な気分がまぎれる	1	2	3	4	5

第7章　子どもとふれ合うことによる高齢者の感情体験　231

(5) 自分の健康の維持に役立つ	1	2	3	4	5
(6) 日常の嫌なことを忘れられる	1	2	3	4	5
(7) 自分が持つ知識や技術を伝えられる	1	2	3	4	5
(8) 年配者として社会に貢献できる	1	2	3	4	5
(9) うれしい気分を感じる	1	2	3	4	5

引用・参考文献

1) 世代間交流プロジェクト「りぷりんと・ネットワーク」編『子どもとシニアが元気にな
る絵本の読み聞かせガイド：現役シニアボランティアが選んだ「何度でも読んであげたい
絵本」101選』ライフ出版社、2008年

2) 大平英樹編『感情心理学・入門』有斐閣アルマ、2010年

3) Ostir GV, Markides KS, Peek MK, et al. The association between emotional well-being
and the incidence of stroke in older adults. Psychosomatic Medicine, 2001; 63, 210-215.

4) Cohen S, Doyle WJ, Tumer RB, et al. Emotional style and susceptibility to the common
cold. Psychosomatic Medicine, 2003;65:652-657.

5) Benyamini T, Idler L, Leventhal H, et al. Positive affect and function as influences on
self-assessments of health: expanding our view beyond illness and disability, Journal of
Gerontology, 2000; 55B:107-116.

6) Ostir GV, Markides KS, Black SA, et al. Emotional well-being predicts subsequent
functional independence and survival. Journal of American Geriatric Society, 2000; 48:473-
478.

7) Lowton MP, Kleban MH, Rajagopal D, et al. Dimensions of affective experience in
three age groups. Psychology & Aging, 1992; 7:171-184.

8) 藤原佳典, 西真理子, 渡辺直紀, 他「都市部高齢者による世代間交流型ヘルスプロモー
ションプログラム："REPRINTS"の1年間の歩みと短期的効果」日本公衆衛生雑誌 2007
年:53(9):702-714頁

9) 亀井智子, 糸井和佳, 梶井文子, 他「都市部多世代交流型デイプログラム参加者の12か
月間の効果に関する縦断的検証：Mixed methodsによる高齢者の心の健康と世代間交流の
変化に焦点を当てて」老年看護学 2010年;14(1):16-24頁

10) Weintraub APC, Killian TS. Perception of the impact of intergenerational programming on the physical well-being of participants in adult day service. Journal of Intergenerational Relationships, 2009; 7:355-320.

11) Chung JCC. An intergenerational reminiscence program for older adults with early
dementia and youth volunteers: values and challenging. Scandinavian journal of caring
sciences, 2009; 23(2):259-264.

12) 村山陽, 竹内瑠美, 大場宏美, 他「世代間交流事業に対する社会的関心とその現状：新聞

記事の内容分析および実施主体者を対象とした質問紙調査から」日本公衆衛生雑誌 2013 年; 60(3):138-145 頁

13) 村山陽, 高橋智也, 村山幸子, 他『高齢者における「世代間のふれ合いにともなう感情尺度」作成の試み』高齢者の心身の健康との関連：厚生労働統計協会、厚生の指標 2014 年, 61(13), 1-8 頁

14) 村山陽, 長谷部雅美, 山口淳, 他 (2016). 地域高齢者における子どもとのふれ合いに伴う感情体験と精神的健康との関連. 日本老年社会科学会第 58 回大会論文集.

15) 古田加代子, 流石ゆり子, 伊藤康児「在宅高齢者の外出頻度に関連する要因の検討」日本老年看護学会誌 2004 年; 9(1):12-20 頁

16) 藤田幸司, 藤原佳典, 熊谷修, 他「地域在宅高齢者の外出頻度別にみた身体・心理・社会的特徴」日本公衆衛生雑誌 2004 年; 51(3):168-180 頁

17) Davidson KW, Mostofsky E, Whang W. Don't worry, be happy: positive affect and reduced 10-year incident coronary heart disease: the Canadian Nova Scotia Health Survey.

Chapter 7

Emotional Experiences of Elderly through Intergenerartional Exchange with Children

Yoh Murayama

This chapter describes the positive emotional experiences of elderly people through the intergenerational exchange with children. Over the last several decades, in Japan, as a result of the rapidly increasing aging population, increasingly more attention is being placed on maintaining interpersonal relationships among the elderly. In the social background, intergenerational program have been developed over the past several decades in Japan. However, very few studies have investigated the mechanism of intergenerational exchanges. Therefore, we focused on the emotional process of elderly people through exchange with children and try to construct an Intergenerational Exchange Emotional Scale (IEES) for elderly. To construct the scale, we gathered episode on positive emotional experience of intergenerational exchange through interview research for 47 elderly people, and classified 15 categories. And then, we conducted questionnaire survey for 291 elderly people to construct IEES and investigate the reliability and validity with 15 categories. The result indicated that the scale consisted of 3 factors: approval feeling, self-sufficiency feeling, and self-enhancement feeling, and elderly with a history of heart disease feel less approval and self-enhancement. Furthermore, we developed a revised version of IEES (IEES-R) and conducted questionnaire survey for 275 elderly people to investigate the relation between positive emotional experiences of intergenerational exchange and the mental health of elderly people. Structural equation modeling clarified that approval feeling have positive effect on the mental health of elderly. These results suggest that positive emotional experience of intergenerational exchange with children may be effective for the health of elderly.

第8章　リ・ラーニングをひらく学校

溝邊　和成

1．はじめに

　近年、中教審第二次答申（1997）の「高齢社会に対応する教育の在り方」や「少子化と教育について」（2000）に見られるように、成熟された社会での教育に関心が寄せられている。最近の第2期教育振興基本計画（文科省 2013）においても、ライフステージに応じた「縦」の接続が一つの共通理念とされ、「世代間交流の促進」が掲げられている。「一人一人が多様な個性・能力を伸ばし、充実した人生を主体的に切り開いていくこと」ができ、「個人や社会の多様性を尊重し、それぞれの強みを活かして、ともに支え合い、高め合い、社会に参加すること」のできる生涯学習社会の実現に向けて、世代間交流の活動は、確かな広がりを見せ始めている。その取り組みの一つに「聴講生制度」がある。一般に「聴講生制度」は高等教育において導入され、科目等履修生と同様に、特定科目について受講することができる制度である。本稿では、そのシステムの初等・中等教育段階での試みと定義付け、異世代の地域住民と児童・生徒がともに授業を受ける異年齢同居型の授業に焦点付けている。いわゆる就学期を終えた地域住民の「学び直す：re-learning」機会としてひらかれた試みを取り上げ、紹介する。

2．愛知県（扶桑町）

　愛知県丹羽郡扶桑町のホームページ記載内容によれば、本町は、2001年度から小・中学校で学校評議委員制度を導入したほか、2002年度末までに地域住民の参加も得た学校評価制度を取り入れることを各小・中学校に求めるなど「開かれた学校づくり」を積極的に進めてきた。その一環として、「学びたいと

きに、いつでも学べる生涯学習社会を推進する」(2001年)ことが提案され、小・中学校で町民を対象とした「聴講生制度」が全国初で始まった（2002年9月）。ここでは、扶桑町総合計画（第3次：1996～2005，第4次：2008～2017）と連動し、設定された扶桑町生涯学習基本構想（2012）には「独自の文化があふれる生涯学習の町づくり」が謳われ、生涯学習社会における町づくりが志向されている。この聴講生制度の導入は、家庭の事情などで十分な学校教育を受けられなかった町民に学習機会を提供するとともに、異なる世代との交流の促進、町民への学校の開放、生徒の学習意欲の向上、教員の緊張感ある授業の展開にもつながることを期待している。すなわち、生涯学習の場として、小中学校で行われている授業、行事等の教育活動の場を広く町民に開き、町民と児童生徒の共生と協力、競争の中に、より質の高い教育活動の展開を期待するとともに新しい学校のあり方を模索することを目的とした。この制度の基本的な考えは、表1のように示されている。また、制度実施上の具体的な留意点は、表2の通りである。

さらに聴講生の募集要項では、「1学級2名までとする。」「自分の孫、子の在籍する教室は避ける。」や「遠足、運動会、体育大会なども希望により参加可能。」「希望により、給食も実費で用意。」のほか、「児童生徒の教育に支障を

表1　基本的考え
学校教育を生涯学習の基礎基本を学ぶ場ととらえ、町民の希望者にも生涯学習確立のための再教育の機会とする。
完全に地域に開かれた学校の姿を求め、学校が地域をつくり、地域が学校をつくるという関係を醸成する。
町民と児童生徒が共に生活する場や学び合う場を持つことで、高齢者には生きがいを提供し、児童生徒には思いやりと学習意欲の向上を期待する。
学習活動の場面によっては、聴講生も指導者として知識技能を生かすことができ、より質の高い学習活動が可能になる。
授業に適度な緊張感を与え、教員の意識改革をもたらす。

表2　実施上の留意点
扶桑町民または近隣市町の住民を対象とし、学校、学年、教科は自由選択とする。
1年間の聴講を原則とするが、前期・後期だけでも受け入れる。
聴講料は無料であるが、教科書は自分で購入。教材費は実費徴収する。
学校も聴講生も気遣いは無用とする。
学校でのケガなどについては、「国民健康保険」などで対応する。
1年1回、結核検査の結果を提出。
3月には『修了証』を授与する。

きたす行為があった場合には、受講を断る。」も記されている。またこの制度の長所は次のようである（本町教育委員会）。

（1）地域の人が日常的に入ることで、開かれた学校づくりができる。普段の様子を見てもらうことで、学校理解につながっている。

（2）顔見知りの大人たちが学校にいることで、不審者への対応など安全面の強化につながっている。

（3）児童生徒以外の大人に教えることで、教師にとってはいい緊張感が生まれ、授業の向上につながっている。

（4）核家族が多い子どもたちにとって、祖父母世代の学ぶ姿勢を見たり、時には人生の先輩としてよき相談相手にもなったりして、異世代交流ができている。

（5）子どもたちと学び合うことで、聴講生にとっても貴重なふれあいの場、生きがいの場となっている。

　このように聴講生制度は、「地域の学校理解」「地域の安全強化」「授業の質の向上」「よき相談者」「ふれあい・生きがいの場」がキーワードになる世代間交流として受け止められていることが推察される。聴講生の参加状況は、表3のように、年度によってばらつきがあるものの、平均して6.8名／年となっている。また小学校11名に対して中学校への聴講生の数は71名にのぼり、中学校への関心が高いことがわかる。

表3　聴講生の参加状況

年度	人数（小・中）	年度	人数（小・中）	年度	人数（小・中）
2002	5（0，5）	2006	6（1，5）	2010	4（1，3）
2003	11（0，11）	2007	10（1，9）	2011	7（2，5）
2004	6（1，5）	2008	9（2，7）	2012	5（1，4）
2005	5（1，4）	2009	10（1，9）	2013	4（0，4）

3. 福岡（那珂川町）

　福岡県筑紫郡那珂川町の聴講生制度は、全国初となる扶桑町の聴講生制度を参考に、2005年度から全国で2番目にスタートしている。那珂川町立学校（小・中・高等学校）の授業・行事等の教育活動を広く町民に生涯学習の場として開き、町民と児童生徒の共生・協力により、質の高い教育活動を展開することを目的としている。制度の基本的な考えや実施上の留意点を表4および表5のように述べている。

　また募集は、町立学校を対象に聴講生の希望により学校教育活動の一部又は全部を児童生徒とともに学習する場として提供される。聴講の期間は、教育委員会の許可した日から学年末までとされているが、次年度についても応募することは可能である。学年末には修了証が聴講生に交付される。学級編成において、聴講生は学級定員数外とし、原則として各学級2名以下とし、学級人員を多くならないように配慮するとともに聴講生の子または孫と同学級にならないよう編成する。聴講生の受け入れ状況ならびに選択された教科は、表6、7の通りである。

表4　基本的考え
学校教育を生涯学習の基礎を学ぶ場ととらえ、生涯学習としての再教育の機会とする。
完全に地域に開かれた学校の姿を求め、学校が地域を作り、地域が学校を作るという関係を醸成する。
聴講生と児童生徒が共に生活する場や学び合う場を持つことで、聴講生には生きがいを提供し、児童生徒には思いやりと学習意欲の向上を期待する。
学習活動の場面によっては聴講生も指導者として知識や技能を生かすことができ、より質の高い学習活動が期待できる。
授業に適度な緊張感を与え、教員の意識改革を図る。

表5　実施上の留意点
年齢や国籍などの資格制限はない。町外在住者の方も受講することも可能。町外在住者は通学できる人のみ。
福岡女子商業高等学校の申込みは「女性」のみ。
受講科目は、学校で教えられている教科が基本。全教科を受講することも、希望する科目のみを1つ以上選択して受講することも可能である。
受講料は無料。受講する際に必要な教科書や教材、上履きなどの日常品は自己負担である。実費を支払うことで、児童生徒と一緒に給食を食べることもできる。
事故などの補償制度はなく、事故が生じた場合は、すべて本人の責任として対応。

表6　聴講生の受け入れ（複数校種を含）

年度	人数（性別）	年齢			校　種		
		80歳以上 50歳～	70歳～ 40歳～	60歳～ 30歳以下	小	中	高
2005	5（男2女3）	2 2	1 0	0 0	1	5	0
2006	5（男1女4）	2 2	0 0	1 0	1	5	0
2007	12（男3女9）	2 1	2 2	4 1	2	10	0
2008	16（男3女13）	1 3	2 5	3 2	2	9	5
2009	10（男3女7）	2 1	3 3	1 0	4	3	5
2010	8（男2女6）	2 1	2 2	0 1	3	2	5
2011	6（男4女2）	1 0	4 0	0 1	2	0	4
2012	2（男1女1）	1 0	0 0	0 1	1	0	1
2013	3（男2女1）	0 0	1 1	1 0	2	1	1
2014	5（男3女2）	1 0	1 1	2 0	1	3	1
計	71（男24女48）	14 10	16 14	12 6	19	38	22

表内の数値は人数を表す。

　年度によってばらつきが見られるものの、平均7人／年となり、男女比は1：2で、聴講する学校として中学校が多いことがわかる（表6）。

　科目別に見ると、小学校においては、国語と音楽、中学校では英語に人気があり、高校では情報処理をトップに書道や英語、数学が選択されていたことがわかる（表7）。

表7 選択した教科

年度	小学校			中学校				高等学校				
	国社	算音	理図	国英	数音	理美	社	書音	珠簿	情社	数	英
2005							1					
	1			2	2							
2006												
	1			2	2	1						
2007	1				1	1	1					
	1	1		5	2	1						
2008	1		1				1	3	1	2	1	
	1	1		5	1	1						
2009	1							1		1	1	1
	2	1		1		2		1				
2010	1				2		2	1		1	1	1
	1	2						1				
2011	1				1					2	1	1
	1			1								
2012	1											1
2013	1	1		1	1	1	1					
				1								
2014	1			1	2	1	1					
				2				1 (日本史)				
計	8	1	1	1	7	3	7	5	1	6	4	4
	1	9	3	18	7	6		1	1	1		

表内の数値は人数を表す。

4．福岡県（須恵町）

　須恵町教育委員会資料「須恵町聴講生制度推進事業実施要項」によれば、聴講生制度は、2005年3月の定例教育委員会、校長会で「須恵町聴講生制度推進事業実施要綱」（案）が提示された。その後、教育委員会としての「聴講生制度推進事業」実施の可否を決定し、校長会に再説明を行い、協力・推進体制を整えた（4月）。同年6月には「広報すえ」などで須恵町聴講生制度推進事業を公表し、社会教育課で聴講生を募集した。8月になって、教育委員会と学

校とで聴講生候補者を選考し、本人に受講の意思を再確認するとともに聴講生の学級配置を決定し、公表（紹介）した。同年、後期開始の10月、職員と生徒に聴講生が紹介され、受講が始まった。このようにして成立した本町の聴講生制度は、「須恵町立中学校で実施されている授業、行事等の教育活動の場を生涯学習の場として広く町民に開き、町民と生徒とがふれあい、共生、協力し、学習することの喜びを味わい、より質の高い教育活動を展開しながら、地域に開かれた新しい学校のあり方を模索することを目的とする」と定められている。また、この聴講生制度を「生涯学習・リカレント教育の場の一つ」とし、「『地域に開かれた学校づくり』の一環とし、学校から地域へ、地域から学校への双方向から学校を開き、学社融合、校区コミュニティづくりに資する」点や「学校教育が地域の『ひと・もの・こと』を活用すること」、さらには「学校の安全確保」の一助としている。事業のねらいとして表8に同様の内容を挙げ、再教育の場の提供や町民と生徒がともに学び合う場、聴講生参加による生徒の学習の質向上を目指している。また、表9のように事業の推進として「本事業の目的及びねらいを理解し、積極的に学習しようとする須恵町民で、聴講中（登・

表8　事業のねらい
学校教育を生涯学習の基礎を学ぶ場ととらえ、町民の学習ニーズに応える再教育（リカレント教育）の機会とする。
「地域に開かれた学校」の姿を求め、学校が地域をつくり、地域が学校をつくるという関係（住民参加型学校）を醸成する。
町民と生徒がともに生活する場や学びあう場を持つことで、高齢者には生きがいを提供し、生徒には思いやりと学習意欲の向上を目指す。
学習活動の場面によっては、教員の求めに応じ、聴講生も指導者として知識・技能・人生経験を生かし、より質の高い学習活動の展開を図る。
教員は授業に適度な緊張感をもち、授業計画・授業評価を含む授業改善と意識改革を資する。
聴講生は学校教育の現状を知り、町民の学校教育に対する理解と協力を高める橋渡しとなる。
聴講生など町民が頻繁に学校へ出入りすることで、学校の安全確保の一助とする。

表9　事業の推進
教育委員会が、町民の希望を取りまとめ、町内中学校との調整を図る。
聴講生は、原則として各学級に2名までとして、聴講生の子や孫が活動する学級は避ける。
健全な教育活動に支障をきたすような行為があった場合には、聴講生の身分を取り消す。
受講料は無料であるが、教材費等の実費は聴講生の自己負担とする。
聴講期間は、4月～翌年3月までの各学期単位とする。
受講資格は、本事業の目的及びねらいを理解し、積極的に学習しようとする須恵町民とし、事故等があった場合、学校、教員、生徒への責任を求めることなく、自らの責任において処理するものとする。
募集規定については別に定める。

下校中を含む）に事故等があった場合、学校、教員、生徒への責任を求めることなく、自らの責任において処理できる者」が資格とされている。加えて「聴講を希望する者は、学校、学年、教科を指定して申し込むことができる」が、学校での影響を配慮し、「子どもや孫が在籍する学級を指定することはできない」としている。聴講費用はただし書きがあるものの、無料として聴講生の負担を軽減している。

　なお聴講生の参加人数は、7名（2005年）、8名（2006年）であったものの、2007、2008年では、2名に落ち込んだ。その後、4名（2009年）、5名（2010年）と上向き傾向となったが、ここ数年は、1名（2011、2012、2013、2014年）と少なくなってきている。

　溝邊ら（2015）の調査では、聴講生受け入れ経験のある生徒27名中、24名が肯定的な意見（自由記述）を述べていたことがわかった。また聴講生（2011年より中学校で英語を3年間受講中）へのインタビューから、学び直しができる機会ととらえており、生徒には学習面のみならず心の成長や生き方など、聴講生から良い影響がもたらされると考えていたことがわかった。「どんなに年をとった人でも学びたいと思っていることがある」という受講生が語る表現には、生涯学習社会での生き方を示していることが読み取れる。受講生を担当している教員への質問紙調査では、聴講生は、学ぶ喜びを感じ、生徒とのふれあいを楽しんでいるととらえ、聴講生の参加により緊張感を感じるが、授業を乱されることはないと回答している。むしろ聴講生から学ぶことが多くあると思っていることがわかった。さらに個人情報流出・漏洩については、学校側としてそれほど心配しておらず、聴講生への信頼度の高さが読み取れた。

5．おわりに

　今回取り上げた事例では、いずれも町行政は、聴講生制度を生涯学習社会における地域に開かれた学校づくりの一つとしており、かつ町民の学習ニーズに応えるリカレント教育の一環として位置付けていることがわかった。また、1

クラスに2名までの受け入れなど類似したルールを設け、取り組んでいること
も明らかとなった。しかしながら、聴講生制度の利用者数の減少傾向は一つの
課題として受け止められる。扶桑町（2014）の高齢者を対象にした調査報告は、
課題に対して示唆的であろう。そこでは、対象者は趣味や経験を中心に人的交
流や地域貢献を希望していると推察され、また、世代差を気にせずにコミュニ
ケーションを行う土壌も形成されていると考えられる。これらの点を参考にす
れば、趣味とされる内容をも取り入れた幅広く柔軟性のある聴講生学習プログ
ラムの作成が必要となるだろう。クラスでの授業科目をはじめ、部活や教養講
座、ボランティア活動などへの参加も可能となる多様な学習選択型プログラム
が今後の聴講生制度に有効かもしれない。

引用・参考文献

溝邊和成・田爪宏二・吉津晶子・矢野真（2015）小中学校の聴講生制度に見られる世代間交
　流，日本世代間交流学会誌，Vol.5 No.1,pp.47-55.

文部科学省（1997）21世紀を展望した我が国の教育の在り方について（中央審議会第二次答申）
　http://www.mext.go.jp/b_menu/shingi/old_chukyo/old_chukyo_index/toushin/1309655.
　htm

文部科学省（2000）少子化と教育について（中央教育審議会報告）http://www.mext.go.jp/
　b_menu/shingi/old_chukyo/old_chukyo_index/toushin/1309769.htm

文部科学省（2013）第2期教育振興基本計画 http://www.mext.go.jp/a_menu/keikaku/de-
　tail/__icsFiles/afieldfile/2013/06/14/1336379_02_1.pdf

扶桑町

扶桑町民聴講生制度推進事業実施要領

　http://www.fuso.ed.jp/kyouiku/tyoukousei.htm

　http://www.fuso.ed.jp/tyoukousei_bosyuu.htm

　聴講生募集　http://www.fuso.ed.jp/

財団法人長寿社会開発センター（2007）ひょうひょう，Vol.106, pp.1-3

小嶋紀行（2003）内外教育2003年1月24日，時事通信社，pp.8-9.

河村共久（2003）生涯学習リポート，週間教育資料2003年9月15日号，No.817, p.30.

毎日新聞2008年12月4日夕刊

日本経済新聞2009年11月20日夕刊

扶桑町（2014）扶桑町高齢者等実態調査報告書 http://www.town.fuso.lg.jp/kaigo/docu-
　ments/koureisyajittaityousa.pdf

第8章　リ・ラーニングをひらく学校　243

須恵町

「広報すえ（http://www.town.sue.fukuoka.jp/site/kouhou/）」および下記の内容の資料を参
　照した。
　須恵町聴講生制度推進事業実施要綱、須恵町聴講生制度応募規定、聴講生制度の位置づけ、
　期待されるメリット・デメリット、聴講生制度発足までの日程

那珂川町

http://www.town.fukuoka-nakagawa.lg.jp/soshiki/20/tyoukousei.html

http://www.town.fukuoka-nakagawa.lg.jp/uploaded/attachment/2472.pdf

（注）本稿は、科学研究費助成事業：基盤研究（B）（課題番号：26285176、研究代表：溝邊和成）
　（平成 26 ～ 28 年度）の助成を受けて行われた研究をもとに作成されている。

Chapter 8

Re-Learning System for the Elderly
in the Elementary/Junior High School

Kazushige Mizobe

In the second recent education promotion basic plan (Ministry of Education, Culture, Sports, Science and Technology 2013), vertical connections according to the life stage are regarded as one common philosophy, and "promotion of intergenerational contact" is raised. The activities of intergenerational exchanges are showing steady spread for the realization of a lifelong learning society that each person can develop diverse individualities and abilities and can independently open up a fulfilling life, and that respects the diversity of individuals and society, utilizes their respective strengths.

One of the actions is "a system that the elderly can learn with young students". I introduce an open trial as re-learning opportunity for the local inhabitants who finished so-called attendance at school period.

2 Aichi(Fuso cho)

According to the homepage mention contents of Fuso cho, Aichi, it was suggested, "We promoted a lifelong learning society which they could learn anytime they want to " (2001). It was the first time in Japan that "a system to learn with young students" for townsman began at an elementary and a junior high school (September, 2002).

An operational important matter;

Target: the Fuso townsman or the residents of neighboring city towns

A school, a grade, and a subject: free choice

Period: one year, but auditors have classes only in the previous term or the latter term.

Admission fee: free, textbook: by yourself, material: actual expenses.

Auditors can have a "completion certificate" in March.

More information;

- Up to 2 students per class.

- Avoid classes where auditor's grandchildren or children are enrolled.

- Auditors can participate in excursions, sports festivals, etc. and eat school meals with actual expenses, if they wish.

3 Fukuoka (Nakagawa-cho)

The system of Nakagawa Town in Fukuoka Prefecture began in FY 2005, with reference to the system of Fuso-cho, which was first conducted in Japan. This is the second system in Japan. The recruitment method is in accordance with the system in Fuso-cho.

Although there are variations from year to year, the average is 7.2 people / year, the ratio of male and female is 1: 2, and there are many middle schools willing to accept elderly students. In elementary schools there were many elderly students who learn national languages and music, and it was popular to learn English for them at junior high schools. In high school, information processing was the most popular subject and some elderly students chose to learn calligraphy, English, and mathematics.

4 Fukuoka (Sue-cho)

The system in this town, which began in October 2005, is regarded as "a place for life-long learning and recurrent education" as well as others.

In the survey of Mizobe (2015), it was found that 24 of the 27 students, who had experience of accepting elderly students, expressed positive opinions to the system. From an interview with a female elderly student, we found that she understood the system as an opportunity of re-learning. She said young students could receive positive influence from elderly students not only about learning contents but also mental growth and way of life.

In another survey for a female teacher who taught elderly students, she realized that elderly students felt great on learning and enjoyed the contact with students. She also felt a sense of tension due to the participation of the elderly students, but she reassured that the lesson was never disturbed, and there were many things to learn from the elderly student.

おわりに

　周知のように、日本においては、古くから世襲制・徒弟制によって技の伝承が行われたり、地域の祭りや行事を通して世代が交わり、世代を超える文化の継承・発展が行われたりしてきた。しかし、その学究的検討については、いくつかの研究分野で行われてきたものの、一つの組織として集約的・継続的な取り組みが始まったと言えそうなのは、数年前に成立した日本世代間交流学会の活動からだろう。そうした史的背景を踏まえれば、本書の編集意図として、新しい学問的潮流が日本に生まれたことを世界に発信する点に加え、関係諸賢とともにこれからの社会創造に参加・参画する一歩と主張しても許されるのではないだろうか。その趣旨に賛同し、寄稿してくれた第一線で活躍中の外国研究者諸氏に厚く御礼を申し上げるとともに日本においても先進的研究に挑戦する研究者らが声を上げ、熱いメッセージを投げていただけたことに深く感謝の意を表したい。

　ここでは、本書編著者を代表し、そのベースともなった日本世代間交流学会の学会誌紹介を通して、応援いただいた方々へのお礼と刊行できた喜びの気持ちを伝えたい。

　2010年に日本世代間交流学会が成立した。その目的を草野篤子氏（初代会長：2010〜現在）は、次のように述べる。

　　　あらゆる世代が心身ともに健全に育つことが出来る家庭や地域を作り出すことは、社会全体に課せられた責務です。この責務を果たすために、学問の領域を超えて、あらゆる世代を取り巻く問題に関心や係わりのある研究者や実践者が集い、共に研究し、提言をし、実践してゆくなかで、あらゆる世代の健康と人間発達に寄与する総合科学を確立し、あらゆる世代のためのよりよい家族や地域社会を実現することが、『日本世代間交流学会』の目的です。

さらに、このような表現が続く。

　世界各国において、子ども・青年・中年世代・高齢者を取り巻く生活環境は異なっていますが、あらゆる世代の健全な人間発達とその地域作りは共通の課題であり、各国の研究者や実践者が連携して研究や実践の上で協力し合うことが重要であるので、そういった機会を本学会が提供していきたいと考えています。(http://www.jsis.jp/introduction.html)。

　そして、上記のような目的を達成する方法の一つとして、本学会は年1回学会誌を発行している。

　学会誌（Journal of Japan Society for Intergenerational Studies : ISSN2185－7946）は、写真1・2のように発刊当初より和文（表）と英文（裏）表記となっており、国際的な文化のつながりと広がりをイメージしている。表紙左部分は、紐（ひも）が結び合って世代を繋ぐイメージを表している。日本文化の一つ「組み紐」を象徴化したと解釈してもよいだろう。冊子全体の色合いは、伝統的な「藍」色を基調とし、すっきり感が感じられる。学会名左にあるマークは、本学会のシンボルマークで地球上の様々な世代の者たちが互いに手を取り合って「和」をつくり、現在から未来社会を創造していく姿を表している。こちらの色合いは存在感がありながら、重さを感じさせない工夫が受け取れる。

　一般的にどの学会誌もそうであるように、本学会誌も投稿規定、倫理規定、執筆要領、学会論文テンプレートに加え、投稿登録用紙ならびに著作権譲渡同

　　写真1　（学会誌：表）　　　　　　写真2　（学会誌：裏）

意書の準備がなされている。特に投稿規定は、内容を整備する目的に毎年検討がなされ、現在では、英文表記を用意し、国際化に対応してきている（HPに記載されている規定は、2013年改定）。

学会誌の内容は、研究論文（Original Article）、資料（Research Report）、研究ノート（Research Note）の他に招待論文（Invited Paper）や展望論文・総説（Prospective Overview/ Review Article）で構成されている（2015年現在）。2011 ～ 2014年までの論文数及びその分類を示すと、平均論文数は13.5／年で研究論文や資料が主となる。外国研究者についても、招待論文：2、展望論文：3、研究ノート：11（その内、外国人投稿数3）を数え、国内外の研究者の参加が認められる。掲載された54編に見るキーワードは、その数の多い順に「世代間交流：30」、「高齢者：14」、「子ども：10」、「高齢者のイメージ：8」となる。これらは、単に偶然性を表すのではなく、世代間交流の枠組みを議論する内容や、高齢者と子どもの実際的な関わりをターゲットとして論究する内容の重要性を物語っていると推察できる[註]。

註）2015年ハワイで開催された Generations United のラウンドテーブル：Uchida, H. & Mizobe, K.(2015), Progress of Japan Society for Intergenerational Studies Since its Start in 2010, Generations United, Roundtable Sessions で用いた筆者の発表資料 Journal of Japan Society for Intergenerational Studies より引用

今後もこの学会誌は、国際的な動向を反映させながら、その時々のホットな話題を提供していくだろう。また、本書のように、学会誌とシンクロしグローバル化を意識した出版物が次々と世に出され、日本における研究も世界標準に近づいていくと期待される。少し余談になるが、それまでわずかな発表しか見られなかったGU（Generations United）の国際的なカンファレンスにも2015年には、例年以上の数のポスター発表に加え、シンポジウム、ワークショップやラウンドテーブルなどにも日本人の参加が見られるようになった。それらのメンバーの多くが、日本世代間交流学会員であったことは言うまでもなく、国際的な視野に立った研究が盛んに行われ始めてきたことの証左である。その点でも二ヶ国語併記タイプのユニークな本書出版は、国際化への引導あるいは後押しの役割を演ずる意義があると自負する。

https://guconference.wordpress.com （2016.6.12 アクセス）

　最後になりましたが、本書出版に際し、草野博志・ヨシエ記念財団の援助を受けましたことに厚くお礼申し上げます。また、寄稿くださった方々をはじめ、翻訳、編集作業等に深くかかわっていただい皆様に、心より感謝の意を表します。合わせて、このたびも多大な尽力を賜りました本出版社の中桐様にお礼申し上げます。ありがとうございました。

2017 年春
編著者代表して　溝邊　和成

Afterword

As is well known, for a long time in Japan, cultural tradition has been in many ways tied to a great deal of human efforts and lineage such as apprenticeship. Also, cultural succession and development beyond generations have been strengthened through local festivals and events.

Intergenerational studies have been conducted in several fields such as sociology and medicine.

It can be also said that intensive and continuous efforts have been contributed by Japan Society for Intergenerational Studies (JSIS) established in 2010. Dr. Atsuko Kusano, the first and current president of JSIS, made the following emphasis or objective of JSIS.

-------- It is the responsibility of the whole society to create a home and community that every generation can grow healthily in the mind and body.

In order to fulfill this responsibility, researchers and practitioners who are interested in the intergenerational issues shall gather, study, and make recommendations. In practice, they shall establish a science for all generations in terms of health and human development as well as achieve a better family and community.

Journal of JSIS is published for the above purpose every year. This journal will provide the occasional hot topic in future while letting you reflect an international trend.

Given such a historical background, we would like to have the opinion that we will inform the world of Japan's new academic trend, and this can be meant a collaboration with the rest of the world.

In addition, we hope to get the official journal of a scientific society, this book and articles of Japan closer to the global standards.

We would like to express our deep gratitude to foreign researchers who work at the forefront and to Japanese researchers who keep taking up the challenges of advanced research work.

At last, we would like to thank all of you from the bottom of our hearts again.

Kazushige Mizobe
Editor

著者プロフィール一覧（Authors）

第1部（Part.1）

第1章（chapter.1）

Donna M. Butts

Generations United, 25 E Street NW, Third Floor, Washington, DC, 20001, USA

Executive Director, Generations United

Donna Butts has been the Executive Director of Generations United since 1997. Previously she served in leadership positions at several youth serving organizations including the YWCA, National 4-H Council, and Covenant House. An internationally known speaker, author and advocate, Butts frequently addresses intergenerational connections, grandparents raising grandchildren and policies effective across the lifespan. She has served on four United Nations expert panels. She served as an at large delegate to the 2005 White House Conference on Aging and attended the 2015 conference. Butts is a graduate of Stanford University's Executive Program for Nonprofit Leaders. She was recognized three years in a row by The Nonprofit Times as one of the Top 50 most powerful and influential nonprofit executives in the nation. In 2015 she was named one of the Top 50 Influencers in Aging by Next Avenue. Butts serves on several boards including the Journal of Intergenerational Relations.

第2章（chapter.2）

Ann-Kristin Boström

Rindögatan 15, vån. 8 115 36 Stockholm, Sweden

Dr. Ann-Kristin Boström, is affiliated researcher in Encell (National Centre for Lifelong Learning), at the School of Education at Jönköping University in Sweden. Her research interests are theory, concepts and contexts of lifelong learning and intergenerational learning as well as how this can be explained using the concepts of social capital, well-being and quality in life. She has a broad international network within this area and is a board member of the Journal of Intergenerational Relationships, where she is guest editor for a special issue concerning lifelong learning and intergenerational learning. Parallell with her research she has been working as a Director of Education for the Swedish Ministry of Education and Research and as a Special Advisor for the Government Offices in Sweden. She has been representing Sweden in the European Council, within OECD and the EU.

第 3 章 (chapter.3)

Michelle C. Carlson

Dr. Carlson is an Associate Professor in the Department of Mental Health at the Johns Hopkins Bloomberg School of Public Health in Baltimore, MD, core faculty member in the Center on Aging and Health, and holds joint appointments in the Department of Epidemiology and the School of Nursing. Dr. Carlson leads these investigations using both observational studies and pharmacologic and behavioral intervention trials. She currently serves as the Johns Hopkins site principal investigator of the Cardiovascular Health Study, now entering its 29th year and led the Johns Hopkins site of the Ginkgo Evaluation of Memory (GEMS) randomized, controlled trial. She pioneered the incorporation of functional neuroimaging as an outcome in the first social engagement trial among older adults, entitled the Baltimore Experience Corps Trial (BECT). Dr. Carlson continues to innovate in the evaluation of the mechanisms through which social engagement impacts neurocognitive health using neuroimaging, GPS, and accelerometery. She also serves on the AARP Global Brain Health Initiative (GBHI) on social engagement and is a Fellow of the Gerontological Society of America.

Linda P. Fried

Linda P. Fried, MD, MPH, is Dean of Columbia Univeristy's Mailman School of Public Health, where she is the DeLamar Professor of Public Health, Professor of Medicine and Senior Vice President of Columbia University Medical Center. Previously, and until 2008, Dr. Fried served as Director of the Johns Hopkins Center on Aging and Health and of the Division of Geriatric Medicine and Gerontology. Dr. Fried is co-designer and co-founder of Experience Corps, and led the creation of the evidence-based model that has been implemented and tested in Baltimore, MD and throughout the US. Dr. Fried is the President of the Association of American Physicians, and member of the National Academy of Medicine, where she is an elected Council member. She co-chairs the World Economic Forum's Global Futures Council on Human Enhancement. The recipient of numerous awards and honors, she most recently received the Inserm 2016 International Science Prize.

George W. Rebok

Dr. George W. Rebok received his Ph.D. in life-span developmental psychology from Syracuse University, with a specialization in gerontology and did post-doctoral training in the dementias of aging at the Johns Hopkins School of Medicine. He is a Professor in the Department of Mental Health in the Bloomberg School of Public Health at Johns Hopkins

著者プロフィール一覧（Authors） 253

University and holds joint faculty appointments in the Department of Psychiatry and Behavioral Sciences, the Johns Hopkins Center on Aging and Health, and Center for Innovative Care in Aging. His research includes studies on cognitive interventions with the elderly and the effects of aging and dementia on driving and other everyday functional tasks. Dr. Rebok has served as PI of two large NIA-funded intervention trials, the ACTIVE trial, and the Baltimore Experience Corps® trial. Dr. Rebok is a Fellow of the Association for Psychological Science, American Psychological Association, and Gerontological Society of America.

第 4 章（chapter.4）

Daniel R. George
Department of Humanities, H134
Penn State College of Medicine Milton S. Hershey Medical Center
500 University Drive, Hershey, PA 17033, USA
　Dr. Daniel R. George is Associate Professor in the Department of Humanities at Penn State College of Medicine. He earned his Ph.D and M.Sc in medical anthropology from Oxford University in 2010. Dr. George is co-author of The Myth of Alzheimer's, which was published by St. Martin's Press in 2008, and has been translated into 4 languages. He has over 90 professional peer-review publications, and his research on intergenerational issues in dementia care has been recognized by the global advocacy group Alzheimer's Disease International. In addition to teaching and research at Penn State, Dr. George has co-founded the Farmers Market in Hershey, and a Community Garden on the hospital campus. He serves as a member of the Alzheimer's Association Regional Board in Central Pennsylvania.

第 5 章（chapter.5）

Nancy Henkin
606 Zollinger Way, Merion, PA 19066, USA
nzhenkin@gmail.com
　Dr. Henkin is the founder and former Executive Director of the Intergenerational Center at Temple University. She is currently serving as a Senior Fellow at Generations United. A leading authority in the fields of intergenerational practice and lifelong civic engagement/learning, she has given presentations at numerous national and international conferences as well as written a myriad of journal articles, manuals and books.
　Dr. Henkin serves on the editorial board of the International Journal on Intergenera-

254

tional Relations and is a member of the Mayor's Commission on Aging in Philadelphia. She is the recipient of numerous awards, including the Jack Ossofsky Award from the National Council on the Aging (2005), the Maggie Kuhn Award from the Gray Panthers (1988), the Marjorie Cantor Leadership Award from Elders Share the Arts (2013) and the Intergenerational Champion Award from Generations United . In 2006, she was elected into the Ashoka Fellowship, a global community of social entrepreneurs, for her efforts to build *Communities for All Ages.*

第 6 章 (chapter.6)

Alan Lai

12E, Seaview Crescent, Tung Chung, Hong Kong.

　Associate Professor of Applied Psychology in the Dept. of Applied Psychology.

　He completed his doctorate at the University of Technology, Sydney. His graduate training is in the intersection of Ecological Psychology, Applied Linguistics, and ESL (English as a Second Language) Education. His research lies in the areas of curriculum design, program implementation, project leadership, and evaluation of intergenerational programs. Dr. Lai is the founder and director of the Intergenerational-ESL Program in Hong Kong.

第 7 章 (chapter.7)

Maeona Sachie Mendelson

18 South Kalaheo Avenue, Kailua, Hawaii 96734, USA

　　Previous Professional and Educational Experience Director and Professor in Residence, Intergenerational Center at Chaminade University. Consultant to the Executive Office on Aging (EOA), State of Hawaii for the creation and implementation of the Alzheimer's State Plan. Received Ph.D in the Philosophy of Social Welfare, University of Hawaii. Graduated with a BA from the School of International Service, American University, Washington, D.C. and received an MSW from the School of Social Work, University of Hawaii.

(Current Publications)

Published two articles for the Japanese journal, Gendai no Esupuri, *"Communication Challenges in a Community Network and Using Intergenerational Models to Meet the Needs of At-risk Children and Youth.* Published essays in two anthologies: *Sixty-five Things to Do When You Retire: Travel (2013) and Seventy Things to Do at 70 (2013).*

　　Co-editor of the Journal of Intergenerational Relationships (JIR). Previous and Current Volunteer Activities Co-founded with Peace Child International (1999), the Hawaii based Millennium Young Peoples' Congress (MYPC). This event began the World Youth Con-

著者プロフィール一覧（Authors）　255

gress series that has convened international youth in Morocco (2003), Scotland (2005), Quebec (2007), Istanbul (2010), Rio (2012).

The next congress will be held in Honolulu in 2017. National Board member of AARP, Chair of the AARP Foundation, and President, AARP-Hawaii, (2004-2012).

National Board member, Help Age USA/International (2013 – 2015).

(Awards)

Resolution and Commendation from the House of Representatives, State of Hawaii for contributions to international affairs, culture, education and trade on behalf of Hawaii, 2004.

Award from the Moroccan Youth Forum of the Third Millennium (youth parliament), May 2005.

Social Worker of the Year Award in Gerontology, NASW, 2007.

第 8 章（chapter.8）

Pablo Galindo-Calvo

Departamento de Sociología　Facultad de CC. de la Educación

Universidad de Granada

Campus de Cartuja 18071 – Granada, Spain

　Pablo Galindo-Calvo, Associate Professor of Sociology at the University of Granada, and Tutor-Professor of Sociology and Social Work at the Distance Education National University in Spain. Dr. Galindos' research develops around social and cultural diversity, as well as in the area of education, employment and educational systems. He is a member of the research group "Social Problems in Andalusia".

Mariano Sánchez-Martínez

Departamento de Sociología Facultad de CC. Políticasy Sociología Universidad de Granada Rector Logía Universidad de Gran– Granada, Spain

　Associate Professor of Sociology at the University of Granada in Spain and International Affiliate in the Center for Healthy Aging at the Pennsylvania State University, has been technical coordinator of the Spanish Social Network of Experiences with Intergenerational Relations in the period 2005-2012, former co-editor of the Journal of Intergenerational Relationships, and member of the Management Committee of the International Consortium for Intergenerational Programmes. He has co-authored chapters on intergenerational relationships in two recent White Papers on Active Ageing published in Spain. Professor Sanchez co-directs Certificate in Intergenerational Projects, an online training initiative for intergenerational practitioners. His most recent book in the intergenerational field has been Intergenerational Pathways to a Sustainable Society, published by Springer in 2016, in co-

256

authorship with Dr. Matt Kaplan and Dr. Jaco Hoffman.

第 9 章（chapter.9）

Leng Leng THANG

Dept of Japanese Studies, National University of Singapore
AS8, 10, Kent Ridge Crescent, Singapore 199260

Associate Professor, Head of Department of Japanese Studies, National University of Singapore

Field: anthropology, Research interest: Aging, intergenerational programs and relationships, family, gender.

Dr. Thang Leng Leng is a socio-cultural anthropologist with research interests on ageing, intergenerational approaches and relationships, gender and family. She has numerous publications, including "Generations in Touch: Linking the old and young in a Tokyo neighborhood" (Cornell University Press, 2001), "Ageing in Singapore: Service needs and the state" (co-author, Routledge, 1996, 2012), and "Experiencing Grandparenthood: An Asian perspective" (co-editor, Springer, 2012). Dr. Thang is also active in community to promote intergenerational approaches. She is co-editor-in-chief of the Journal of Intergenerational Relationships (Taylor and Francis, USA). She is currently Associate Professor and Head of the Department of Japanese Studies, Deputy Director of the Centre for Family and Population Research and Honorary Fellow with the College of Alice and Peter Tan, National University of Singapore.

第 10 章（chapter.10）

Alan Hatton-Yeo

Strategic Development Manager Volunteering Matters Cymru
07702 583584

Alan worked for 16 years as CEO of the Beth Johnson Foundation and retired in January 2014 to focus on his interest in Intergenerational work and Age-Friendly Communities. He has an international reputation for his work in the fields of Intergenerational Practice and Ageing and has written extensively. His current roles include:

Strategic Development Manager for Volunteering Matters Wales

Member National Partnership Forum for Older People for Wales

Chair and expert lead of the Age-Friendly Communities network Wales.

Honorary Research Fellow University of Keele

Associate Editor Journal for Intergenerational Relationships

著者プロフィール一覧（Authors）　257

Chair Generations Working Together Scotland

Chair International Consortium for Intergenerational Programmes.

In 2012 he was awarded Doctor of University by the University of Keele in recognition of his contribution and leadership in the field of ageing and an MBE for his contribution to the development of intergenerational practice.

第 11 章（chapter.11）

Peter Whitehouse

Professor of Neurology and current or former Professor of Psychiatry,

Neuroscience, Psychology, Cognitive Science, Bioethics, Nursing, History,

and Organizational Behavior,Case Western Reserve University

Strategic Advisor in Innovation Baycrest Health Center and Professor of Medicine and Institute of Life Course and Aging, University of Toronto

President, Intergenerational Schools International

Mailing Address: 2895 Carlton Road, Shaker Heights, OH 44122

Tel: 216-752-8155

Email:peter.whitehouse@case.edu

Peter is a Professor of Neurology and former or current professor of Psychiatry, Psychology, Cognitive Science, Neuroscience, Bioethics, History, Nursing and Organizational Behavior at Case Western Reserve University, Professor of Medicine at the University of Toronto, and President of Intergenerational Schools International. He is also currently a strategic advisor in innovation at Baycrest Health Center. He received his undergraduate degree from Brown University and MD-PhD (Psychology) from The Johns Hopkins University (with field work at Harvard and Boston Universities), followed by a Fellowship in Neuroscience and Psychiatry and a faculty appointment at Hopkins. In 1986 he moved to Case Western Reserve University to develop the University Alzheimer Center. In 1999 he founded with his wife, Catherine, The Intergenerational School, a unique public multiage, community school (www.tisonline.org).He is a geriatric neurologist, cognitive scientist, environmental ethicist, and photographer. He is active in visual arts, dance and music organizations globally, including the National Center for Creative Aging and Dance Exchange. He is a transdisciplinarian and loves metaphors. He is coauthor of "The Myth of Alzheimer's: what you aren't being told about today's most dreaded diagnosis." (www.themythofalzheimers.com) and hundreds of academic papers and book chapters. He is part of the reimagine aging movement personally and culturally. He claims to have led the invention of two words: intergenerativity and ecopsychosocial (models of health). He is a futurist with a deep interest in historical roots.   He also occasionally performs as Tree Doctor, a metaphorical creature who educates humans about being healthy from the perspective of a tree.

Yachneet Pushkarna

MBA (Grande Ecole in Paris France)

Yachneet Pushkarna is Vice President Global Strategies and Operations for Intergenerational Schools International and Head of Strategy for an Educational Group. Yachneet has extensive corporate exposure over 14 years in pharmaceutical, media and consulting industries Hong Kong, Paris, Singapore and New York. He has worked on multimillion dollar projects end to end from conceptualization to delivery. He has very successfully taken the Intergenerational School model and reengineered into Intergenerational Digital Knowledge Center for International implementation based on GLOZON strategies in which a global concept is modified into a zonal need making maximum impact within its area of operation. 1st project of its kind is coming up in India (state of Himachal Pradesh) he has managed to get backing from one of the largest organizations within the United States of Indian American origin. National Federation of Indian American Associations (NFIA). As well as creating a powerful strategic base in India with one of world's largest Media group Times of India (Foundation), Top engineering schools of India IIT (Indian Institute of Technology), one of the world's prominent medical establishment AIIMS (All India Institute of Medical Sciences) on board.

Qinghong Wei

Dr. Wei is the Executive Director of Community Performance International, Vice President for Art and Community of Intergenerational Schools International, and Co-Founder of pARTicipate, an award-winning social enterprise based in China. Dr. Wei conducted original research on community development through the arts which is a significant contribution to the field. She has over a decade of diverse development planning experience working with local governments, international corporations and communities. From 2011 to 2013, Dr. Wei had an exceptional opportunity to serve as the President & CEO of Overseas China Education Foundation (OCEF), winners of multiple national and international giving challenges. OCEF has an asset of over $1 million and over 5,000 registered volunteers worldwide. At OCEF, she designed and launched the first online education program, the Internet School, for rural China which now has benefited thousands of rural students and teachers. Dr. Wei is the co-artistic director of The *Intergenerativity* Project in Cleveland, Ohio which celebrates the 15 year history of the Intergenerational Schools. She is also the co-producer, co-director, and author of *Songs of Tang Hulu*, a social theater project in Beijing, China.

著者プロフィール一覧（Authors） 259

Richard Owen Geer

Community Performance, International7481 Teller St.Arvada, CO 80003

Tel: 303-907-7081

Dr. Geer received his doctoral degree in performance studies from Northwestern University. He is an esteemed director and scholar in community performance and the co-founder of Community Performance, International (CPI). Dr. Geer developed Community Performance, a theater genre that celebrates ordinary people and their communities. His Story Bridge Method uses theater as a catalyst for peace building and community change. Dr. Geer founded more than 40 Community Performance projects worldwide, one of which is Swamp Gravy, the official Georgia Folklife Play and a participant in the Cultural Olympiad of the Atlanta Olympics. Dr. Geer co-hosts the annual Building Creative Community Conference. His recent keynote at the Brushy Fork Institute presented his vision for the arts-transformation of challenged communities. With Qinghong Wei he regularly directs here and in China. His publications include *Story Bridge: From Alienation to Community Action*.

第 2 部（Part.2）

はじめに（Preface）第 2 章（chapter.2）

草野篤子（Atsuko Kusano）

白梅学園大学子ども学部〒 187-8570 東京都小平市小川町 1-830

白梅学園大学名誉教授、博士（医学東北大学）。日本世代間交流学会（JSIS）会長、特定非営利活動法人日本世代間交流協会（JIUA）理事、International Consortium for Intergenerational Programs（ICIP）運営委員、Journal of Intergenerational Relationships 編集委員。米国テンプル大学世代間学習センター上席研究員、信州大学教育学部教授を経て、白梅学園大学教授。著書には、『インタージェネレーション：コミュニティーを育てる世代間交流』（現代のエスプリ NO.444）　至文堂、" Intergenerational Programs: Support for Children, Youth, and Elders in Japan" State University of New York Press, "Linking Lifetimes: A Global View of Intergenerational Exchange", University Press of America,『グローバル化時代を生きる世代間交流』、明石書店、『世代間交流効果：人間発達と共生社会づくりの視点から』三学出版、『世代間交流学の創造—無縁社会から多世代間交流型社会実現のために』　あけび書房、『世代間交流の理論と実践シリーズ 1 —人を結び未来を拓く世代間交流』　三学出版他多数。

Faculty of Child Studies, Shiraumegakuen University

1-830 Ogawacho, Kodairashi Tokyo, 187-8570 JAPAN

260

Tel: +81-42-346-5639 Fax: +81-42-346-5644 E-mail:kusano@shiraume.ac.jp

Dr. Atsuko Kusano, Ph.D, is a Professor Emeritus of Shiraumegakuen University and a chair of Japan Society for Intergenerational Studies(JSIS), Ex-chair of Japan Intergenerational Unity Association (JIUA), Member of Managing Committee of International Consortium for Intergenerational Programs (ICIP), Editorial Member of Journal of Intergenerational Relationships etc.

第 1 章（chapter.1）

牧野　篤（Atsushi Makino)

東京大学大学院教育学研究科

〒 113 - 0033　東京都文京区本郷 7 - 3 - 1

　東京大学大学院教育学研究科教授・東京大学高齢社会総合研究機構副機構長（兼任）　博士（教育学）。専門は生涯学習・社会教育および中国近代教育思想。全国各地の基礎自治体及び基層の住民コミュニティとともに「学び」を通した新たな関係の形成とまちづくりの実践を進める。またそれらの実践を通して「学び」概念の再検討も進めている。『生きることとしての学び』（東京大学出版会、2014)、『人が生きる社会と生涯学習』（大学教育出版、2012）など著作多数。

Graduate School of Education, The University of Tokyo

7-3-1 Hongo, Bunkyo-ku, Tokyo, 113-0033 JAPAN

Tel & Fax: +81-3-5841-3974 E-mail: makino@p.u-tokyo.ac.jp

Dr. Atsushi Makino is a professor of Graduate School of Education and a vice-director of Institute of Gerontology at The University of Tokyo. He received his PhD degree in Education in 1992 from Nagoya University, Japan. His major is Social Education, Lifelong Learning and Educational Thought in Modern China. He is now promoting the development of grassroots communities run by local residents and trying to rebuild the concept of learning through these practices.

He has many writings like as follows:

Makino, A., Learning as Creating the Place to Live in: Theory and Practice for Revitalizing Local Community through Lifelong Learning (Ikiru Koto to shiteno Manabi: 2010nendai Jisei suru Komyunity to Kyohenka suru Hitobito), University of Tokyo Press (Tokyo Daigaku Shuppan-kai), Tokyo, 2014

Makino, A., Lifelong Learning in the Society in which We Live: Making Weak Tie among People (Hito ga Ikiru Shakai to Shogaigakushu: Yowakuaru Watashitachi ga Musubitsuku koto), University Education Press (Daigaku Kyoiku Shuppan), Okayama, 2012

Makino, A., Essays on the Possibility of Desire for Co-recognition and Excessive Self-narratives: For Encountering Myself through Past and Others in This Sullen and Intolerant Society (Mitomeraretai Yokubo to Kajo-na Jibun Gatari), University of Tokyo Press (Tokyo Daigaku Shuppan-kai), 2011

第 2 章（chapter.2）

佐々木剛（Tsuyoshi Sasaki）

第一幼児教育専門学校

〒 170-0013 東京都豊島区東池袋 3-20-15

　都築教育学園第一幼児教育専門学校・副校長。子ども学修士。公立学校教員を経て東京都教育委員会指導主事、東京都立特別支援学校副校長、東京都稲城市教育委員会特別支援教育スーパーバイザー等を歴任後、現職に至る。星槎大学非常勤講師。専門は学校教育相談、特別支援教育、障害福祉研究、子ども学。主な論文「地域の共生・協働意識に支えられた世代間交流プログラム－東京都 A 小学校が独自に実践する「里孫制度」からの検討－」（日本世代間交流学会誌 Vol.6 No.1 2016 年 11 月）。「ソーシャル・キャピタルとしての世代間交流プログラム - 持続可能な開発のための教育 (ESD) の実践との関連を通して -」（日本世代間交流学会誌 Vol.5 No.1 2016 年 9 月）ほか。

Daiichi Nursery Teachers College

15-20-3 higashiikebukuro, Toshima-ku Tokyo,170-0013, JAPAN

Tel: +81-3-5957-5511 Fax: +81-3-5957-5512

E-mail:t.sasaki@dnc.tsuzuki-edu.ac.jp

　Vice-principal of Daiichi Nursery Teachers College：Tsuzuki Education Group, Lecturer of Seisa University,

Master of Child Studies. He wrote The Intergenerational Program Supported bythe Consciousness of Symbiosis and Cooperation in a Community: An Examination of "Foster-Grandchildren System" in A Elementary School in Tokyo. *Journal of Japan Society for Intergenerational Studies, Vol.6 No.1 2016.* The Intergenerational programs as Social Capital: Through the context of the practice of Education for Sustainable Development (ESD). *Journal of Japan Society for Intergenerational Studies, Vol.5 No.1 2015.*

第 3 章（chapter.3）

内田勇人（Hayato Uchida）

兵庫県立大学環境人間学部

〒 670-0092 兵庫県姫路市新在家本町 1-1-12

　兵庫県立大学・大学院教授。博士（医学）（岡山大学）。専門は健康教育学、人間発達学。

2002 年から 2003 年までジョンズホプキンス大学公衆衛生大学院疫学科にて在外研究（ポストドクトラルフェロー）。同大学 Center on Aging and Health に在室。現在、児童養護施設入所児童と高齢者との交流効果やバーチャルリアリティ技術を用いた高齢者の生活支援・転倒予防プログラムの開発等に関する研究等に従事。「世代間交流の理論と実践（1）人を結び、未来を拓く世代間交流」（編著），三学出版（2015 年）ほか。

School of Human Science and Environment, University of Hyogo
1-1-12, Shinzaike-honcho,
Himeji, Hyogo, 670-0092, JAPAN
Tel&Fax: +81-79-292-9367 E-mail: uchida@shse.u-hyogo.ac.jp

　Dr. Hayato Uchida is Professor of the School of Human Science and Environment at the University of Hyogo, Japan. He received his PhD in Medical Science in 1996 from Okayama University, Japan. His major is Health Education and Human Development. He was a postdoctoral fellow in the Department of Epidemiology of the Bloomberg School of Public Health at the Johns Hopkins University, from 2002 to 2003. He spent one year in the Center on Aging and Health, JHU. His latest research is about the educational support program for the children in a child welfare institution offered by the senior volunteers. He also works on the programs to support the elderly's daily life and prevent them from falling by using virtual reality technology. Atsuko Kusano, Kazushige Mizobe, Hayato Uchida, Masashi Yasunaga, Toshiko Yamanokuchi (2015)(Eds.) *The theory and practice for Intergenerational exchange activities*, Sangaku Co., Japan. etc.

第 4 章 （chapter.4）

高橋知也（Tomoya Takahashi）
東京都健康長寿医療センター研究所　社会参加と地域保健研究チーム
〒 173-0015 東京都板橋区栄町 35-2
　横浜国立大学大学院環境情報学府博士課程在籍。修士（教育学）。専門は発達心理学、社会老年学。現在は、高齢者と子どもとの「絵本読み聞かせボランティア活動」を通じた世代間交流による効果や、子育てサロンをはじめとする多世代交流の活動拠点づくりに関する研究のほか、高齢者の援助要請に関する研究等にも従事している。

Research Team of Social Participation and Community Health, Tokyo Metropolitan Institute of Gerontology
35-2, Sakae-cho, Itabashi, Tokyo, 1730015, Japan
Tel: +81-3-3964-3241 ext.4255 Fax:+81-3-3579-4776
　Tomoya Takahashi is in a PhD program in Environment and Information Sciences,

著者プロフィール一覧（Authors）　263

Yokohama National University, Japan. He received his Master of Education in 2013 from Yokohama National University, Japan. His major is Developmental Psychology and Social Gerontology. His latest researches are about the effect of intergenerational interaction with picture books between the elderly and children, the strategy of making a center for intergenerational activities and help-seeking preferences among the elderly.

第5章（chapter.5）

安永正史（Masashi Yasunaga）

東京都健康長寿医療センター研究所　社会参加と地域保健研究チーム

〒 173-0015　東京都板橋区栄町 35-2

　東京都健康長寿医療センター研究所・社会参加と地域保健研究チーム研究員。子ども学博士（白梅学園大学）。専門は教育心理学、社会老年学。2009 年より高齢者の学校支援ボランティア「りぷりんと」プロジェクトに参加し、高齢者と子どもの間の世代間交流が双方に与える効果に関する研究に参画。著書：『世代間交流の理論と実践 1—人を結び、未来を拓く世代間交流—』. 三学出版（編者）

Research Team of Social Participation and Community Health, Tokyo Metropolitan Institute of Gerontology

35-2, Sakae-cho, Itabashi, Tokyo, 1730015, Japan

Tel: +81-3-3964-3241 ext.4255 Fax:+81-3-3579-4776

E-mail: yasunga9@tmig.or.jp

　Masashi Yasunaga is Researcher of the Research Team of Social Participation and Community Health, Tokyo Metropolitan Institute of Gerontology. He received his PhD in Child Studies in 2013 from Shiraume Gakuen University, Japan. His major is Educational Psychology and Social Gerontology. He have participated in REPRINTS program since 2009. His latest research is about the effect of intergenerational interaction on both the elderly and children. Atsuko Kusano, Kazushige Mizobe, Hayato Uchida, Masashi Yasunaga, Toshiko Yamanokuchi (2015)(Eds.) *The theory and practice for Intergenerational exchange activities*, Sangaku Co., Japan. etc.

第6章（chapter.6）

藤原佳典（Yoshinori Fujiwara）

東京都健康長寿医療センター研究所　社会参加と地域保健研究チーム

〒 173-0015 東京都板橋区栄町 35-2

　東京都健康長寿医療センター研究所社会参加と地域保健研究チーム研究部長（医学博士）、

東京都老人総合研究所研究員、ジョンズ・ホプキンス大学／加齢健康研究所訪問研究員などを経て平成23年より現職。多世代共生の地域づくりの視点から高齢者の社会参加と健康に関する研究を進めている。日本世代間交流学会副会長、日本老年医学会評議員、日本老年社会科学会理事や多数の自治体審議会委員長を兼務している。特定非営利活動法人日本世代間交流協会（JIUA）理事、著書には、『子どもとシニアが元気になる絵本の読み聞かせガイド』ライフ出版、『世代間交流学の創造』あけび書房、『ソーシャルキャピタルで解く社会的孤立』ミネルヴァ書房『世代間交流効果』三学出版、『世代間交流学の創造』あけび書房、『シニアボランティアハンドブック』大修館『何歳まで働くべきか？‐高齢期の就業と健康』社会保険出版他多数。

Research Team of Social Participation and Community Health, Tokyo Metropolitan Institute of Gerontology

35-2, Sakae-cho, Itabashi, Tokyo, 1730015, Japan

Tel: +81-3-3964-3241 ext.4255 Fax:+81-3-3579-4776

Email; fujiwayo@tmig.or.jp

Dr.Yoshinori Fujiwara is a team-leader of Tokyo Metropolitan Institute of Gerontology and a co-chair of Japan Society for Intergenerational Studies(JSIS). He has engaged in promoting a intergenerational volunteer program "REPRINTS" in school setting.

第7章（chapter.6）

村山　陽（Yo Murayama）

東京都健康長寿医療センター研究所　社会参加と地域保健研究チーム

〒173-0015 東京都板橋区栄町35-2

東京都健康長寿医療センター研究所　社会参加と地域保健研究チーム　非常勤研究員博士（社会学）。慶應義塾大学大学院社会学研究科後期博士課程単位取得満期退学。2009年より東京都健康長寿医療センター研究所の非常勤研究員として世代間交流に関する研究にたずさわっている。現在は、地域における世代間援助の検証に取り組むとともに、その実現に向けたアクションリサーチを進めている。専門は、社会心理学、老年学、世代間交流学。著書：『コミュニティの社会心理学』（共著）、『地域を元気にする世代間交流』（共著）他。

Research Team of Social Participation and Community Health, Tokyo Metropolitan Institute of Gerontology

35-2, Sakae-cho, Itabashi, Tokyo, 1730015, Japan

Tel: +81-3-3964-3241 ext.4255 Fax:+81-3-3579-4776

E-mail:yhoyho05@tmig.or.jp

Dr.Yoh Murayama is an adjunct Researcher of Tokyo Metropolitan Institute of Gerontol-

著者プロフィール一覧（Authors） 265

ogy. He has engaged in studying an intergenerational support in local communities.

第 8 章（chapter.7）おわりに（Afterword）

溝邊和成（Kazushige Mizobe）
兵庫教育大学大学院学校教育研究科
〒 673-1494 兵庫県加東市下久米 942-1
　兵庫教育大学大学院学校教育研究科教授。博士（学術）。専門は、小学校生活科・理科・総合学習実践論・カリキュラム論。最近では、世代間交流の視点から見た教育実践に注目している。日本世代間交流学会副会長・学会誌編集委員長・学会事務局担当。「多様化社会をつむぐ世代間交流次世代への『いのち』の連鎖をつなぐ」（編著），三学出版（2012 年），「世代間交流の理論と実践（1）　人を結び、未来を拓く世代間交流」（編著），三学出版（2015 年）ほか。

Graduate School of Education,Hyogo University of Teacher Education
942-1,Shimokume, Kato,Hyogo, 673-1494,JAPAN
Tel&Fax: +81-795-44-2197 E-mail: mizobek@hyogo-u.ac.jp
　Dr. Kazushige Mizobe is Professor of Hyogo University of Teacher Education, Japan. His major is the curriculum and practice for Living Environment Studies, primary science, and the integrated study of elementary school. Recently, he is interested in the educational research at the view of intergenerational exchange. He is a vice president of Japan Society for Intergenerational Studies (JSIS), a chairman of journal editorial board of JSIS, and the Secretary-General.
　Atsuko Kusano, Kazushige Mizobe, Hayato Uchida, Masashi Yasunaga, Toshiko Yamanokuchi (2015)(Eds.) *The theory and practice for Intergenerational exchange activities*, Sangaku Co., Japan. etc.
　Atsuko Kusano, Hayato Uchida, kazushige Mizobe, Masako Yoshizu (2012)(Eds.) *Intergenerational exchanges to tie diversified society-Connect chain of "life" to next generation*, Sangaku Co., Japan.

編著者一覧

草野篤子（Atsuko Kusano）
溝邊和成（Kazushige Mizobe）
内田勇人（Hayato Uchida）

安永正史（Masashi Yasunaga）以上前出

＜翻訳協力者＞
奈良勝行（Katsuyuki Nara）白梅学園大学教育・福祉研究センター研究員
大島　真（Makoto Oshima）都留文科大学名誉教授・元信州大学教授
谷本泰子（Yasuko Tanimoto）信州大学名誉教授
倉岡正高（Masataka Kuraoka）東京都健康長寿医療センター研究所研究員
岡野聡子（Satoko Okano）　奈良学園大学講師
山本美穂（Miho Yamamoto）愛徳学園中学校教諭
ジニータ・グラント（Juanita Grant）ESL teacher

世界標準としての世代間交流のこれから

2017 年 10 月 16 日　初版発行

著　者　草野篤子・溝邊和成・内田勇人・安永正史
発行者　中桐十糸子
発行所　三学出版有限会社
　　　　〒 520-0013　大津市勧学二丁目 13-3
　　　　　　（TEL/FAX 077-525-8476）
　　　　　　http://sangaku.or.tv

モリモト印刷（株）印刷・製本